A Chanticleer Press Edition

Taylor's Guide to Water-Saving Gardening

Houghton Mifflin Company Boston

Library of Congress
Cataloging-in-Publication Data
Taylor's guide to water-saving gardening.
1st ed. — (Taylor's guides to gardening)
Based on: Taylor's encyclopedia of gardening.
4th ed. 1961.
ISBN 0-395-54422-X : $16.95
1. Landscape architecture in water
conservation. 2. Plants, Ornamental—Water
requirements. I. Taylor's encyclopedia of
gardening. II. Title: Water-saving
gardening. III. Series.
SB475.83.T39   1990   635.9'8—dc20
89-71750

Prepared and produced by Chanticleer Press,
New York
Typeset by Graphic Arts Composition,
Philadelphia
Printed and bound by Dai Nippon, Tokyo
Cover photograph by Robert Heapes

Series designed by Massimo Vignelli

First Edition.

DNP   10   9   8   7   6   5   4   3   2   1

Contents

Contributors

Ken Ball, co-author of the essays on fundamentals and design and general consultant for this guide, is a conservation specialist for the Office of Water Conservation at the Denver Water Department. He has been involved with conservation and resource management programs for over twenty years, serving as executive director for the Clean Denver Program, head of the Denver Water Department's Environmental Planning program, and a member of the Keep America Beautiful, Inc., national training team, among other endeavors. He was responsible for bringing the Xeriscape concept to national attention in the early 1980s and played a key role in the founding of the National Xeriscape Council, Inc., serving on its board of directors. Mr. Ball is also on the board of Xeriscape Colorado!, Inc., and has been consultant to developers, cities, and universities on conservation and resource management issues. In recognition of his efforts, he has received the Irrigation Association's National Water and Energy Conservation Award and the Iron Eyes Cody Peace Medal for Environmental Improvement.

Ann Reilly, who compiled the list of plants included in this guide and wrote the descriptions in the Encyclopedia, is also the author of the essay about choosing plants. She was consulting editor for ten volumes in the Taylor's Pocket Guide series and has written all or parts of over thirty-five garden books. She is a horticultural photographer as well as a writer; some of her work appears in the color plates.

Gary O. Robinette, co-author of the essays on fundamentals and design, is Director of Landscape Architecture at the University of Texas at Arlington. He is the author of eighteen books and numerous articles about landscape architecture and horticulture, including *Water Conservation in Landscape Design and Management,* and he lectures frequently across the country.

The illustrations in the essay called Choosing the Right Plants are by Dolores R. Santoliquido; those in the other essays and in the chart on irrigation methods are by Edward Lam. The drawings in the Encyclopedia of Plants are by Daniel Allen, Robin Jess, Margaret Kurzius, Edward Lam, Dolores R. Santoliquido, Aija Sears, and Mary Jane Spring; the three maps in the Appendices are by Paul Singer.

Preface

Although most of the earth is covered with water, only 3 percent of that water is available for human consumption and use in agriculture, industry, recreation, and gardening. And it is a simple scientific fact that there is no practical means to create more water. Essentially all the water that exists on the earth has been here for eternity. In fact, one of the most significant results of the American space effort has been to show that "Spaceship Earth" is a closed environmental system, with water naturally cycled from sea to atmosphere to rainfall to river to sea, over and over again.

While the supply remains constant, the demand for water will only grow in the future, as development takes place, agricultural irrigation needs increase, and industry implements water-intensive environmental protection programs. Add to this the fact that humans continue to contaminate supplies of potable water, and you will see a very real decline in the amount of water available for landscaping and other human needs.

If global warming is indeed a reality, the next 40 to 50 years could witness greater reductions in supply and even greater competition for what's left. We must find more efficient ways to use water—in the home, the garden, and elsewhere.

Gardening has long been the most popular leisure-time activity in America. Only recently, gardeners have become concerned about environmental protection and improvement, sparking interest in the challenge to save water in landscaping. The goal of water-saving gardening is to create surroundings that look beautiful and require the least possible water to remain that way. The process calls for only a bit more planning than conventional gardening, and you will find that fitting together the pieces that will realize the most savings can be an enjoyable challenge.

In some regions of the United States, water-saving gardening is an absolute must. The arid Southwest and the semiarid High Plains receive fewer than 14 inches of precipitation each year and experience summer temperatures that regularly exceed 100 degrees. Very few ornamental plants can withstand such conditions without extra water, but it makes economic and ecological sense to keep the extra water to a minimum. In less arid portions of the country, expensive water rates and fluctuating levels of yearly rainfall make conservation desirable. In any region, it is a good idea to create a water-saving landscape around a summer home, because it will be able to survive neglect during times when the home is unoccupied. Wherever you live, designing a garden to use little water can increase the value of your property, help improve environmental conditions, and introduce you to some attractive new plants and economical gardening techniques.

How to Use

Gardening to save water is a relatively new activity, especially in areas of the country where drought is not a fact of life. Fortunately, in recent years gardeners have come to realize that the basis of water-saving gardening — choosing plants whose needs are closely met by the conditions in their landscapes — makes sense no matter where they live. Such plants not only have a very good chance of thriving, but they also require little maintenance to keep them looking well. They can survive unexpected periods of drought as well as unavoidable periods of neglect by busy homeowners.

Whether you are planning a water-saving garden out of necessity, concern for the environment, convenience, or a combination of all three, this book will help you through the entire process. The result will be a beautiful, functional landscape that you and your family can enjoy for years to come.

How This Book Is Organized

This guide contains three types of material: color plates, plant descriptions, and articles by experts to guide you through every aspect of creating a water-saving garden.

Color Plates

Ten beautifully landscaped gardens and more than 320 attractive plants that thrive on little water are shown in the color plates. The plates are divided into five groups: gardens, flowers, ground covers, shrubs, and trees. In the first group, each water-saving garden is shown in a double-page photograph, illustrating how appropriate plants can be selected and arranged to offer beauty as well as economy. Within each of the following groups, photographs of individual plants are arranged by color and shape, making it easy for you to find the plant that will create the effect you desire.

The captions that accompany the color plates provide essential information at a glance. In the first section, they identify the type of garden, its location, and important features of the landscape design. The caption for each plant photograph offers scientific and common names, plant height, flower or fruit size, bloom time, hardiness information, and a reference to the relevant page in the Encyclopedia of Plants. There is also a description of the plant's relative drought tolerance, ranging from extremely to slightly drought-tolerant. The five terms used translate roughly as follows:

- Extremely drought-tolerant: Needs less than 14 inches of water per year
- Very drought-tolerant: Needs about 16 inches of water per year
- Moderately drought-tolerant: Needs about 18 inches of water per year
- Fairly drought-tolerant: Needs about 20 inches of water per year
- Slightly drought-tolerant: Needs about 22 inches of water per year

By comparing a plant's water needs to the average amount of annual rainfall in your area (as shown on the precipitation map in the

This Guide

appendices) you can determine about how much, if any, extra water
it would need in order to thrive in your garden.

Encyclopedia of Plants
Here you will find full descriptions of the plants featured in the color
plates. Entries are arranged alphabetically by genus and cross-
referenced to the color section. If you are unfamiliar with scientific
names, look up a plant by its common name in the index.
Each description begins with the genus name, followed by the
common and scientific family names. A guide to the pronunciation
of the scientific name precedes a brief overview of the genus. The
How to Grow section provides specific information about what type
of soil, light, and fertilizer the plants need and tells you how to start
them in your garden. It offers tips on pinching, pruning, watering,
propagating, and other chores that will help the plants thrive. The
section called Uses describes some of the best situations in which to
grow the plants, such as in a rock garden or near the sea.
Next you will find descriptions of, and page references to, the species
shown in the color plates. These tell you about the particular
characteristics of each plant and often list the names of popular
varieties. Finally, they give information about the plant's hardiness
so that you can determine if it is likely to do well in your region.

Essays
Written by experts in the fields of water conservation, landscape
design, and horticulture, the essays in the front of the book explain
all aspects of water-saving gardening—altering existing sites,
planning new gardens, selecting appropriate plants, choosing
irrigation methods, and maintaining a beautiful and economical
garden. After you've read about the fundamentals, the design
process, and the special characteristics of drought-tolerant plants,
turn to the case study. It describes, in step-by-step fashion, the
redesign of a suburban landscape that resulted in a 75 percent drop in
water use.

Appendices
The appendices contain useful maps—of average yearly rainfall, first
frost dates, and USDA hardiness zones; a chart delineating the pros
and cons of eight different irrigation methods; lists of plant sources
and of publications that offer further information; and a directory of
organizations throughout the country that promote water saving
efforts on the local level.

Water-Saving

Successful water-saving gardening is simple if you follow seven fundamentals. Through effective planning and design, soil improvement, appropriate use of turf, efficient irrigation, use of mulches, a well-informed selection of plants that require little water, and a good maintenance program you can achieve a significant savings of water, money, and time. The actual amount of water you save will vary with the amount and spread of natural precipitation, temperature, and other regional elements, but for much of the nation a 50 percent savings is very possible. Specialists generally agree that even just fine-tuning your irrigation practices and equipment can produce savings of 20 or 30 percent. Another bonus is that your garden will be less subject to environmental stress, less likely than your neighbors' to suffer if you suddenly find yourself unable to care for it.

Planning and Design

Of course, all of the aesthetic principles of design—form, function, proportion, style, color, texture—that underlie any attractive landscape apply to water-saving gardens, too. If you've never planned a garden before, you may wish to refer to some of the many books available on the subject, including *Taylor's Guide to Garden Design*. In this book, we focus on adapting traditional design considerations to help reduce the need for water and to use existing water more efficiently—that is, working with nature rather than trying to change it.

Your water-saving garden design should take into account the other six fundamentals, discussed in some detail below. It should also serve your personal goals and life style, and make realistic use of your space. Here are a few questions to ask yourself as you plan:

1. What is the actual amount of water you now use for landscape maintenance, and by how much would you like to reduce it? It is easy to compute these figures using a water-demand analysis form like the one completed on page 46. The figures will enable you to establish goals for savings and to measure your results as the garden grows.

2. How much land do you have, and what portion of it is open—that is, not covered by buildings, driveways, walks, patio areas, or other such features? You'll need to compute this figure for both existing and planned landscapes. Your goal will be to reduce the open space somewhat, to analyze the water use in various parts of the garden, and to find better ways to organize and plant the garden so that some or all areas can be watered more efficiently.

3. Where are the problem areas? Every landscape contains potential problem areas, which can be made less troublesome with a more effective design. Narrow areas, steep slopes, and hot, sunny exposures are some examples. Look for places that are hard to water or maintain, or that have never looked attractive or often appear to be suffering from drought. Work on those first. In designing new landscapes, always plan carefully in order to prevent the creation of such areas from the beginning.

Fundamentals

4. What is the price of water? Whatever water may cost in your area, it is certain that the cost will only go up. In some places, the price is so high that the cost of converting to a lower-water-use garden is quickly repaid. In other areas, the return will come more slowly, so you may decide to convert small areas one at a time.

5. Are your present irrigation methods as efficient as they could be? Often substantial savings are possible by simply making adjustments in existing irrigation systems and practices. Merely changing your watering schedule so that it coincides more closely with your plants' natural water loss can reduce water use by up to 20 percent. Fine-tuning an irrigation system so that it covers all areas equally can extend water savings to 30 percent or even more.

6. Can the planted area be reduced in size? Introducing functional zones such as decks and patios can increase enjoyment of your yard as well as decrease the amount of water it needs. A bonus is that water will tend to run off these structures into planted areas.

7. Can problem slopes be altered? Slopes and gravity cause water to run off before it can soak in and benefit plants. The steeper the slope, the greater the problem. If your yard contains steep slopes, consider terracing (see the illustration on page 28) as a way to save runoff water. Avoid making steep berms of soil—that is, creating mounds for plantings—because water runs off of berms too quickly, causing an increased need for irrigation.

Soil Improvement

Making sure you provide the best soil for your plants is the most important of the seven fundamentals. Soil types vary greatly, even within a given site, so you may need to employ special techniques or planting schemes. Check with your state college, cooperative extension office, or a soil-testing lab to determine the best soil improvements for your site and chosen plants.

An ideal soil for water saving is a deep, friable loam—a mixture of sand, organic matter, and clay that crumbles easily. The components of loam are balanced in a way that permits air and water to penetrate to the root zones of plants. The organic materials provide nutrients to the plants and beneficial microorganisms to the soil.

Unfortunately, loam does not exist naturally around most homes. When your house was built, the soil around it was probably disturbed and compacted. In some instances, the organically rich topsoil may have been stripped from the site. Your native soil may be too sandy or light and unable to hold water around the roots of plants. To illustrate, 100 square feet of sand will hold only 60 gallons of water, while loam will hold 90 gallons and clay 160 gallons. However, if your soil contains too much clay, it will be too dense to allow water to penetrate to the roots of plants. One inch of water will penetrate 12 inches in sand, 6 to 10 inches in loam, but only 4 to 5 inches in clay soil. In any case, taking the time to correct these problems before planting or altering your garden is essential.

Methods of soil conditioning vary from region to region. For example,

Water-Saving Fundamentals

bedrock in San Antonio, Texas, is so close to the surface that gardeners joke that they need to haul in about 18 inches of soil before they can plant anything. Generally, though, organic material of any kind is helpful — good choices are compost, sawdust, and decomposed waste products such as cottonseed hulls, manure, shredded and partially composted tree and garden trimmings, and the like. Peat moss, especially sphagnum peat moss, is ideal. Avoid black meadow peat, however, because it has already decomposed naturally and will provide only short-term benefits. Organic matter helps break up heavy and/or compacted soil and adds bulk and water-holding capability to otherwise loose, sandy soils.

Some products have come onto the market recently that help water seep into and stay in the soil for plant consumption. Wetting agents, technically referred to as surfactants, act to lubricate soil particles by breaking down surface tension, which permits the water to penetrate more easily and deeply into the soil. Products called polyacrylamides absorb water that has made its way into the soil and retain the water for plant roots to tap. They are new to the gardening market and still relatively expensive, but you may want to buy a small packet from your garden center and experiment with it. Just remember that the best possible way to make your garden take and hold water is still old-fashioned tilling and working in good amounts of organic material from the start.

You may not need to work the soil to a uniform depth over the entire garden. Determine the approximate depth to which the majority of plant roots will reach in certain areas, and till accordingly. Lawns need soil modified from 6 to 8 inches deep; annual beds, from 8 to 10 inches deep, and perennial beds and shrub borders, from 18 to 24 inches.

There are two schools of thought about preparing the soil for trees and large shrubs. One view is that you should replace as much of the soil you removed as possible, to give the plant the best start in loosened but natural soil. The other is that you should put back a mixture containing about two-thirds to three-fourths original soil and one-third to one-fourth organic material. The theory behind the second method is that the roots may be shocked if they grow directly from the very good soil of the container or rootball into the soil already on the site; the mixture helps the tree adapt to the native soil. The "mixture" method probably works best if you're planting regionally specific native plants. Be sure to ask the plant supplier for suggestions on correct soil treatment for the particular plant you're buying.

Appropriate Use of Turf

Americans have a fascination with turf. Neighborhood competition for the greenest lawn has been characteristic of suburbia for generations. It is true that turf can add distinctive color, texture, and function to a landscape. On the other hand, formally maintained, highly manicured areas of turf are the most water- and maintenance-demanding elements of any landscape. In some regions of the country, the turfgrasses commonly planted require two, three, or more times the number of inches of rainfall expected. Obviously, decisions about how much and what type of lawn to plant can greatly affect water savings.

There are three basic actions any property owner can take to use turf more efficiently. The first is to consider alternative grass species. The most important characteristics of a lawn grass are color, texture, blade thickness, sod-forming capability, and water requirements. For a water-saving lawn, narrow your choices by selecting a species whose water requirements come close to being met by the amount of precipitation in your region. Investigate using grasses native to your region. Many are being improved and hybridized so that little, if any, additional irrigation is needed, and they function quite well as lawns. In addition to the savings, your new lawn will be less likely to suffer or die during a drought because it will adapt easily.

You should be aware that, depending on where you live, you may need to alter your vision of the perfect lawn. Choosing a water-saving species may mean moving away from the closely cropped, deep green blades seen in lawn-mower ads. But it allows you to experiment, to create a landscape more in harmony with your natural surroundings. And, imagine being able to sit in the hammock while your neighbors spend their weekends watering, reseeding, and fertilizing. Your lawn may actually look better than theirs during long hot spells.

It is always wise to check with a knowledgeable turf horticulturist to determine the ideal water-saving turf for your garden. There are some general guidelines based on the fact that grasses are divided into two types, warm-season and cool-season. Generally, cool-season grasses grow best in northern latitudes and at higher elevations, where temperatures are cool for most of the growing season. Warm-season grasses usually do better where the climate is hot the entire year long. Some of the best choices among the cool-season grasses are the turf-type tall fescues. There are many water-saving varieties, which have been bred for fine blade texture in order to make them competitive with the more water-demanding bluegrass that many Northerners are used to seeing. Fescue grows well in sun or shade and keeps its green color during a long growing period. It grows in clumps but will produce a rich, thick mat if seeded densely. It should be mowed to between 3½ and 6 inches tall.

In warm-season areas, there is a wider range of choices. Bermuda grass is a popular, low-growing grass with a fine texture and medium green color. It forms a dense sod because it increases by stolons that spread across the soil and root. There are many useful hybrids on the market. The growth habit of St. Augustine grass is similiar to that of Bermuda, but St. Augustine is lighter in color and somewhat coarser in texture. Its vigorous growth necessitates more frequent mowing, but it survives well on little supplemental irrigation. Buffalo grass, which grows naturally in the High Plains and Great Basin regions, has a medium-fine texture and a grayish-green color. Use it in areas of full sun and be careful not to over-water it. Buffalo grass survives cold winters better than St. Augustine or Bermuda grasses.

Water-Saving Fundamentals

At right is an example of an "ET" (evapotranspiration) curve. It illustrates how the level of a plant's natural need for water changes during the growing season.

There are transition areas where either warm- or cool-season grasses may be grown. In such areas, choose a grass whose water requirements will be met closely by your area's normal precipitation.

Another way to save water in the lawn is to irrigate more efficiently. Learn the needs of your type of grass and meet them without over-watering. It helps to be aware of the lawn's evapotranspiration (or "ET") curve. Evapotranspiration refers to two ways in which moisture is lost to plants. Evaporation is the natural loss of water to the air from the soil, water surfaces, and other nonliving materials. Transpiration is water loss by plants themselves—through their leaves and stems, primarily—during their natural life and growth processes. A sample ET curve is shown above. Although curves vary from plant type to plant type, species to species, and region to region, they are generally higher during warm, dry seasons. You can see from the illustration how watering at a constant, high rate (a) throughout the growing season can be wasteful. The plants cannot use as much water during spring and fall as they need at the height of summer. But watering at a constant, low rate (b) would be inadequate during the hottest summer months. Thus, changing your irrigation schedule can help you capture savings that might otherwise be missed.

ET rates are often available from a local university, parks department, or cooperative extension office. Water departments in some regions publicize ET data to promote water savings. Researching the bio-logical requirements of your turfgrass over the seasons can help you alter your irrigation schedule accordingly.

The third water-saving action to take is to reduce the area of turf in your landscape. Consider other plant materials, such as ground covers, perennials, and shrubs, or hard surfaces. Or limit more water-intensive turf types to small areas and plant grasses with lower requirements in the rest of the landscape. For example, plant a play area with "thirsty" grass, but sow an area beyond it with a native or adapted grass that is either allowed to grow tall and wave in the wind or is mown periodically for a more controlled appearance.

Efficient Irrigation

Most gardens have to be irrigated at some time in some way. The key is to know how much water to use, where to apply it, and during which season or time of day it will do the most good. Also, make sure your basic garden design and irrigation design are fully integrated. If you understand the characteristics and limitations of various methods, you can design your garden to take advantage of them. Some irrigation systems are automated, saving you time that would otherwise be spent setting the hose and changing it yourself; they also remember to water when you might not. Others are less convenient but cost less to install. Study the alternative methods in the chart beginning on page 422 to decide which would be best for you.

It may help you to sketch the plan of your garden, labeling areas that need special attention—such as lawn, rose garden, vegetable patch, or shrub border—and think about which method would best serve each

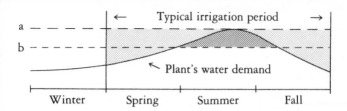

space. Remember that whatever irrigation system you choose, it should provide water at or near the rate at which your soil will absorb it and only as frequently as the plants really need water.

There are several ways to find out how well your irrigation methods are working. The first, and easiest, is to make a visual assessment of your plants' water needs. Learn to recognize signs of water deficiency, such as drooping or falling leaves and lack of new growth or vigor. Your turf needs watering if the blades do not spring back after you step on them, or if the turf has changed color from deep green to dull gray-green. Strolling around your garden to check for such signs can solve problems before they start.

Another test is to check the soil on the surface and in the root zones of your plants. Push a screwdriver into the soil, dig a small hole, or use a soil-core sampler to determine if the soil is moist enough near the plant roots.

Measuring the rainfall in your garden and comparing it to the needs of various plants can help you determine how much supplementary irrigation to provide. Use a rain gauge to determine not only how much water has fallen naturally but also how much water your irrigation system is providing. Or try the less formal "tuna can" system. Set a series of identical containers with straight sides throughout the irrigated zone. Compare the amounts of water they collect to determine if adjustments should be made to insure optimum coverage in each area.

Tensiometers are devices you can install permanently or use periodically to measure soil moisture at different depths in your garden. Although they are expensive and are used most often by professionals, they are becoming more effective and may become more practical for homeowners in the near future. Computerized irrigation control systems are now available to the home gardener as well. They measure rainfall, local evapotranspiration (ET) rates, and the amount and timing of irrigation water applied, and then help evaluate what changes may be required. With the growing use of computers in the home, such systems will probably become more moderately priced in the near future.

In some drought-prone areas, homeowners install two water-meter systems to measure water use — one for indoor and the other for outdoor consumption. That way they know exactly how much water they use outdoors each month. Some communities and water authorities have staff members who will come to your home and perform "water audits" to show you how you are using water and suggest ways you might improve your water-use habits. Others offer short courses or seminars in which you can learn more about low-water-use garden design in your locale. See the Network List at the back of this book for some keys to locating these programs. Finally, an increasing number of Xeriscape or other water-saving demonstration gardens have been developed in arboreta, parks, and around public buildings throughout the United States. Visit the nearest one to learn more and to see what your own results could be.

Section of a front lawn before water-saving improvements.

One of the best ways to save water in the landscape is to reduce the turf area. The drawings below illustrate how replacing part of a lawn with ground covers, flowers, small trees, and decorative boulders can increase its beauty as well as its water efficiency.

Same area after improvements. New plantings include Himalayan Fleece-flower, thyme, coreopsis, daylilies, vinca, and small hawthorn trees.

Use of Mulches

If you could invent the perfect water-control device for your garden, it might involve a series of louvers that would open up to let water into the soil around your plants and then close to keep the water from evaporating out of the soil. That is, in effect, what mulches do in the garden. The concept is that if a blanket of organic, inorganic, or man-made material is placed to varying depths over the soil and around the roots of a plant, it will keep the heat of the sun from causing evaporation and also help control weeds. Mulches also control erosion of the soil around the base of plants and, if organic, can improve the quality of the soil as well. They help prevent soil from compacting, allowing moisture to move easily to the plant roots. What is more, they can make your garden neater and more attractive. Organic mulches consist of vegetative materials, such as wood chips, bark, straw, peat moss, pine needles, and even rice hulls, nut hulls, or cotton-gin waste. Inorganic mulches are derived from natural, non-plant materials such as rock, gravel, decomposed granite, brick chips, or coarse sand. Man-made mulching materials include polyethylene, glass fiber, plastic, and paper. (Look for plastic and polyethylene products that are woven or spun-bonded. They allow air and moisture into the soil; solid sheets of plastic do not.)

In order to conserve the most water in your garden, you should try to use thick layers of mulch; apply mulch in more areas, such as in shrub beds and perennial borders; and relate the type of mulch to the requirements of various areas of the landscape. Remember, however, that vast areas of mulch can become monotonous.

In hot regions, be cautious about using large expanses of rock mulch near buildings. The radiant and reflective heat from rock can raise indoor temperatures by 10 to 15 degrees. In cooler regions, however, rock mulch near buildings can work like a passive solar collector to help warm the structure. In such places, a good idea is to use rock mulch around a planting of deciduous shrubs. The summer shade will keep the mulch from raising indoor temperatures, but in winter the rocks will be exposed to the sun's warmth.

Perhaps the best "mulch" of all is a very drought-tolerant ground cover, which will perform all the functions of other mulches and also lend beauty, color, and interest. Take a look at the many possibilities in the color section of this book. You may want to apply mulch under new plantings of spreading ground covers to keep the landscape looking nice until the plants fill in. If so, apply the mulch only about an inch deep so as not to interfere with the spread of the plants. In areas of high wind, use long, stringy wood mulch because it will not be blown around your yard easily. Avoid bark nuggets, which, besides being expensive, are very easily moved by air and water.

Selecting Plants That Require Little Water

Some plants, such as willow trees, naturally grow in areas where there is a great deal of water. It stands to reason that when these plants are used in a garden, they require heavy watering to keep them healthy and attractive. Selecting plants for a water-saving garden involves avoiding these types of plants in favor of those that naturally thrive in dry conditions. The challenge is to work in harmony with your regional environment, considering high and low temperatures, soil types, available sunlight, humidity, and—most important—natural precipitation.

Plants that require little water are not necessarily desert plants, as a glance through the photographs in this book will prove. They simply have characteristics that help them survive without receiving large amounts of moisture at regular intervals. There are several categories of these plants (described in greater detail in the essay "Choosing the Right Plants"). Degrees of drought-tolerance vary from site to site, species to species, and plant form to plant form.

It is also wise to consider growing plants that are native to your area. Since they have existed in your geographic region for hundreds of years without irrigation, they will probably do well in your garden without a lot of extra attention or water. But before you decide to "convert" to native plants, there are a few things you should know.

Most native plants are growing in complex relationships with other plants and have been doing so for centuries. It is virtually impossible to reconstruct all of those relationships in your garden in a short time, but you should be aware of them if you do want to come close. For instance, Flowering Dogwood *(Cornus florida)* is an understory tree, growing in the shade of a larger canopy tree in the forest. If you put it in full sun and treat it as a canopy tree, the dogwood will not do well and will use more water than you would expect. Also, the soil in your garden has been conditioned and is not like the soil in which native plants naturally grow. Be sparing in your use of soil conditioner and fertilizer if you wish to grow native species.

Do not assume that more care is always best. This story will help illustrate: In some parts of the Southwest, newcomers from the North are intrigued by the native Mesquite *(Prosopis juliflora),* which Southwesterners treat as a weed. The new homeowners add Mesquite trees to their gardens and, desiring them to look nice, water and fertilize them "well." The gardeners are confused and disappointed when the trees die. The moral of the story is that a native species that thrives on neglect may be killed by kindness in a garden.

The best selection of plants for your water-saving garden will include a mixture of drought-tolerant and native plants, plus many plants "adapted" from other geographic regions. (The term "xeric-adapted" is sometimes used to describe plants that are able to survive and flourish with limited water.) The nursery trade has found and propagated a wide range of plants that may not necessarily be native to your area but that can work given the appropriate care. Ask your local nursery professional to let you know you what is available.

The way you group plants can also make a big difference in your water use. Landscape professionals use the term "zoning the landscape" to describe dividing the garden according to the water needs of plants. Zoning is a simple way to manage water use and maintenance more effectively. Plants with like water needs are grouped together so that you can irrigate them with nearly the same amount of water. Those that take a great deal of water are separated from those that take less. For example, you might designate the turf area as a water-intensive zone and divide the balance of the garden into moderate, low, and very low water-use zones. Then you would develop four different watering schedules and avoid the nightmare of trying to irrigate one water-loving plant right in the middle of a mass of very drought-tolerant types. It also helps to match your zones with the conditions on your site. If possible, put water-loving plants in the wettest area and those with limited water needs in the naturally hot and dry areas.

A Good Maintenance Program

A garden you've created based on the six preceeding fundamentals will be the envy of the neighborhood. It will continue to look well in almost any circumstance, and you will enjoy the extra time that its easy care affords you. A water-saving garden, because it is more natural and more regionally appropriate than many other kinds of gardens, tends to require minimal maintenance. However, because no garden is ever totally maintenance-free, here are some tips on how to keep your new landscape healthy, starting with the grass.

Ornamental grasses in the landscape require minimal attention. You need only remove old seed heads and grass blades if they are unattractive, or prune occasionally to renew the plants. If properly selected, ornamental grasses may require no irrigation. Natural stands of grass (grass that grew in a spot on its own) or a native or adapted species you have planted for a naturalistic effect may require mowing only once each year. On the other hand, a grass used in a highly traveled area or a play area needs more maintenance and water to heal damage to its tissues from use. If you mow these grasses to a taller height than usual, they will need less irrigation and will grow deeper roots. Always mow regularly enough that you need to remove only 30 percent of the blade in any one mowing, and catch or collect the clippings so you can compost them.

Aerating turf and removing thatch will help water make its way through the soil to the plant roots. Aeration, sometimes referred to as coring, is accomplished by punching deep holes in the turf root zones. You can rent a machine for aerating, or do it manually with a special device that pulls plug holes from the turf. Turf specialists recommend aerating lawns at least once a year—and more often in high-traffic areas. Aeration is particularly helpful on slopes, where water loss by runoff is greatest.

Thatch is the dead, concentrated plant material that accumulates just above the soil line in a lawn and impedes its growth. Periodic raking will suffice to remove thatch, but there are power machines that make tough jobs easier. There is also a machine called a vertislicer, or verticutter, which accomplishes aeration and dethatching at the same time by cutting vertically into the soil zone.

Since water-saving gardening is based on working with nature, the goal is to introduce as few chemicals as possible into the soil. Overusing certain chemicals can be hazardous to the garden, and there are certain products, such as soil sterilants and other powerful herbicides, that you should never use. They may drift in the wind and cause damage to adjacent landscapes, or they may contaminate nearby water sources or destroy beneficial microbes in the soil. Of course, overuse and misuse of any chemicals and fertilizers can cause pollution of nearby streams and lakes. Your goal in fertilizing, then, should be to do so as infrequently as possible, and, when you do fertilize, to use the right type, in the correct form, at the proper time in the plant's growing cycle.

The best fertilizer for a drought-resistant garden is low in nitrogen and high in potassium, which encourages root growth. Using a high-nitrogen-based fertilizer encourages a plant's top growth to increase, creating a need for both more water and more frequent mowing or pruning; high-water-use zones in your garden may still require more traditional fertilizing. Fertilizers generally do the most good if you apply them in the fall. Fertilizer must act with water to dissolve and distribute its stimulators—another reason to limit its use in a water-saving garden. Often gardeners waste both fertilizer and water by applying them at the wrong time in the growing cycle of the plant. Certain varieties of turf, shrubs, and ground covers begin growing at one time of year, maintain that growth for a while, and then become dormant. Adding fertilizer and water while plants are dormant or nearly dormant does them little good. To avoid making this mistake, learn about the life cycles of your plants and irrigate and fertilize them accordingly.

You may also unwittingly waste water and fertilizer if the chemistry of your soil is not correct. Soil pH (a measure of the acidity or alkalinity of soil) affects the way nitrogen is released from the soil for plant use. If your soil is very acid, you can adjust the pH easily; the common procedure is to add lime to the soil, but use a testing kit or ask your local specialists to examine a sample of soil before you change the chemical balance.

Other Maintenance Tasks

Weeds take a great deal of water from the soil and compete with landscape plants. Therefore you should weed your water-saving garden often and carefully, especially during the first growing seasons. Once the plants become established, there will be fewer weeds.

Keeping your irrigation system in good repair can save you gallons of water, quite a bit of money, and several plants—which may be getting too much or too little irrigation. Take special care to see that all parts of your system are functioning properly, especially during times when water is scarce. Pruning can reduce your plants' demand for water because it removes excess growth. Do not go overboard by shearing, topping, or pollarding; simply remove vegetation selectively, thinning to promote the natural shape and form of the plant or to remove any dead or diseased growth. Correct pruning will also strengthen the plant; reducing the top mass of trees and shrubs lessens stress on their roots as well.

Another important maintenance task is to protect your plants from dehydration during especially dry periods. Each plant is, in essence, a water pump, bringing water out of the soil, moving it through the plant, and transpiring oxygen and water out of the microscopic openings, or stomata, in the leaves, needles, or blades. The loss of water through the stomata can be controlled to some extent by anti-transpirants—wax-based or paraffin-based materials applied to the leaves. These are sometimes used on plants in cold climates to protect them from freezing or drying out during the winter. You can buy an anti-transpirant at a garden center and spray it on selected plants during transplanting or during dry periods to protect them from dehydration. Just remember that using anti-transpirants is not a substitute for watering plants; it will simply lock in whatever moisture is already there.

Part of your original garden design should be a schedule of specific water needs for each species of plant. The schedule should allow enough water for the plant's early establishment and change as the plant matures. Following this schedule, and checking periodically to see that it remains effective, will ensure the health of your water-saving landscape.

Knowing the seven fundamentals should set you well on your way to saving water in the garden. The challenge of planning carefully, making informed decisions, and coordinating your efforts can be fun, and you will enjoy the attractive, economical results for years to come.

Garden Design

Thoughtful, sensitive design and planning make all the difference in controlling water use in a garden. In fact, creating an efficient garden plan can save more water than any other single action you may take. Whether you are designing an entire landscape or just altering one area, it pays to make a detailed plan, put it on paper, and follow it through.

Taking Inventory

No design can be created in the abstract; any plan must be tied to a particular site. So the first step in designing or redesigning a garden is to take inventory of what currently exists. Here is a list of characteristics to note:

• Solar patterns—How does the sun move across your site seasonally? Daily? Where are the areas of deep shade, light shade, and full sun?

• Wind patterns—What are the speed and direction of prevailing winds? How do they change daily or seasonally?

• Topography and orientation—Where are there slopes? How steep are they? In what direction do they slope? What are the natural drainage patterns?

• Existing vegetation—What types of plants are on the site now? How old are they and in what condition? What are their ecological relationships to one another?

• Soils—What types exist? How deep are they? In what condition?

• Precipitation—What is the total annual amount, and how is it spread over the year?

• Water data—Are there records of water use? These should show the amount and price of water used for irrigation, so that you can determine how much you have been spending to irrigate the present landscape.

• Landscape purpose—How are various areas used? Heavily or lightly? For what activities or what types of plants? Are there areas that have been underutilized or that have presented traffic-flow problems?

• Irrigation needs—Are there perpetual dry or wet spots? Are plants grouped according to their water needs? Are all zones being covered adequately? Are there problem areas or leaking systems?

Ideas for dealing with some of these points have been discussed in the previous pages. The case study beginning on page 39 will show you how some of those ideas can be put into effect. If you need more information on the fundamentals of design, consult *Taylor's Guide to Garden Design* or another basic landscaping book; some helpful titles are listed at the back of this book.

How Much Can You Save?

The next phase in the design process is to analyze the data you collected during the site inventory. Your goal is to discover the opportunities and constraints to making the landscape more water efficient. What can you do to save water? What may be too ambitious? What can you do at minimal cost? What will require significant cost?

Garden Design

Performing a water-demand analysis may help you at this stage. This involves figuring the amount and cost of water used in various areas of the landscape so that you can determine where changes might be made. You'll find a sample analysis completed on page 46, in conjunction with a case study about redesigning a "typical" landscape. The sample illustrates how reorganizing a space and using different plants can create dramatic savings of water, money, and maintenance time.

It is usually quite realistic to plan to reduce water demand by 40 to 50 percent, especially if your current landscape includes large areas of turf. If such a goal seems too ambitious, start by working with a small area of the yard. In either case, it is very possible to pay for your conservation improvements with savings derived from lower water bills, fewer purchases of chemicals, and lower maintenance costs. For example, a recent redesign of a garden in the San Francisco Bay area changed a yard covered with lawn into a beautiful, functional garden with mass plantings of ground covers, perennials, shrubs, and trees. After the plants became established, the new landscape required only one-tenth the water and one-fifth the maintenance time that the old design had used.

Developing Your Design

Once you've analyzed your site and set some preliminary goals for water savings, it's time to draw up a plan. Start by looking at your space with a fresh eye. Gaze out the windows of various rooms, determining which views you want to preserve or enhance and which you'd like to screen out. Consider the views of your property from different outdoor vantage points as well. Sketch some alternative plans on tracing paper and place them over a base drawing of your site to see how each would fit. Using tracings will help you visualize your plans and save time by showing you quickly which of them may not be practical. Doing much of the design work on your own requires some time, learning, and effort, but your reward will be a thorough understanding of how your new garden works. In addition, you could save yourself hundreds of dollars in design services. Nonetheless, especially if you are a beginner, you may wish to have a professional landscape architect or designer review your plans and provide suggestions before you begin construction. Look for a professional who has experience in developing water-saving gardens.

Improving Existing Gardens

It may not take a complete redesign to make your yard more water efficient. Just a few changes could create sizable savings. For instance, if your site analysis reveals that a certain plant has been using quite a bit of water, you may decide to replace it with one that requires less. Or you may discover that some plants have been competing with others in the same area for available water. Removing them could solve this problem. Perhaps you could rearrange or reorganize a small planting area, grouping the plants according to their water requirements. It may make sense to provide windbreaks for some small plants that have been losing water through evaporation caused by strong winds. Or you could add a new bed of shade-loving plants in an area where existing plants cast shadows.

Providing Protection from Sun and Wind
The last two suggestions above — providing windbreaks and shade — are too often overlooked in garden design. Fast-moving dry winds blowing across the hard surface of moist soil actually "pull" water out of the ground. As moisture leaves the top layer of soil, more water comes up from the root zone to replace it. Thus, a plant that is continuously exposed to high winds will dry out easily, and the top level of soil around it will dry out as well. Erecting barriers to reduce wind speed will lessen these effects and save on irrigation.

In regions of heavy snows, windbreaks also help by causing snow to pile up on their leeward (downwind) side. As the snow melts, it provides extra moisture, sometimes enough to eliminate any need for irrigation the following spring.

Most windbreaks have an effective area of from one to three times their height on the leeward side. Thus, to create wind protection for a six-foot area, you would need a two- to three-foot-high windbreak. It could consist of an architectural device — such as a freestanding wall or retaining wall, a solid fence, or even a building. Large plants can also act as windbreaks for smaller plants, adding beauty at the same time. A disadvantage of using living windbreaks is that they can compete for moisture with the plants they are protecting. But if you study the needs of different species, you can find compatible combinations.

When the hot sun of a summer afternoon strikes a plant or the bare soil, its heat causes moisture to move out of the soil and into the atmosphere. Therefore, a plant growing in the shade requires less water than it would if it were exposed to the sun. You can create microclimates in your own garden by using shade selectively so that it benefits plants at certain times of the day or during certain seasons of the year.

First, determine the sun's path across your yard in summer. Then place a tree or large shrub so that it will cast a shadow to protect a particular planting. (Remember to check the plants' needs first, since many plants do not thrive in shade. The captions in the color section of this book tell you if the plants pictured will tolerate shade.) In addition to trees or shrubs, try using vines grown on trellises or canopies, or architectural elements such as fences or walls, to provide the shade you desire.

Directing Water Flow
To maximize your water savings, you may find it beneficial to modify the shape of the land, causing water to flow to areas where it can do the most good. Land surfaces around new homes are usually graded by the builder, but most of these conventional grading practices are rudimentary, serving mainly to direct rainfall or irrigation away from

Garden Design

your house and prevent flooding. For a water-saving garden, it often pays to develop a more sophisticated, fine-tuned grading plan that will direct water toward or through planting beds, or around the base of a large tree. (See the case study on pages 39–48 for a detailed example of how to change water flow to your advantage.)

There are several methods of grading that cause soil to hold falling water rather than drain it off. One is to provide a "catchment area," which consists of a series of holes filled with gravel and covered with soil and ground cover. During rainstorms, or when the area is irrigated, the holes fill up with water. The water then filters slowly into the surrounding soil to irrigate the roots of nearby plants. Catchment areas are actually required in some communities where water shortages are a fact of life.

Often, lawn irrigation water penetrates to the roots of turf and small shrubs, but not to the roots of trees. The drawing at right shows how you might use a variation of the catchment-area concept to provide more water to a large tree that has been suffering from drought stress. It involves capturing rainfall in plastic pipe sumps or filling them periodically by hand. Another way to trap water for trees is to construct a permanent "saucer" of soil that extends a few feet out from the trunk and collects rain or water from an irrigation system.

You can also use your rooftop and other hard surfaces on your property to serve as rainfall collectors. Impervious materials such as concrete and blacktop are the best choices, because water tends to run off of them rapidly and can be directed toward plants that need it. Paving materials such as gravel, crushed stone, or brick on sand allow water to penetrate into the soil, where it may run into nearby planted areas. You may want to try some of the newly developed pavers called "Grass-crete," which allow for increased traffic on turf but also provide for percolation of water into the soil. They are square, flat, plastic or concrete grids with holes that you fill with soil and grass seed. The grass grows and covers the exposed grid, but the pavers remain structurally sound enough to support even vehicular traffic.

In some instances, it is possible to design or install curbs that conduct water into a planted area. They serve to slow, channel, or direct water so that it does not cause erosion or damage to the plants it passes through.

Terracing

If you have a sloping yard or garden, consider grading the slope into a series of level planted areas. When water is applied at the highest level, it filters down to be used over and over again in the lower stages. Terracing is a must on steep slopes, especially those with more than one foot of drop over two feet of horizontal distance. The illustration on page 29 will help you visualize slope steepness and learn how best to handle various degrees of slope. Turn to page 62 to see an excellent example of how terracing can make a steep hillside beautiful as well as more effective in water and soil conservation.

The system shown below serves to catch and hold water so that it can benefit tree roots. Two perforated PVC pipes, 4 inches wide and 24 inches long, are buried at the tree's dripline and filled with crushed rock. Water drips in and percolates out through the rocks and perforations, becoming available to tree roots.

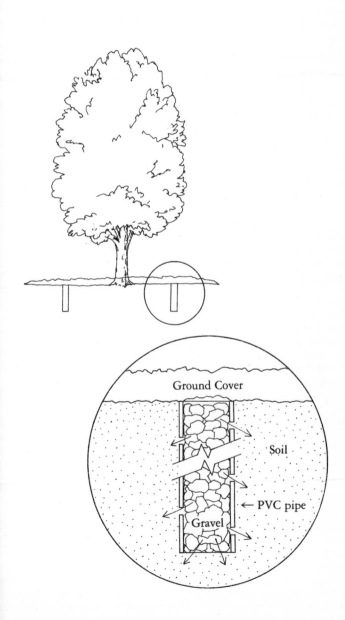

Garden Design

Slopes can be treated in several ways to reduce runoff. A 45° slope (a) should be stabilized with rocks or terraced, as shown below. Slopes described as 1 in 2 (1 foot of rise over 2 feet of length) as in (b) or 1 in 3 (c) should be planted in ground covers. A 1 in 4 slope (d) can be planted in turf.

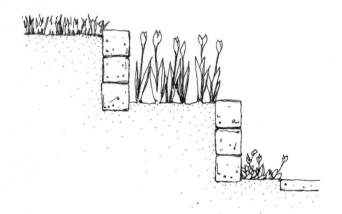

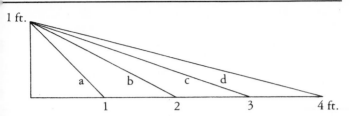

1 ft.

a b c d

1 2 3 4 ft.

Reusing Water

Purifying water costs a great deal of money, and garden plants do not require pure drinking water to survive. In fact, in certain parts of the country, partially treated waste water is used to irrigate forests and golf courses. The water presents no health hazards; in fact, the treatment process is completed by soil microbes that consume nutrients in the waste water as it moves through the soil. In California during a major drought local residents were encouraged to use "gray water" to keep their plants alive. Gray water is water left over from rinsing dishes or clothes, or even from taking a bath or shower; the main caution is that any soap in the water should be low in phosphates and biodegradable. It may never be necessary for you to use gray water in your yard, but it is good to know that you can do so in emergencies. Always check with local health offices for more particular recommendations before going ahead.

A Few Warnings

There are several "don'ts" to be aware of when it comes to altering the shape of your land. Don't mound earth into berms between curbs and walks; irrigation water will easily run off and be wasted. Instead, channel or scoop out these areas so they will retain excess water and filter it slowly into the soil. If channels make the strip too hard to mow, simply dig out a bit of soil so that the planted area will lie somewhat lower than the sidewalk or curb and therefore catch extra water before it runs off.

Another caution: Some people believe that a good way to save water is to remove most of the plants that require it and replace them with decorative stones or even concrete or blacktop. Such a radical approach actually does very little to save water, but it does succeed in reducing the beauty and value of property. A properly designed water-saving landscape, filled with attractive plants that require only minimal irrigation, should be your goal. Coordinate the planning and design techniques with the other six water-saving fundamentals; you will save money and time, as well as contribute to the health of our environment.

Choosing the

Some gardeners may be surprised to learn how many attractive plants will thrive in relatively dry conditions. A glance through the color section of this book should prove that the range of choices is indeed vast and varied. There you will see 259 species of flowers, ground covers, shrubs, and trees that are adaptable to the water-saving garden. Many of them are familiar garden plants that also appear in other Taylor Guides; some are more strictly suited to dry environments. Additional possibilities exist, of course, beyond these suggestions, but they may be available only where they are native.

The easiest way to determine how much water a particular plant requires and whether it will thrive in your garden is to ask an experienced local nurseryman. Your neighborhood garden center and your cooperative extension agent may also be able to help you put together a list of drought-tolerant plants that will grow in your area. But there are clues to be found in the plants themselves. Once you know a bit about the natural habitats and physical characteristics of drought-resistant plants, you will be able to make an educated selection for your water-saving garden.

Natural Habitats

The first clues to a plant's drought tolerance are the characteristics of its natural habitat—that is, where it grows best in the wild. Natural habitats are listed for many plants in this book, and they can also be found in *Hortus Third,* the ornamental horticulturist's bible, and in other books on native plants and wildflowers. If a plant is native to a dry climate, it is probably resistant to drought. So, if you live in a naturally dry area, or can match the growing conditions of our driest regions, look for plants native to those regions for the highest assurance of success.

The driest areas of North America include the cold desert of Utah, Nevada, and parts of Colorado, where sagebrush *(Artemisia tridentata)* is a dominant plant; the hot desert of Arizona and New Mexico, where cacti and yucca abound; and the coastal areas of California, which have wet, mild winters but very dry summers. The climate of coastal California is said to be Mediterranean, a term also applied to parts of Australia and South Africa (not to mention the Mediterranean region itself). You will notice as you study drought-resistant plants that many are indigenous to regions with a Mediterranean climate.

The amount of rainfall is an important factor in determining whether an area's native plants are drought resistant, but other elements must be considered as well. Even when annual rainfall is plentiful, high temperatures will cause great water loss to evaporation. In the desert, high evaporation rates and porous sandy soil, from which water drains quickly, combine to create an arid environment. On mountainsides and slopes, water may run off before it penetrates into the root zone, leaving plants dry even after a heavy rain. In areas with a thin layer of topsoil over rock formations, water retention is usually low. Another important influence on vegetation is the pattern of the rainfall— whether it rains year-round or seasonally.

Right Plants

Deserts

During the brief period of spring rains, desert plants burst into bloom and set seeds, which may lie dormant until enough rain falls again the following year to support germination and growth. The cacti and succulents native to deserts have the most remarkable mechanisms for surviving dry heat. Because this book's aim is to go beyond the scope of desert gardens, it does not include a large number of desert plants. It is nonetheless worth knowing something about their water-saving characteristics, because these mechanisms illustrate dramatically how plants adapt to harsh environments.

Most cacti have thick, pulpy stems that are ribbed or somewhat segmented. The stems expand when water is available and shrink slowly as the weather becomes dry. Photosynthesis takes place in the thick skin of these stems, obviating the need for large, sun-catching leaves. This is just as well, because herbaceous leaves are easily desiccated and wouldn't survive in the desert. Instead, cacti have modified leaves, which we call spines. They protect the plants from predators, prevent water loss by shading the stem, and trap water in the form of morning dew.

Seashores

Although seashores, like deserts, offer sand and sun, they support different kinds of vegetation because their climate is different. At the seashore, rainfall is more abundant and fog is frequent, but the sand is so porous that water filters away from the plants quickly. The hot sun and sea breezes dry out both soil and plants.

A variety of defense mechanisms help coastal plants combat these dry growing conditions. Sea lavender (*Limonium* species), for example, has wide-spreading roots that grow deeply to collect water from a large area. Other seaside plants have thick, hard stems and leaves that resist desiccation. The ground-hugging habit of some plants helps shelter them from drying winds. Some grasses and grasslike plants have leaves that fold up on dry, windy days. Many beach plants have white, silver, or gray leaves that reflect the strong sunlight and heat.

Rugosa, or Saltspray, Rose *(Rosa rugosa),* many grasses, thrift (*Armeria* species), sea lavenders, and saltbush (*Atriplex* species) are only a few of the plants that seem to defy nature by growing on pure, dry, infertile sand. Off the dunes, but still near the beach, you are apt to find bayberry *(Myrica pensylvanica),* whose aromatic, waxy leaves prevent it from drying out, and bearberry *(Arctostaphylos uva-ursi).* On the West Coast, you are likely to see the California Poppy and its relatives *(Eschscholzia* species) growing on sand dunes.

The Far North

The far north has a harsh climate with long, cold winters and short summer growing seasons. Rainfall is relatively sparse. The Quaking Aspen *(Populus tremuloides)* and many conifers have adapted to this difficult environment. Some conifers have small, hard needles that are resistant to drying out. Others, junipers in particular (*Juniperus*

Choosing the Right Plants

species), have tiny scalelike leaves that overlap one another to protect against the drying effects of the wind and sun. Conifers vary greatly in their needs for water; for use in a water-saving garden, look for conifers native to coastlands and dry, rocky slopes.

Thin-Soil Areas

Conditions similar to those in seaside areas exist in places where topsoil is spread very thin over rock formations. Even if the rainfall is adequate, the shallow soil retains so little water that plants must be able to tolerate drought. Ground Pink *(Phlox subulata)* is native to thin-soil areas, as are some members of the genus *Cerastium,* such as *C. tomentosum,* Snow-in-Summer.

Open Fields and Other Microclimates

Even if you don't live in one of the typically dry regions, you have probably seen water-conserving processes at work in your own area. Abandoned fields and dry, sunny roadsides are microclimates that sometimes approximate drought conditions. Knowing about the progression of plants that typically appears in abandoned fields in your own region can give you good clues to which plants will survive sunny, dry conditions without watering.

In general, the most common plants of dry, open fields in the northern temperate regions belong to three important families—the grasses (Gramineae), the pea family (Leguminosae), and the daisy family (Compositae or Asteraceae). The first perennials to pop up are Black-eyed Susans *(Rudbeckia fulgida),* goldenrod *(Solidago* species), Butterfly Weed *(Asclepias tuberosa),* and Common Yarrow *(Achillea millefolium).* As abandoned fields mature, woody plants start to dominate. In the East, plants in the genera *Rubus* (bramble), *Rhus* (sumac), and *Lonicera* (honeysuckle) are the first to appear.

In time, if left alone, the field will develop into woods, and the complexion of the planting will change again. Shade will be cast by large trees, often oaks *(Quercus),* and decaying leaves will increase the humus content of the soil, causing it to retain more water. Oaks fare especially well in dry woods because they have deeply penetrating roots and can adapt to a wide range of soil conditions. Dry woods contain other plants with abilities to withstand drought, many of which can be used in the garden—plants of the heath family (Ericaceae), such as blueberries *(Vaccinium)* and bearberry *(Arctostaphylos uva-ursi),* spicebush *(Lindera benzoin),* and some viburnums. In the South and West, a similar progression of plant types will occur, although the species may be different ones.

Collecting Plants from Their Native Habitats

It is always a good idea—and especially if you are trying to save water—to use nature's suggestions in determining which plants your local microclimate will support. But before you go out and begin digging up plants from the wild to transplant into your garden, a word of warning must be given. Some plant species are endangered and must not be moved or dug up; many are protected by law, and tampering with them will bring a stiff fine or other penalty. The best way to guarantee these plants their longevity is to collect seeds for yourself; but take just a few, and leave enough behind for the plant to continue flourishing.

In addition, moving plants can be quite disruptive. If you cannot collect seeds, you may want to take a cutting. But do not take cuttings from protected species. Finally, be aware that a native plant may not do well in your garden if you cannot give it conditions similiar to those in which it grew originally.

Many of our "native" field plants were spread by the European settlers as they migrated across the country. Sometimes this dispersal was deliberate, but often seeds simply traveled on clothing, in hay, on wagon wheels, or in animal hair. Now these thriving plants are widespread, quick to germinate, and need little help from us. Many have been adapted for home gardens and are perfect for use in water-saving landscapes; some good examples include flax (*Linum* species), tansy *(Tanacetum vulgare)*, sunflowers (*Helianthus* species), evening primroses (*Oenothera* species), asters (*Aster* species), pussytoes *(Antennaria dioica)*, spurges (*Euphorbia* species), and daylilies *(Hemerocallis* species), to name a few. Some genera include both eastern and western native species.

Types of Drought-Tolerant Plants

Just as plants indigenous to certain environments promise greater success in the water-saving garden, so too, you will find, certain families or types of plants do better with little water. Some of the major groups are described below.

Succulents

The plants we call succulents usually have thick, fleshy stems and leaves, which are coated with a waxy substance that prevents them from drying out and are filled with sap that retains moisture. Most are native to areas that are arid or semiarid for at least part of the year. Most cacti grow in deserts, but there are many other succulents and a few cacti that will do well in a variety of garden situations. Some are quite winter hardy, although they must have dry soil with excellent drainage all year round. Some succulents well suited for cultivation — many of which you will see in the color plates — include the so-called ice plants in the genera *Mesembryanthemum* and *Delosperma;* many spurges in the genus *Euphorbia;* purslane *(Portulaca)* and rock purslane *(Calandrinia);* and the milkweeds, including *Asclepias* species and other members of the Asclepiadaceae family. The sedums *(Sedum)* are also very popular succulents; they are biologically distinctive in that the pores in their leaves open at night to admit the carbon dioxide needed for growth, but close during the day to conserve moisture.

Grasses
The family Gramineae — the grasses — is the largest family of flowering plants in the world. It is also one of the most useful, as it contains all of the grain crops, lawn grasses, and ornamental grasses. In nature, grasses are the first plants to sprout on barren, burned, or poor soils. Their roots, which can grow quite deep to seek out water, prevent soil from being washed or blown away. Many grasses grow quickly in spring when rain comes, but as the hot summer moves in, they go dormant. You have probably seen lawn grass turn brown over summer and then turn green again with the cooler, damper days of fall. This ability to "shut down" during especially dry seasons is what helps grasses survive. Native grasses can store enough food in their roots to tolerate several years of drought.

Legumes
Many members of the pea family — Leguminosae (sometimes called the bean) family — are not only decorative but are also important food plants for people and animals. The legumes "fix" nitrogen — that is, they take it from the air and, through a reaction with soil bacteria, convert it to a form that provides important nutrition to plants. Because they manufacture their own fertilizer, so to speak, the Leguminosae can grow in the very poor soil that often exists in drought-prone areas. Many legumes have long taproots, which grow deep into the soil seeking water. These include the brooms from the genera *Cytisus, Genista,* and *Spartium,* among many other plants.

Poppies
Plants in the family Papaveraceae survive in dry conditions because they have deep taproots. This characteristic makes them hard to transplant or divide, but is the reason for their drought tolerance. Many poppies also go dormant in summer, their foliage disappearing after they bloom, as a mechanism to combat heat and lack of water. Most poppies have divided leaves; this arrangement results in a smaller surface area from which water can transpire. The family includes the true poppies of the genus *Papaver* and their relatives in the genera *Eschscholzia* (California poppy) and *Romneya* (California tree poppy).

Specific Plants
It is not always possible to make broad statements regarding the drought resistance of a particular family or genus, so you must often look to the species level, to a particular plant's natural habitat and other features, to determine drought tolerance. For instance, most members of the family Ranunculaceae — which includes the buttercups and their relatives — are native to moist and marshy places; there are a few exceptions, however, such as some of the clematises, which thrive in dry conditions. A large percentage of meadow flowers are from the daisy family, although not all members of the daisy family are drought resistant. Many of the drought-resistant types have hairy leaves, which trap moisture and prevent the plants from drying out.

*Fleshy roots (top) and
deep taproots (below)
help some plants resist
drought by storing water
or reaching deep into the
soil to locate water.*

Hemerocallis
species (Daylily)

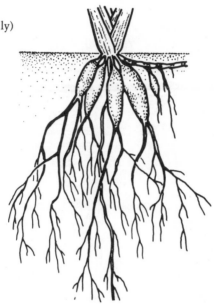

Romneya coulteri
(California Tree
Poppy)

Choosing the Right Plants

Two characteristics of
Dusty Miller help it
resist drought: divided
leaves and tiny hairs
covering the plant.
There is less leaf area
from which moisture can
evaporate, and the hairs

Senecio cineraria
(Dusty Miller)

Phlox subulata
(Ground Pink)

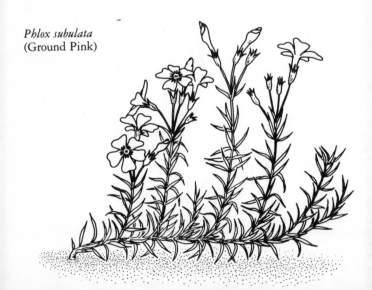

*trap water and hold it
close to the leaf surface.
The creeping growth
habit of Ground Pink
keeps it close to the moist
soil and out of drying
winds.*

Physical Characteristics

In addition to its natural habitat and genus or family, a plant's physical characteristics can also give you clues about its ability to conserve water or survive in dry conditions. Drought-tolerant plants have evolved certain types of roots, leaves, and other mechanisms to help them survive.

Roots

Many drought-resistant plants survive because their roots are long enough to reach water that is unavailable to other plants. Such a plant may have a taproot, which is a long, thick, single root, something like a carrot, or it may have wide-spreading roots, like those of many trees, that reach out in all directions seeking moisture. Besides the members of the poppy and pea families already mentioned, some plants of the carrot family (Umbelliferae), such as goutweed *(Aegopodium podagraria)* and sea holly *(Eryngium* species), also have deep taproots. Daylilies *(Hemerocallis* species), Red-hot Poker *(Kniphofia uvaria),* and lily-turf *(Liriope* species), all members of the lily family, have thick, fleshy roots that store large quantities of water.

Foliage

Some plants adapted to dry climates have small or divided leaves; the reduced area of leaf surface allows less water to transpire. The leaves of other plants curl under when moisture levels are low to conserve the water within them.

Although there are exceptions to every rule, it is safe to say that plants with gray, silvery, or white foliage tend to be drought resistant. The leaves of many of these pale-foliaged plants are actually green, but they are so densely covered with hairs that they appear light. The hairs protect the leaves from sun and wind exposure; help them collect and retain moisture; and reflect sun and heat. Some other plants have hairy leaves but still retain their green color. The hairs shade the leaves, keeping them cool; trap water, in the form of drops of morning dew; and protect the leaves from drying winds.

For the garden, the most popular hairy-leaved plants, in addition to members of the daisy family (Compositae), are *Arabis* species (rock cress), *Aurinia saxatilis* (Basket-of-Gold), *Achillea tomentosa* (Woolly Yarrow), *Artemisia* species (wormwoods), *Senecio cineraria* (Dusty Miller), *Lavandula* species (lavender), *Rosmarinus* species (Rosemary), *Stachys byzantina* (Lamb's Ears), and *Thymus* species (thyme).

Like hairy foliage, aromatic leaves have also evolved moisture-retaining properties. The aromatic oils in the leaves are volatile; in heat, they react by generating a protective haze around the plant that prevents it from drying out. Eucalyptus and lantanas have wonderfully pungent aromas that add an interesting element to the water-saving garden. Many other species with aromatic leaves are plants of choice for herb gardens; because the plants are drought-adapted, herb gardens usually need dry soil. The list includes lavender, Hyssop *(Hyssopus officinalis)*, Chamomile *(Matricaria recutita)*, bergamot *(Monarda* species), rosemary, thyme, and others.

Plant Habit

The way a plant grows—upright or trailing, open or compact—is called its "habit." The habit of a plant can be a factor in its ability to survive dry conditions. Some drought-tolerant plants have a creeping or spreading habit. They may have ground-hugging foliage that sends up flowers on leafless or nearly leafless stems. The foliage stays close to the ground, closer to the source of moisture and out of drying winds. Treasure Flower *(Gazania rigens)*, Ground Pink *(Phlox subulata)*, and Avens *(Geum reptans)* are typical ground-hugging drought-resistant plants. (There are also some moisture-loving plants that grow in this form, so don't choose a plant for your water-saving garden based on habit alone.)

Plant Names

A final clue in identifying drought-resistant plants can be found in their Latin names. Plants with the species name *tomentosum, tomentosus, pubescens, villosus,* or *mollis* have hairy leaves; those designated *argentea* have silvery leaves; the name *glauca* implies a white or gray bloom on the leaves; and those called *hirsuta, hirta,* or *hispida* have coarse or stiff hairs. These are all characteristics of drought-resistant plants. The species name *angustifolia* means the plant has long, narrow leaves, while *filamentosa* means it has threadlike leaves; these are often characteristics of plants with good drought resistance. The Latin names *repens, reptans, horizontalis, patens, procumbens,* and *divaricatus* mean creeping or spreading, a characteristic of many, although not all, drought-tolerant plants. Meadow and field plants are sometimes called *pratensis* or *campestris.* The names *arenaria* and *arenarius* mean growing in sandy places, and *maritimus* means native to seashore areas. Plants native to dry mountains may be designated *alpina* or *alpinus.* Those with aromatic leaves are sometimes named *aromatica.* Stay away from plants whose species name is *aquatica* or *palustris,* as the names indicate that these are plants for wet places.

Choosing your plants well is a vital aspect of successful water-saving gardening. Now that you know a bit about drought-tolerant plants, you can begin selecting the species for your garden, with the help of the color plates and the plant descriptions in this book. With careful planning, you can design and maintain a lovely, colorful garden while helping to conserve one of our most valuable natural resources, water.

A Case Study

The following case study will take you through a five-year plan to make a traditionally designed landscape more water efficient. It should help you visualize how the seven fundamentals can be put into effect and give you some clues to altering your own landscape.

The Site

The home illustrated on pages 42–45 is about 30 years old; the grounds had been landscaped in various ways over the years, as the owners' budgets and interests allowed. The design was neat and attractive, but it lacked any special interest, and it required quite a bit of water and maintenance to keep it looking nice. The land was covered almost totally with bluegrass turf, interrupted occasionally by a large shrub or tree, and the foundation plantings were predictable and somewhat overgrown. The shrubs flanking the front walk had grown so large that the owners had to prune them to maintain an entryway, thereby destroying the shrubs' natural shape.

This home is located in a region of the U.S. that receives about 50 inches of rainfall each year. Temperatures are moderate, but winter lows can go below 0° F and summer highs can pass 90° F. Water prices are moderate as well, but apt to go higher in the near future.

Making Changes

The owners wanted to modify the landscape so that it would require less water and less maintenance—weeding, pruning, fertilizing, mowing, etc. They also wished to solve these specific problems:

- It was very difficult to water and mow the steep bank along the front walk.
- The patio was too small for outdoor entertaining.
- There was little privacy in the front or back yard.
- The steps in the front walk made it difficult for a handicapped neighbor to visit.

The owners also wanted to improve the appearance of the landscape in order to increase the resale value of their house. To make the most efficient use of time and money, they planned to spread the work over five years, beginning in the front yard.

The First Steps

In fall, the owners measured the property and drew a map, to scale, of the existing conditions. (See the small map on page 42.) Using tracing paper placed over this base map, they sketched in the water-use zones shown on the larger map on page 43. The zones divide the property according to the amount of extra water that will be needed to sustain the plants in various areas. Turf areas use the most water, so they were planned first. Then three additional zones were sketched in, based on the needs of plants already there and the anticipated needs of the plants the owners wanted to add.

The next step was to indicate on the map the types of plants—trees, shrubs, ground covers, perennials—chosen, and to sketch new structures, such as the modified front walkway, deck, side-yard paths, and a rock garden. Together, all of these changes would work to solve the problems that had been identified and to add beauty to the landscape.

To check their plan for water efficiency, the owners completed the water-use analyses shown on pages 46–47. They revealed that their plan would indeed save water—approximately 40,000 gallons per growing season. As a final precaution, they had a local landscape architect review their plan and suggest improvements in both layout and plant choices. By early spring they were ready to begin construction.

Year One

Work began in the front yard with the removal of the walk, the foundation plantings (which had required large amounts of water), and the lawn between the curb and the sidewalk. To speed up the process and reduce the work load, the owners hired a demolition contractor to perform these tasks. The 30-year-old tree was saved, and a catchment system was devised to reduce its water demand. The contractor also regraded the walkway area, making the slope gentler and removing the need for stairs. To the south of the walk, he created a slight mound to set off the plants that would be installed there.

Some of the soil taken from the walkway site was used to change the grade near the northeast corner of the house. Now water from the downspout will run near the new and existing trees and toward the new rock garden. To create the rock garden, the contractor loosened the soil along the embankment and regraded it slightly. The large boulders weigh up to 1,500 pounds each; a boom truck delivered them and deposited them in place as the owners instructed. Where no regrading was needed, the contractor simply dug up the existing sod and turned it over in order to suffocate the grass.

Another contractor was hired to build the new walkway—a wide, curving series of squares and rectangles—and to create the new wider step-out area near the curb. Within a week, the concrete had cured, the area had been cleaned up, and the contract work was done.

Soil Improvement and Irrigation

At this point, the owners had their soil tested and learned that it was low in nitrogen. They bought some nitrogen-enriched wood shavings at the local nursery, spread them two inches deep over the entire area, and tilled them into the soil with a rented Rototiller. Then they raked and hand-graded the site to give it a final contouring.

The next step was to begin installing the irrigation system. Although simple hose-end irrigation would have sufficed to keep the new landscape healthy, the homeowners opted for the convenience of a permanent in-ground system, which they installed themselves with some help from the supply company. The water-control valves were plumbed together into a manifold and buried near the house in a box with a removable lid. The controller and supply pipe were situated in the basement nearby, with wires strung from the controller to each valve. From each valve a distribution pipeline, leading to each water-use zone, was laid at a depth of about eight inches.

The supply lines for the turf area were placed first. They carried four-inch pop-up spray heads to distribute the water above the new tall fescue grass, which would be mown to about three-and-a-half inches high. Four hundred square feet of sod was delivered and placed, and a thick vinyl edger was installed to reduce trimming time.

Over the next four weekends, the other, lower-volume irrigation supply lines were placed and the new shrubs and trees installed.

Filling In

In early June, the owners planted ground covers and perennials in the front yard. They chose some large container-grown plants, that would give instant results, and many smaller ones, which cost less but would fill in nicely over the next few years. They spread mulch under and around the new plants and watched and watered them carefully to see that they became established.

In the fall, they turned their attention to the backyard, where they dug up and turned over the turf. It would die over the winter, leaving the area ready to work the next spring.

Year Two

Plans for the second year called first for altering the area in the back-yard nearest the house. This included removal of the old concrete patio and construction of a new redwood deck in its place. Some of the thirsty shrubs were removed, and irrigation lines were laid. The new turf and plants were installed in the same manner as for the front yard.

Years Three and Four

The side yards and the perimeter of the backyard were completed during these years. A walkway was added leading from the driveway to the deck, past a new flower and vegetable garden on the south side of the house. Tall shrubs made the backyard more private. This work was done at a leisurely pace so that expenditures of time and money were spread over a manageable period.

Year Five and Beyond

The main task of the last year was to fill in plantings of flowers and ground covers. Most of the first year's plantings were established, and the turf had taken hold well.

The new landscape needs 80 percent less water than the old one did. It also requires less of the owners' time for mowing and fertilizing turf areas; and the changes increased the resale value of their home by 15 percent. Best of all, the owners enjoy their property much more now. It is a recreation area and private enclave, rather than an ordinary-looking source of endless weekend work. The plan worked so well, in fact, that some of the neighbors have been inspired to try their hands at water-saving gardening.

A Case Study

The plan at left shows the landscape described on page 39 before the owners began a 5-year program of water-saving alterations. Among other problems, large areas of bluegrass turf *required large amounts of water and a steep slope to the sidewalk encouraged runoff. The changes made to save water are shown in the larger plan. They include reducing turf*

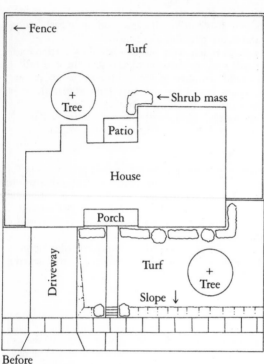

Before

Planned Water-Use Zones

■ High (turf areas)

▤ Moderate

▥ Low

□ Very low

After

→ N

area by substituting ground covers, shrubs, and trees and adding a large deck. The slope was regraded and made into a rock garden.

Plantings are grouped in zones according to their water needs.

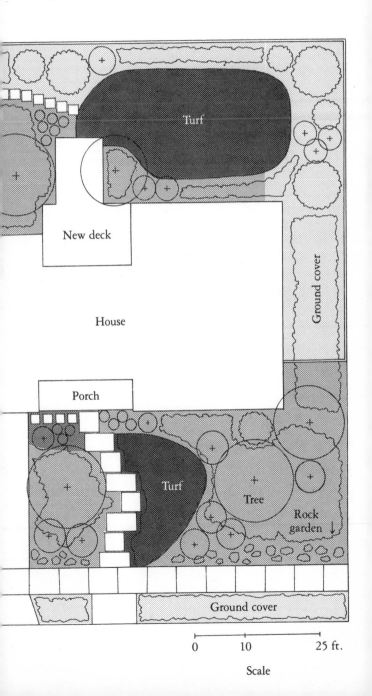

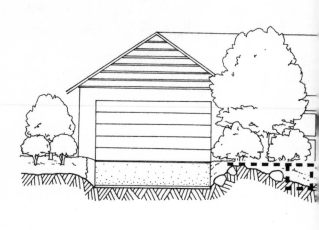

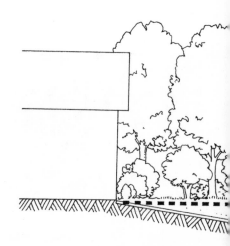

The elevations below are based on the After plan on page 43. The top drawing illustrates the front yard as seen from the street. The one below shows the same area as seen from the driveway, looking north.

The dotted lines indicate the original level of the land, before regrading.

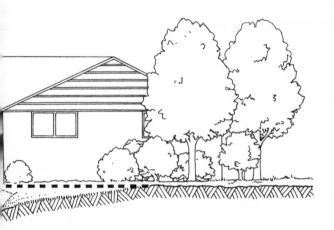

A Case Study

Water-Demand Analysis
The calculations below and on the facing page describe conditions in a
sample landscape before and after a water-saving plan was instituted.
(The particular lot and changes made are described in detail in the case
study beginning on page 39.) Read through the figures to find out
how you can analyze your own property for water efficiency. If you are
considering changes, complete a hypothetical "after" analysis to see
how much water—and maintenance time—it would save.

Before Water-Saving Alterations
These figures are based on the small plan shown on page 42. A similar
outline will work in analyzing any landscape.

1. Site description
a. Lot size   9990 square feet
b. Area covered by structures   2282 square feet
c. TOTAL open space (1a − 1b)   7708 square feet

2. Open-space use
a. Hard surfaces (walks, driveway, patio)   1250 square feet
b. TOTAL plantable area (1c − 2a)   6458 square feet

3. Plantable-area use
a. Turf (bluegrass)   6458 square feet
b. Shrubs and trees (included in 3a because they
are irrigated at the same time and rate as the turf)

4. Water demand
a. Turf (2b × 8* gallons/sq. ft./growing season)   51,664 gallons
b. Steep slopes and narrow turf strips[†]   924 gallons
c. TOTAL water demand   52,588 gallons/
                                                     growing season

5. Water cost (@ $1.50 per 1,000 gallons) $78.90

[†]These areas require more water than the level ground because water is
wasted as it runs off or misses the targeted irrigation area. For such
inefficiencies, add 30 percent to the water-demand figure. Determine
the amount of problem area and multiply it by .30 times the water-
demand figure—in this case, 385 square feet × .30 × 8 = 924.

NOTE: It was also determined that this landscape required 60 hours of
mowing and trimming time per growing season to maintain.

After Water-Saving Alterations
The large map on page 43 indicates the changes that were made in the
landscape analyzed on the facing page. The following figures show
that 80 percent less water will be needed to maintain the new
landscape. It will be more attractive and functional as well.

1. Site description	
a. Lot size	9990 square feet
b. Area covered by structures	<u>2282 square feet</u>
c. TOTAL open space (1a − 1b)	7708 square feet
2. Open-space use	
a. Hard surfaces	<u>1729 square feet</u>
b. TOTAL plantable area (1c − 2a)	5979 square feet

3. Plantable-area use
(The area has now been divided into zones based on
four levels of water needs.)

a. Turf zones (tall fescue)	1190 square feet
b. Moderate water-need zones	188 square feet
c. Low water-need zones	1994 square feet
d. Very low water-need zones	2607 square feet

4. Water demand	
a. Turf grass zones (1190 × 4.5* gallons/sq. ft./ growing season)	5355 gallons
b. Moderate zones (188 × 3* gallons/sq. ft./ growing season)	564 gallons
c. Low zones (1994 × 1.5* gallons/sq. ft./ growing season)	2991 gallons
d. Very low zones (2607 × 0.5*gallons/sq. ft./ growing season)	1304 gallons
e. TOTAL water demand (sum of figures in 4, above)	10,214 gallons

5. Water cost (10.2 thousand gallons × $1.50 per thousand)	<u>$15.30</u>

*These figures should be available from local horticulturists or
nurseries. They are based on type of plants grown and climatic
conditions in your region. If the data you receive is expressed in terms
of the number of inches of extra irrigation needed, figure that there
is .62 gallon of water to each inch. In the case study, the turf required
13 inches of extra irrigation (13 × .62 = 8.06 gallons).

NOTE: Mowing and trimming time will be reduced by 75 percent,
but an increase in time required for periodic pruning and weeding of
new plants will give a net time savings of 25 percent.

The Color Plates

The plates on the following pages are divided
into five groups: Gardens, Flowers, Ground
Covers, Shrubs, and Trees. The first group
includes examples of beautiful gardens
designed with drought-tolerant plants. In
the sections that follow, you'll see over 300
species of plants from which to choose as you
create your own water-saving landscape.
Within each group, the photographs are
arranged by color and shape. For all of the
trees and some of the shrubs, two
photographs are shown—an overall view and
a detail of flowers or other attractive features.

Captions
The caption for each garden photograph
provides three kinds of information: the type
of area seen—a rock garden or a front-yard
planting, for example; the garden's location;
and some of the most important qualities of
the planting.

Captions for the plant photographs give
scientific and common names of each plant
and offer detailed information about height,
flower or fruit size, bloom time, and
hardiness. They also refer you to the
description given in the Encyclopedia of
Plants. A relative evaluation of drought-
tolerance is also provided; the terms given
express water needs roughly as follows:

Extremely drought-tolerant: Needs less than
14 inches of water per year

Very drought-tolerant: Needs about 16
inches of water per year

Moderately drought-tolerant: Needs about
18 inches of water per year

Fairly drought-tolerant: Needs about
20 inches of water per year

Slightly drought-tolerant: Needs about
22 inches of water per year

Consult the rainfall map at the back of this
book to determine the average amount of
yearly rainfall in your region.

Gardens

*Herb and Flower Gardens
at Herbfarm
Fall City, Washington*

When carefully planned, a water-efficient landscape can provide both food and beauty. This garden includes apple trees and herbs, in the background, as well as drought-resistant flowers, in the foreground. Santolina, coneflowers, verbena, and marigolds are planted between decorative, and useful, pathways.

Foliage Garden
Massachussetts

This naturalistic planting of Russian Olive, Japanese Maple, juniper, Mugo Pine, and cotoneaster needs only occasional pruning and cleaning to keep it looking attractive. It is a good example of how drought-tolerant foliage plants can be selected and arranged to provide beauty and shade with little or no need for irrigation.

Front-Yard Planting
Doylestown, Pennsylvania

A beautiful combination of rudbeckia, alyssum, sedum, and yew, this garden is a welcome alternative to the shrub-and-lawn treatment that is too often used in front yards. It also requires significantly less water and maintenance time to keep it looking attractive.

Perennial Garden
Shelburne Falls,
Massachusetts

This wide herbaceous border consists of lavender, phlox, bee balm, globe thistle, lilies, coreopsis, and gayfeather, among other flowering plants. It is a beautiful and wise use of a large, sunny area— and a water-efficient alternative to a large expanse of lawn. The natural stand of grass in the background requires minimal mowing and watering.

Silver-tone Garden
Chicago, Illinois

The silver color of the Lamb's-Ears, sage, and Snow-in-Summer in this backyard garden comes from tiny hairs on the leaves, which also serve to trap moisture. The stone walkway helps direct water to nearby plant roots, and the bench provides a shady resting place from which to enjoy the view.

Terraced Garden
Berkeley, California

Terracing is a dramatic and practical way to landscape steep embankments. Here, shelves have been dug into the bank and stabilized with rocks. The shelves catch and hold rainwater that would otherwise run off the site. Santolina, fleabane, Basket-of-Gold, gray-leaved euryops, and Dusty Miller are beautifully displayed.

*Seaside Garden
Boothbay Harbor,
Maine*

The daylilies, sumac,
gaillardia, sedum, and
rudbeckia in this pocket
garden will withstand
strong sun and winds
and require no more
than the natural
precipitation in the
area. The planting is
most effective in summer,
but the plants' foliage is
attractive from spring
through fall.

Courtyard Garden
Santa Fe, New Mexico

A su
adob
accen
Fla:
Sum
The
mic
soil

High walls and an
eastern exposure make
this garden cooler,
shadier, and less dry
than the surrounding
landscape so that its
lush-looking, drought-
tolerant plantings can

thrive. Quaking Aspen,
Mugo Pine, sedum,
thyme, and saxifrage
fill the area, with
container plants used as
accent points.

Flowers

Euphorbia epithymoides

Cushion Spurge
Plant height: 12 in.
Flowers: 1-in. clusters
Blooms in late spring
Zones 5–10

Extremely drought tolerant
p. 309

Thermopsis caroliniana

Carolina Lupine
Plant height: 3–5 ft.
Flowers: 10-in. spikes
Blooms in early summer
Zones 3–9

Very drought tolerant
p. 399

| *Solidago speciosa* | Noble Goldenrod
Plant height: 3–6 ft.
Flowers: ¼ in. wide
Blooms late summer to
fall
Zones 6–10 | Very drought tolerant
Tolerates partial shade
p. 392 |

| *Achillea filipendulina* 'Coronation Gold' | Fernleaf Yarrow
Plant height: 3 ft.
Flowers: 5-in. clusters
Blooms in summer and
fall
Zones 4–10 | Very drought tolerant
p. 245 |

Anthemis tinctoria
'Moonlight'

Golden Marguerite
Plant height: 2–3 ft.
Flowers: 2 in. wide
Blooms in summer and
fall
Zones 4–8

Moderately drought
tolerant
p. 251

Dyssodia tenuiloba

Dahlberg Daisy
Plant height: 6–12 in.
Flowers: 1 in. wide
Blooms early summer to
frost
Half-hardy annual

Moderately drought
tolerant
p. 298

Coreopsis verticillata   *Threadleaf Coreopsis*   *Very drought tolerant*
'Golden Shower'   *Plant height: 1–3 ft.*   *p. 287*
                          Flowers: 2 in. wide
                          Blooms summer to frost
                          Zones 4–10

Coreopsis tinctoria   *Golden Coreopsis*   *Very drought tolerant*
                          Plant height: 1½–3 ft.   *p. 286*
                          Flowers: 1¼ in. wide
                          Blooms summer to frost
                          Hardy annual

Oenothera tetragona

Common Sundrop
Plant height: 18 in.
Flowers: 2 in. wide
Blooms early to
midsummer
Zones 5–9

Very drought tolerant
Tolerates partial shade
p. 357

**Eschscholzia
californica**

California Poppy
Plant height: 8–24 in.
Flowers: 2–4 in. wide
Blooms spring to early
summer
Tender perennial grown
as a hardy annual

Extremely drought
tolerant
p. 306

Oenothera missourensis

Missouri Evening
Primrose
Plant height: 12–15 in.
Flowers: 5 in. wide
Blooms in summer
Zones 5–9

Very drought tolerant
Tolerates partial shade
p. 357

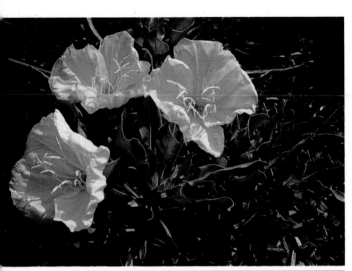

Ratibida columnifera

Prairie Coneflower
Plant height: 1–3½ ft.
Flowers: 1–1½ in. long
Blooms in summer
Zones 4–10

Extremely drought
tolerant
p. 378

Gazania rigens

Treasure Flower
Plant height: 8–10 in.
Flowers: 2–5 in. wide
Blooms late spring to fall
Tender perennial grown
as a tender annual

Extremely drought
tolerant
p. 315

Helichrysum
bracteatum
'Bikini'

Strawflower
Plant height: 1 ft.
Flowers: 1 in. wide
Blooms summer to frost
Half-hardy annual

Very drought tolerant
p. 324

| **Rudbeckia hirta** 'Gloriosa Daisy' | Gloriosa Daisy
Plant height: 1–3 ft.
Flowers: 2–6 in. wide
Blooms summer to frost
Half-hardy annual | Very drought tolerant
Tolerates light shade
p. 387 |

| **Helianthus annuus** hybrid | Common Sunflower
Plant height: to 12 ft.
Flowers: 3–12 in.
Blooms summer to frost
Tender annual | Extremely drought tolerant
p. 324 |

Gaillardia aristata

Blanketflower
Plant height: 2–3 ft.
Flowers: 3–4 in. wide
Blooms early summer to
frost
Zones 3–8

Very drought tolerant
p. 313

Geum reptans

Avens
Plant height: 12 in.
Flowers: 1½ in. wide
Blooms in late spring
Zones 5–9

Moderately drought
tolerant
Tolerates partial shade
p. 317

Papaver nudicaule

*Iceland Poppy
Plant height: 12 in.
Flowers: 1–3 in. wide
Blooms spring to summer
Perennial grown as a
half-hardy annual*

*Moderately drought
tolerant
p. 360*

Arctotis stoechadifolia

*Blue-eyed African Daisy
Plant height: 2½–4 ft.
Flowers: 3 in. wide
Blooms in spring or fall
Tender perennial grown
as a tender annual*

*Very drought tolerant
p. 255*

Erysimum perofskianum

Blister-Cress
Plant height: 2 ft.
Flowers: ½ in. wide
Blooms late spring to early summer
Hardy annual

Moderately drought tolerant
p. 305

Kniphofia uvaria

Red-hot Poker
Plant height: 2–4 ft.
Flowers: 1½–2 in. long
Blooms early summer to fall
Zones 5–10

Moderately drought tolerant
p. 334

sclepias tuberosa   Butterfly Weed   Very drought tolerant
                         Plant height: 1–3 ft.   p. 259
                         Flowers: 2-in. clusters
                         Blooms in midsummer
                         Zones 4–9

ecomaria capensis   Cape Honeysuckle   Moderately drought
                         Plant height: to 20 ft. as tolerant
                         vine or 6 ft. as shrub   Tolerates partial shade
                         Flowers: 2 in. long   p. 398
                         Blooms year-round
                         Zones 9–10

Penstemon pinifolius Pine-leaved Penstemon   Very drought tolerant
                              Plant height: 12–15 in.   *Tolerates partial shade*
                              Flowers: 1 in. long   *p. 360*
                              Blooms in summer
                              Zones 5–9

Helipterum roseum *Everlasting*   *Moderately drought*
                              Plant height: 2 ft.   *tolerant*
                              Flowers: 1–2 in. wide *p. 325*
                              Blooms summer to frost
                              Tender annual

Lychnis chalcedonica

Maltese Cross
Plant height: 18–30 in.
Flowers: 1 in. wide
Blooms early to
midsummer
Zones 4–8

Moderately drought
tolerant
Tolerates light shade
p. 346

Petunia × hybrida
'Flash Series'

Common Garden Petunia
Plant height: 8–18 in.
Flowers: 2–5 in. wide
Blooms early summer to
frost
Half-hardy annual

Extremely drought
tolerant
Tolerates light shade
p. 363

Malva alcea   Hollyhock Mallow   *Slightly drought tolerant*
                 Plant height: 2–4 ft.   *Tolerates partial shade*
                 Flowers: 2 in. wide   *p. 347*
                 Blooms in summer
                 Zones 4–9

Callirhoe involucrata   Finger Poppy Mallow   Extremely drought
                           Plant height: 6–12 in.   tolerant
                           Flowers: 1½–2½ in.   p. 269
                           wide
                           Blooms in summer
                           Zones 4–8

Geranium sanguineum var. *lancastriense*

Blood-red Cranesbill
Plant height: 12 in.
Flowers: 1 in. wide
Blooms late spring to
early summer
Zones 4–10

Moderately drought
tolerant
Tolerates light shade
p. 316

Calandrinia umbellata

Rock Purslane
Plant height: 6 in.
Flowers: ¾ in. wide
Blooms in summer
Half-hardy annual

Extremely drought
tolerant
p. 268

Mirabilis multiflora

Desert Four-O'Clock
Plant height: 2 ft.
Flowers: 1½–2 in. wide
Blooms midsummer to
frost
Zones 6–10

*Extremely drought
tolerant
p. 351*

*Mesembryanthemum
crystallinum*

Ice Plant
Plant height: 8 in.
Flowers: ¾–1¼ in.
wide
Blooms in spring
Tender annual

*Extremely drought
tolerant
p. 349*

Cosmos bipinnatus   Garden Cosmos   Moderately drought
                        Plant height: 3–4 ft.   tolerant
                        Flowers: 3–6 in. wide   p. 289
                        Blooms summer to frost
                        Tender annual

Echinacea purpurea   Purple Coneflower   Very drought tolerant
                         Plant height: 2–4 ft.   Tolerates light shade
                         Flowers: 3–6 in. wide   p. 298
                         Blooms mid- to late
                         summer
                         Zones 4–10

Achillea millefolium
'Fire King'

Common Yarrow
Plant height: 2½ ft.
Flowers: 2- to 3-in.
clusters
Blooms in summer and
fall
Zones 3–10

Very drought tolerant
p. 245

Gomphrena globosa
'Buddy'

Globe Amaranth
Plant height: 8–20 in.
Flowers: 1 in. wide
Blooms summer to frost
Tender annual

Very drought tolerant
p. 320

Armeria maritima   Common Thrift   Very drought tolerant
                            Plant height: 6 in.   p. 255
                            Flowers: ¾-in. clusters
                            Blooms mid-spring to fall
                            Zones 4–9

Dianthus plumarius   Grass Pink   Moderately drought
'Agatha'   Plant height: 9–18 in. tolerant
                            Flowers: 1½ in. wide   Tolerates shade
                            Blooms late spring to   p. 296
                            summer
                            Zones 4–10

Gypsophila repens 'Rosea'

Creeping Baby's-Breath
Plant height: 6–8 in.
Flowers: ¼ in. wide
Blooms in summer
Zones 4–8

Moderately drought
tolerant
Tolerates shade
p. 322

Cleome hasslerana

Spider Flower
Plant height: 4–5 ft.
Flowers: 6–7 in. wide
Blooms summer to frost
Half-hardy annual

Extremely drought
tolerant
p. 285

Coronilla varia

Crown Vetch
Plant height: 18–24 in.
Flowers: ½ in. long
Blooms in summer
Zones 4–8

Extremely drought
tolerant
Tolerates light shade
p. 287

**Brachycome
iberidifolia**

Swan River Daisy
Plant height: 8–18 in.
Flowers: 1–2 in. wide
Blooms late spring to
early summer
Half-hardy annual

Moderately drought
tolerant
p. 266

Aster tataricus

Tartarian Aster
Plant height: 6–8 ft.
Flowers: 1 in. wide
Blooms late summer and
fall
Zones 4–8

Slightly drought tolerant
p. 260

Centaurea cyanus

Bachelor's Button
Plant height: 1–2 ft.
Flowers: 1½ in. wide
Blooms in summer
Hardy annual

Moderately drought
tolerant
p. 277

Catananche caerulea

Cupid's Dart
Plant height: 2 ft.
Flowers: 2 in. wide
Blooms in summer
Zones 5–9 or hardy
annual

Moderately drought
tolerant
p. 273

Centaurea montana
'Violetta'

Mountain Bluet
Plant height: 18–24 in.
Flowers: 3 in. wide
Blooms in late spring
Zones 3–8

Very drought tolerant
p. 278

Monarda fistulosa

Wild Bergamot
Plant height: 3–4 ft.
Flowers: 1½ in. long
Blooms in summer
Zones 4–9

Extremely drought
tolerant
Tolerates partial shade
p. 351

Tradescantia hirsuticaulis

Spiderwort
Plant height: 12 in.
Flowers: 1 in. wide
Blooms late spring to
early summer
Zones 6–9

Moderately drought
tolerant
Tolerates partial shade
p. 401

Anemone pulsatilla   Pasque Flower   Moderately drought
                         Plant height: 9–12 in.   tolerant
                         Flowers: 2 in. wide   Tolerates partial shade
                         Blooms in early spring   p. 250
                         Zones 5–8

Ipomoea tricolor   Morning Glory   Moderately drought
                         Plant height: 10 ft.   tolerant
                         (vine)   p. 332
                         Flowers: 4–5 in. wide
                         Blooms summer to frost
                         Tender annual

Penstemon strictus

Rocky Mountain Penstemon
Plant height: 1–2½ ft.
Flowers: ¾–1¾ in. long
Blooms in summer
Zones 4–9

Very drought tolerant
Tolerates partial shade
p. 360

Baptisia australis

Blue False Indigo
Plant height: 3–5 ft.
Flowers: 1 in. wide
Blooms late spring to early summer
Zones 4–9

Moderately drought tolerant
p. 263

Lavandula angustifolia

English Lavender
Plant height: 1–3 ft.
Flowers: 3- to 8-in. spikes
Blooms early to late summer
Zones 5–10

Moderately drought tolerant
p. 338

Liatris punctata

Dotted Gay-Feather
Plant height: 12–24 in.
Flowers: 6-in. spikes
Blooms in summer
Zones 4–10

Very drought tolerant
Tolerates light shade
p. 340

Hyssopus officinalis Hyssop Very drought tolerant
Plant height: 2–3 ft. p. 329
Flowers: ½ in. long
Blooms summer to fall
Zones 3–10

Limonium latifolium Sea Lavender Moderately drought
Plant height: 1½– tolerant
2½ ft. p. 342
Flowers: ⅛ in. wide
Blooms summer to early
fall
Zones 4–10

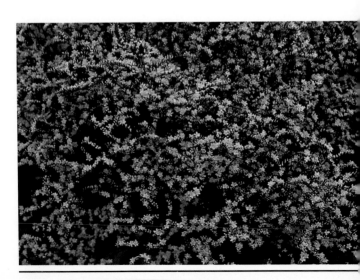

Perovskia atriplicifolia

Azure Sage
Plant height: 3–5 ft.
Flowers: ¼ in. wide
Blooms mid- to late
summer
Zones 5–8

Moderately drought
tolerant
p. 362

Echium lycopsis

Viper's Bugloss
Plant height: 2 ft.
Flowers: ½ in. wide
Blooms in spring
Hardy annual

Moderately drought
tolerant
p. 299

Cynoglossum amabile
'Blanche Burpee'

Chinese Forget-Me-Not
Plant height: 18–24 in.
Flowers: 1/3 in. long
Blooms in spring
Hardy annual

Slightly drought tolerant
Tolerates light shade
p. 293

Gypsophila elegans
'Golden Garden
Market'

Annual Baby's-Breath
Plant height: 10–
18 in.
Flowers: 1/4–1 in. wide
Blooms in summer
Hardy annual

Moderately drought
tolerant
Tolerates shade
p. 322

Linum perenne

Perennial Flax
Plant height: 1–2 ft.
Flowers: 1 in. wide
Blooms late spring to late
summer
Zones 5–10

Very drought tolerant
p. 343

Polygonum aubertii

Silver-Lace Vine
Plant height: to 25 ft.
(vine)
Flowers: ⅛ in. wide
Blooms late summer to
fall
Zones 4–7

Extremely drought
tolerant
p. 371

Clematis
ligusticifolia

Western Virgin's Bower
Plant height: to 20 ft.
(vine)
Flowers: 1 in. wide
Blooms in summer
Zones 4–10

Very drought tolerant
Tolerates partial shade
p. 284

Anaphalis
margaritacea

Pearly Everlasting
Plant height: 20 in.
Flowers: ¼ in. wide
Blooms in summer
Zones 4–9

Moderately drought
tolerant
p. 249

Lonicera japonica
'Halliana'

Hall's Honeysuckle
Plant height: 20–30 ft.
(vine)
Flowers: 1–1½ in. long
Blooms late spring to
early summer
Zones 5–9

Moderately drought
tolerant
Tolerates shade
p. 345

Filipendula vulgaris
'Flore Pleno'

Dropwort
Plant height: 2–3 ft.
Flowers: ½–¾ in. wide
Blooms early to
midsummer
Zones 4–9

Slightly drought tolerant
Tolerates partial shade
p. 312

Gaura lindheimeri *White Gaura* *Very drought tolerant*
 Plant height: 4 ft. *p. 314*
 Flowers: ½–1 in. wide
 Blooms in summer
 Zones 6–9

Matricaria recutita *German Chamomile* *Fairly drought tolerant*
 Plant height: 1–2½ ft. *p. 348*
 Flowers: 1 in. wide
 Blooms in summer
 Hardy annual

Catharanthus roseus
'Albus'

Madagascar Periwinkle
Plant height: to 2 ft.
Flowers: 1–1½ in. wide
Blooms summer to frost
Tender perennial grown
as a tender annual

Very drought tolerant
Tolerates partial shade
p. 274

Dimorphotheca
sinuata

Cape Marigold
Plant height: 4–12 in.
Flowers: 1½ in. wide
Blooms in summer
Tender annual

Moderately drought
tolerant
p. 296

Sedum kamtschaticum

Orange Stonecrop
Plant height: 6–12 in.
Blooms year-round
Zones 4–10

Extremely drought
tolerant
Tolerates partial shade
p. 390

Achillea tomentosa

Woolly Yarrow
Plant height: 6–10 in.
Effective spring to summer
Zones 3–10

Very drought tolerant
p. 245

Aurinia saxatilis   Basket-of-Gold   Fairly drought tolerant
'Citrina'   Plant height: 6–12 in.   p. 261
                             Effective spring to summer
                             Zones 4–10

Eriogonum   Sulphur-Flower   Very drought tolerant
umbellatum   Plant height: to 12 in.   p. 303
                            Effective spring to fall
                            Zones 9–10

Euphorbia myrsinites Myrtle Euphorbia
Plant height: 3–6 in.
Effective spring to fall
Zones 5–10

Extremely drought
tolerant
p. 309

Opuntia humifusa Prickly Pear
Plant height: 12 in.
Effective spring to fall
Zones 5–10

Extremely drought
tolerant
p. 358

Potentilla tabernaemontani

Spring Cinquefoil
Plant height: 2–6 in.
Effective spring to fall
Zones 4–10

Moderately drought tolerant
p. 372

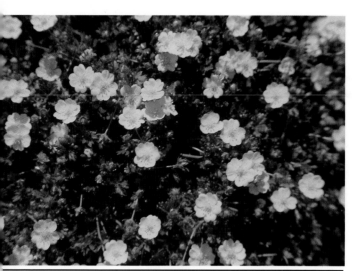

Portulaca grandiflora

Garden Portulaca
Plant height: 4–6 in.
Effective spring to frost
Tender annual

Very drought tolerant
p. 372

Hemerocallis
'Hyperion'

Daylily
Plant height: 4 ft.
Effective spring through fall
Zones 4–10

Moderately drought tolerant
Tolerates partial shade
p. 326

Delosperma
nubigenum

Ice Plant
Plant height: 1–2 in.
Effective year-round
Zones 5–10

Moderately drought tolerant
p. 295

Arctotheca calendula   *Cape Weed*   *Moderately drought*
                       Plant height: to 12 in.   *tolerant*
                       Effective spring to summer   *p. 254*
                       Zones 9–10

Santolina   *Lavender Cotton*   *Very drought tolerant*
chamaecyparissus   *Plant height: 1–2 ft.*   *p. 388*
                       Effective spring to fall
                       Zones 6–9

Helianthemum
nummularium
'Wisley Pink'

Rock Rose
Plant height: 6–12 in.
Effective spring to summer
Zones 6–10

Moderately drought
tolerant
p. 323

Phlox subulata
'Sampson'

Ground Pink
Plant height: 6 in.
Effective spring to fall
Zones 4–10

Fairly drought tolerant
p. 366

Saponaria ocymoides

Rock Soapwort
Plant height: 4–8 in.
Effective spring to summer
Zones 4–9

Moderately drought
tolerant
p. 389

*Lantana
montevidensis*

Weeping Lantana
Plant height: 1–2 ft.
Effective year-round
Tender perennial grown
as a half-hardy annual

Very drought tolerant
p. 337

Sedum spectabile

Showy Stonecrop
Plant height: to 2 ft.
Effective spring to fall
Zones 4–10

Extremely drought
tolerant
Tolerates partial shade
p. 390

**Osteospermum
fruticosum**

Trailing African Daisy
Plant height: 12 in.
Effective year-round
Zones 9–10

Slightly drought tolerant
p. 359

Sedum spurium   Two-row Stonecrop   Extremely drought
                      Plant height: 3–6 in.   tolerant
                      Effective year-round   Tolerates partial shade
                      Zones 5–10   p. 391

Delosperma cooperi   Hardy Ice Plant   Very drought tolerant
                         Plant height: 6 in.   p. 295
                         Effective year-round
                         Zones 7–10

Epimedium grandiflorum 'Rose Queen'

Longspur Epimedium
Plant height: 12 in.
Effective spring to fall
Zones 5–10

Slightly drought tolerant
Tolerates shade
p. 301

Sedum cauticola

Shortleaf Stonecrop
Plant height: 3 in.
Effective spring to fall
Zones 5–10

Extremely drought tolerant
Tolerates partial shade
p. 390

Abronia umbellata   *Prostrate Sand Verbena*   *Very drought tolerant*
    Plant height: 1–2 in.   *p. 242*
    Effective year-round
    Zone 8; or grown as a
    tender annual

Thymus   *Woolly Thyme*   *Moderately drought*
pseudolanuginosus   *Plant height: 1 in.*   *tolerant*
    Effective spring to summer   *p. 400*
    Zones 4–10

Teucrium chamaedrys

Wall Germander
Plant height: 10–24 in.
Effective spring to fall
Zones 5–10

Moderately drought tolerant
Tolerates partial shade
p. 398

Nemophila menziesii

Baby Blue-Eyes
Plant height: 1 ft.
Effective spring to fall
Hardy annual

Moderately drought tolerant
Tolerates shade
p. 355

Campanula
poscharskyana
'E. K. Toogood'

Serbian Bellflower
Plant height: 4–6 in.
Effective spring and
summer
Zones 4–8

Slightly drought tolerant
Tolerates light shade
p. 270

Nemophila maculata

Five Spot
Plant height: 12 in.
Effective spring to fall
Hardy annual

Very drought tolerant
Tolerates afternoon shade
p. 354

Rosmarinus officinalis 'Prostratus'

Trailing Rosemary
Plant height: 6–24 in.
Effective year-round
Zones 7–10

Very drought tolerant
p. 385

Thymus serpyllum

Creeping Thyme
Plant height: to 4 in.
Effective spring to summer
Zones 4–10

Moderately drought
tolerant
p. 400

Iberis sempervirens   *Candytuft*   *Slightly drought tolerant*
Plant height: to 12 in.   *p. 330*
Effective spring to summer
Zones 4–10

Polygonum affine   *Himalayan Fleeceflower*   *Extremely drought*
'Superbum'   *Plant height: to 18 in.*   *tolerant*
Effective year-round   *p. 371*
Zones 4–7

Erigeron compositus
Fleabane
Plant height: 4–8 in.
Effective spring to fall
Zones 4–10

Very drought tolerant
Tolerates light shade
p. 303

Tanacetum vulgare var. crispum
Common Tansy
Plant height: 2–3 ft.
Effective spring to fall
Zones 4–10

Moderately drought
tolerant
Tolerates shade
p. 396

Arabis caucasica
'Snow Cap'

Wall Cress
Plant height: 12 in.
Effective spring to summer
Zones 4–8

Fairly drought tolerant
Tolerates partial shade
p. 252

Vaccinium
angustifolium

Low-Bush Blueberry
Plant height: 1–2 ft.
Effective spring to fall
Zones 3–9

Slightly drought tolerant
p. 403

Baccharis pilularis   Dwarf Coyote Bush
Plant height: 1–2 ft.
Effective spring to fall
Zones 7–10

Slightly drought tolerant
Tolerates shade
p. 262

Microbiota decussata   Siberian Carpet Cypress
Plant height: 1½–2 ft.
Effective year-round
Zones 3–10

Moderately drought
tolerant
Tolerates shade
p. 350

erilla frutescens
tropurpurea'

Beefsteak Plant
Plant height: 1½–3 ft.
Effective spring to frost
Tender annual

Slightly drought tolerant
Tolerates light shade
p. 361

ochia scoparia
ar. tricophylla
hildsii'

Summer Cypress
Plant height: 2–3 ft.
Effective spring to frost
Half-hardy annual

Extremely drought
tolerant
p. 335

Juniperus
horizontalis
'Wiltonii'

Blue Rug Juniper
Plant height: 6 in.
Effective year-round
Zones 3–9

Fairly drought tolerant
p. 333

Arctostaphylos
uva-ursi

Bearberry
Plant height: 2–8 in.
Effective year-round
Zones 3–7

Fairly drought tolerant
Tolerates partial shade
p. 253

Cerastium tomentosum | Snow-in-Summer | Very drought tolerant
Plant height: to 6 in. | Tolerates light shade
Effective spring to summer | p. 278
Zones 4–10

Duchesnea indica | Mock Strawberry | Moderately drought
Plant height: 2–3 in. | tolerant
Effective spring to fall | Tolerates partial shade
Zones 4–10 | p. 297

Epimedium alpinum Alpine Epimedium
Plant height: 10 in.
Effective spring to fall
Zones 4–10

Slightly drought tolerant
Tolerates partial shade
p. 301

Mahonia repens Creeping Mahonia
Plant height: 12–24 in.
Effective year-round
Zones 6–10

Moderately drought
tolerant
Tolerates shade
p. 346

Aegopodium
podagraria
'Variegatum'

Goutweed
Plant height: 6–12 in.
Effective spring to fall
Zones 4–9

Extremely drought
tolerant
Tolerates partial shade
p. 246

Stachys byzantina
'Silver Carpet'

Lamb's-Ears
Plant height: 8 in.
Effective spring to fall
Zones 5–10

Moderately drought
tolerant
p. 394

***Antennaria dioica*
var. *rosea***

Pussytoes
Plant height: 4–12 in.
Effective spring to fall
Zones 4–8

Extremely drought
tolerant
p. 250

***Artemisia
ludoviciana***

Western Sage
Plant height: 2–3 ft.
Effective spring to fall
Zones 5–9

Extremely drought
tolerant
p. 258

Leontopodium
alpinum

Edelweiss
Plant height: 4–12 in.
Effective spring to frost
Zones 4–10

Extremely drought
tolerant
p. 339

Artemisia
schmidtiana
'Silver Mound'

Silver Mound Artemisia
Plant height: 4–12 in.
Effective spring to fall
Zones 4–9

Very drought tolerant
p. 258

Artemisia
absinthium
'Lambrook Silver'

Common Wormwood
Plant height: 2¹/₂–4 ft.
Effective spring to fall
Zones 4–9

Extremely drought
tolerant
p. 258

Senecio cineraria
'Silver Dust'

Dusty Miller
Plant height: 2¹/₂ ft.
Effective spring to fall
Half-hardy annual

Extremely drought
tolerant
Tolerates light shade
p. 391

Artemisia stellerana   Beach Wormwood   Extremely drought
                             Plant height: 2½ ft.   tolerant
                             Effective spring to fall   p. 258
                             Zones 3–9

Artemisia tridentata   Big Sagebrush   Extremely drought
                             Plant height: 4–8 ft.   tolerant
                             Effective spring to fall   p. 258
                             Zones 4–10

Eryngium bourgatii   *Mediterranean Eryngo*   *Very drought tolerant*
Plant height: 2 ft.   *p. 304*
Effective spring to frost
Zones 5–7

Yucca glauca   *Soapweed*   *Extremely drought*
Plant height: 3 ft.   *tolerant*
Effective year-round   *p. 405*
Zones 5–10

Ephedra viridis | Green Mormon Tea | Extremely drought
| Plant height: 4 ft. | tolerant
| Effective year-round | p. 301
| Zones 5–10 |

Yucca filamentosa | Adam's Needle | Extremely drought
'Variegata' | Plant height: 3–5 ft. | tolerant
| Effective year-round | p. 405
| Zones 5–10 |

Cortaderia selloana   *Pampas Grass*   *Very drought tolerant*
                        Plant height: 8–12 ft.   *p. 288*
                        Effective year-round
                        Zones 8–10

Briza maxima   *Quaking Grass*   *Moderately drought*
                        Plant height: 1–2 ft.   *tolerant*
                        Effective spring to fall   *p. 266*
                        Hardy annual

Liriope spicata   *Creeping Lily-turf*   *Slightly drought tolerant*
                             Plant height: 8–10 in.   *Tolerates shade*
                             Effective spring to fall   *p. 344*
                             Zones 5–10

Bouteloua gracilis   *Mosquito Grass*   *Extremely drought*
                             Plant height: 2 ft.   *tolerant*
                             Effective spring to fall   *p. 264*
                             Zones 5–8

Eragrostis trichodes   *Sand Love Grass*   *Very drought tolerant*
Plant height: to 4 ft.   *p. 302*
Effective spring to fall
Zones 5–9

Arrhenatherum   *Bulbous Oat Grass*   *Moderately drought*
elatius bulbosum   *Plant height: 3½ ft.*   *tolerant*
'Variegatum'   *Effective spring to fall*   *Tolerates light shade*
Zones 5–8   *p. 257*

Phalaris arundinacea picta

Ribbon Grass
Plant height: to 3 ft.
Effective spring to summer
Zones 4–10

Fairly drought tolerant
Tolerates shade
p. 364

Festuca ovina glauca

Blue Fescue
Plant height: 12 in.
Effective year-round
Zones 4–9

Extremely drought tolerant
Tolerates partial shade
p. 311

Shrubs

Colutea arborescens
Common Bladder Senna
Plant height: 5–8 ft.
Zones 6–9
Moderately drought tolerant
p. 286

Cytisus scoparius
'Goldfinch'
Scotch Broom
Plant height: 4–9 ft.
Zones 6–10
Moderately drought tolerant
p. 294

Colutea arborescens   *Common Bladder Senna*   p. 286
Flowers: 1 in. long
Blooms in spring and
summer

Cytisus scoparius   *Scotch Broom*   p. 294
Flowers: 1 in. wide
Blooms in mid-spring

Berberis hematocarpa   Red Barberry
Plant height: 3–6 ft.
Attractive fall color
Zones 4–8

Moderately drought tolerant
Tolerates shade
p. 263

Spartium junceum   Spanish Broom
Plant height: 6–8 ft.
Flowers: 18-in. clusters
Blooms summer to fall
Zones 8–10

Very drought tolerant
p. 393

Berberis hematocarpa   Red Barberry   p. 263
                        Flowers: ¼ in. wide
                        Blooms in spring

Chrysothamnus   Rabbitbrush   Extremely drought
nauseosus   Plant height: 2–7 ft.   tolerant
                       Flowers: 4-in. clusters   p. 283
                       Blooms in late summer
                       Zones 3–10

Caragana frutex   *Russian Pea Shrub*   *Extremely drought*
Plant height: to 10 ft.   *tolerant*
Flowers: ¾ in. wide   *p. 270*
Blooms in spring
Zones 2–7

Genista tinctoria   *Woadwaxen*   *Moderately drought*
Plant height: 3 ft.   *tolerant*
Flowers: 1- to 3-in.   *p. 316*
clusters
Blooms in late spring
Zones 5–10

Acacia redolens **var. *prostrata***

Acacia
Plant height: 1–2 ft.
Flowers: 2-in. clusters
Blooms in spring
Zones 9–10

Moderately drought
tolerant
p. 243

Caragana arborescens

Siberian Pea Shrub
Plant height: 7–9 ft.
Flowers: 3/4 in. long
Blooms in spring
Zones 2–7

Extremely drought
tolerant
p. 270

Hypericum calycinum Aaronsbeard St. Johnswort
Plant height: 12 in.
Flowers: 2 in. wide
Blooms in summer
Zones 5–10

Moderately drought tolerant
Tolerates partial shade
p. 328

Cytisus × praecox Warminster Broom
Plant height: 6–10 ft.
Flowers: 1 in. long
Blooms in mid-spring
Zones 7–10

Moderately drought tolerant
p. 294

Hypericum patulum
'Hidcote'

Hidcote Goldencup St.
Johnswort
Plant height: 18–24 in.
Flowers: 2 in. wide
Blooms in summer
Zones 7–10

Moderately drought
tolerant
p. 328

Cassia artemisiodes

Feathery Cassia
Plant height: to 4 ft.
Flowers: 2- to 6-in.
clusters
Blooms early spring to
winter
Zones 9–10

Extremely drought
tolerant
p. 272

Rosa foetida bicolor
Austrian Copper
Plant height: 6–8 ft.
Flowers: 2–2½ in. wide
Blooms in early summer
Zones 6–10

Moderately drought
tolerant
p. 384

Nerium oleander
Common Oleander
Plant height: 8–20 ft.
Flowers: 2½ in. wide
Blooms in summer
Zones 8–10

Extremely drought
tolerant
p. 355

Chaenomeles speciosa
'Phylis Moore'

Common Flowering
Quince
Plant height: 6–10 ft.
Flowers: 1–2 in. wide
Blooms in early spring
Zones 5–10

Moderately drought
tolerant
p. 282

Chaenomeles speciosa
'Toyo Nishiki'

Common Flowering
Quince
Plant height: 6–10 ft.
Flowers: 1–2 in. wide
Blooms in early spring
Zones 5–10

Moderately drought
tolerant
p. 282

Feijoa sellowiana

Pineapple Guava
Plant height: to 20 ft.
Flowers: ¾–1½ in.
wide
Blooms in spring
Zones 8–10

Moderately drought
tolerant
p. 310

Rosa rugosa

Rugosa Rose
Plant height: 4–6 ft.
Zones 3–10

Very drought tolerant
p. 385

| *Leptospermum scoparium* | New Zealand Tea Tree
Plant height: 10–25 ft.
Flowers: ½ in. wide
Blooms in spring or summer
Zones 9–10 | Moderately drought tolerant
p. 339 |

| *Rosa rugosa* | Rugosa Rose
Flowers: 3½ in. wide
Blooms in summer | p. 385 |

Rosa rubrifolia   *Redleaf Rose*   *Moderately drought*
Plant height: 6 ft.   *tolerant*
Zones 2–10   *p. 384*

Kolkwitzia amabilis   *Beauty Bush*   *Fairly drought tolerant*
Plant height: 6–12 ft.   *Tolerates partial shade*
Flowers: ½ in. long   *p. 336*
Blooms in late spring
Zones 5–8

Rosa rubrifolia   *Redleaf Rose*   *p. 384*
                             Flowers: 1½ in. wide
                             Blooms in early summer

Raphiolepis indica   *Indian Hawthorn*   *Extremely drought*
'Rosea'   *Plant height: 3–5 ft.*   *tolerant*
                             Flowers: ½ in. wide   *Tolerates partial shade*
                             Blooms in spring   *p. 378*
                             Zones 8–10

Robinia hispida   *Rose Acacia*   *Very drought tolerant*
Plant height: 3–7 ft.   *p. 382*
Flowers: 3-in. clusters
Blooms in late spring
Zones 5–10

Syringa meyeri   *Meyer Lilac*   *Moderately drought*
'Palibin'   *Plant height: 4–8 ft.*   *tolerant*
Flowers: 4-in. clusters   *p. 395*
Blooms in late spring
Zones 4–8

yringa ✕ *persica*   Persian Lilac   Fairly drought tolerant
                         Plant height: 5–6 ft.   p. 395
                         Flowers: 3-in. clusters
                         Blooms in late spring
                         Zones 4–8

uddleia davidii   Orange-eye Butterfly   Moderately drought
ar. *nanhoensis*   Bush   tolerant
                        Plant height: 6–10 ft.   p. 267
                        Flowers: 12-in. spikes
                        Blooms late summer to
                        fall
                        Zones 5–9

Ceanothus griseus
var. *horizontalis*

Carmel Creeper
Plant height: 1½–3 ft.
Flowers: 2-in. clusters
Blooms in early spring
Zones 8–10

Fairly drought tolerant
p. 275

Buddleia alternifolia
'Argentea'

Alternate Leaf Butterfly
Bush
Plant height: 10–20 ft.
Flowers: ¾-in. clusters
Blooms in early summer
Zones 6–8

Moderately drought
tolerant
p. 267

Caryopteris ×
clandonensis
'Blue Mist'

Bluebeard
Plant height: to 2 ft.
Flowers: ½ in. long
Blooms in summer
Zones 5–10

Fairly drought tolerant
p. 271

Ceanothus cyaneus
'Sierra Blue'

San Diego Ceanothus
Plant height: 10–12 ft.
Flowers: 5-in. clusters
Blooms in early spring
Zones 8–10

Fairly drought tolerant
p. 275

Philadelphus microphyllus

Little Leaf Mock-Orange
Plant height: 4 ft.
Flowers: 1 in. wide
Blooms in late spring
Zones 6–10

Very drought tolerant
Tolerates partial shade
p. 365

Romneya coulteri

California Tree Poppy
Plant height: to 8 ft.
Flowers: 6 in. wide
Blooms in late summer
Zones 7–10

Very drought tolerant
p. 383

Rubus deliciosus 'Tridel'

Rocky Mountain
Flowering Raspberry
Plant height: 6 ft.
Flowers: 2 in. wide
Blooms in late spring
Zones 6–10

Very drought tolerant
p. 386

Nerium oleander

Common Oleander
Plant height: 8–20 ft.
Flowers: 2½ in. wide
Blooms in summer
Zones 8–10

Extremely drought
tolerant
p. 355

Lonicera maackii

Amur Honeysuckle
Plant height: 10–15 ft.
Flowers: ⅔ in. long
Blooms in mid-spring
Zones 3–9

Slightly drought tolerant
Tolerates shade
p. 345

Ribes cereum

Squaw Currant
Plant height: 3 ft.
Flowers: 3-in. clusters
Blooms in early summer
Zones 5–10

Very drought tolerant
Tolerates shade
p. 381

Ligustrum vulgare

European Privet
Plant height: 5–15 ft.
Flowers: 3-in. clusters
Blooms in late spring
Zones 4–10

Extremely drought tolerant
Tolerates partial shade
p. 341

Buddleia davidii hybrid

Orange-eye Butterfly
Bush
Plant height: 6–10 ft.
Flowers: 5- to 12-in.
spikes
Blooms late summer to
fall
Zones 5–9

Moderately drought tolerant
p. 267

Amelanchier alnifolia   Western Serviceberry   Moderately drought
Plant height: 10–12 ft.   tolerant
Flowers: ¾ in. wide   Tolerates partial shade
Blooms in spring   p. 248
Attractive fall color
Zones 3–8

Myrtus communis   True Myrtle   Slightly drought tolerant
'Compacta'   Plant height: 2–3 ft.   Tolerates partial shade
Flowers: ¾ in. wide   p. 354
Blooms in summer
Zones 9–10

Cistus × *hybridus*   White Rockrose   Very drought tolerant
                        Plant height: 2–4 ft.   p. 283
                        Flowers: 1½ in. wide
                        Blooms in late spring
                        Zones 8–10

Fendlera rupicola   False Mock-Orange   Very drought tolerant
                      Plant height: 5–6 ft.   p. 311
                      Flowers: 1½ in. wide
                      Blooms in mid-spring
                      Zones 6–10

Physocarpus opulifolius

Common Ninebark
Plant height: 5–10 ft.
Flowers: 2-in. clusters
Blooms in late spring
Attractive fall color
Zones 3–8

Fairly drought tolerant
Tolerates partial shade
p. 367

Ligustrum japonicum

Japanese Privet
Plant height: 7–10 ft.
Flowers: 4- to 6-in.
clusters
Blooms in spring
Zones 7–10

Extremely drought
tolerant
Tolerates partial shade
p. 341

Aronia arbutifolia   Red Chokeberry   Fairly drought tolerant
                           Plant height: 4 ft.   p. 256
                           Flowers: 1½-in. clusters
                           Blooms in mid-spring
                           Attractive fall color
                           Zones 4–9

Holodiscus dumosus   Rock Spirea   Very drought tolerant
                           Plant height: 3–4 ft.   p. 328
                           Flowers: 7-in. clusters
                           Blooms in summer
                           Zones 6–10

Viburnum lantana
*Wayfaring-tree
Viburnum
Plant height: 10–15 ft.
Flowers: 4-in. clusters
Blooms in late spring
Zones 4–8*

*Very drought tolerant
Tolerates partial shade
p. 403*

Ligustrum vulgare
*European Privet
Plant height: 5–15 ft.
Flowers: 3-in. clusters
Blooms in late spring
Zones 4–10*

*Extremely drought
tolerant
Tolerates partial shade
p. 341*

Chamaebatiaria millefolium

Fernbush
Plant height: 5 ft.
Flowers: 4–6 in.
Blooms in midsummer
Zones 6–10

Extremely drought tolerant
p. 282

Raphiolepis indica

Indian Hawthorn
Plant height: 3–5 ft.
Flowers: ½-in. wide
Blooms in spring
Zones 8–10

Extremely drought tolerant
Tolerates partial shade
p. 378

Cercocarpus montanus   Mountain Mahogany
Plant height: 5–10 ft.
Zones 6–10
Extremely drought tolerant
p. 281

Atriplex canescens   Four-wing Saltbush
Plant height: 3–6 ft.
Zones 4–10
Very drought tolerant
p. 260

Cercocarpus ledifolius   Curl-leaf Mountain   Extremely drought
                              Mahogany   tolerant
                              Plant height: 20–30 ft.   p. 281
                              Zones 4–10

Cercocarpus   Mountain Mahogany   Extremely drought
intricatus   Plant height: to 10 ft.   tolerant
                              Zones 5–10   p. 281

Fallugia paradoxa
Apache-Plume
Plant height: 3–7 ft.
Fruits: small, with 1½-in. plumes
Fruits in fall
Zones 5–10

Extremely drought tolerant
Tolerates partial shade
p. 309

Cotinus coggygria 'Purpureus'
Common Smoke Tree
Plant height: 10–15 ft.
Fruits: 7- to 10-in. clusters
Fruits in summer
Attractive fall color
Zones 5–9

Slightly drought tolerant
p. 290

Cotinus coggygria

Common Smoke Tree
Plant height: 10–15 ft.
Fruits: 7- to 10-in.
clusters
Fruits in summer
Attractive fall color
Zones 5–9

Slightly drought tolerant
p. 290

Rhamnus frangula
'Asplenifolia'

Feathery Buckthorn
Plant height: 10–18 ft.
Fruits: ¼ in. wide
Fruits in summer
Zones 3–9

Fairly drought tolerant
Tolerates partial shade
p. 379

Forestiera neomexicana

Desert Olive
Plant height: to 10 ft.
Zones 5–10

Extremely drought tolerant
p. 313

Myrica pensylvanica

Northern Bayberry
Plant height: 3–10 ft.
Zones 3–9

Very drought tolerant
Tolerates partial shade
p. 353

Cotoneaster adpressus   *Creeping Cotoneaster*   *Moderately drought*
Plant height: 12–18 in.   *tolerant*
Fruits: 1/4–3/8 in. wide   *Tolerates partial shade*
Fruits in fall   *p. 291*
Zones 7–9

Cotoneaster   *Spreading Cotoneaster*   *Moderately drought*
divaricatus   *Plant height: 3–7 ft.*   *tolerant*
Zones 5–9   *p. 291*

Ilex vomitoria *Yaupon* *Extremely drought*
Plant height: 15–25 ft. *tolerant*
Zones 7–10 *Tolerates partial shade*
p. 331

Xylosma congestum *Xylosma* *Slightly drought tolerant*
Plant height: 8–10 ft. *Tolerates partial shade*
Zones 9–10 *p. 404*

Berberia thunbergii
'Aurea'

Japanese Barberry
Plant height: 4–6 ft.
Attractive fall color
Zones 4–8

Moderately drought
tolerant
Tolerates shade
p. 264

Ilex cornuta
'Rotunda'

Chinese Holly
Plant height: 6 ft.
Zones 7–9

Moderately drought
tolerant
p. 331

Berberis
× mentorensis

Mentor Barberry
Plant height: 5–7 ft.
Zones 4–8

Moderately drought
tolerant
Tolerates shade
p. 263

Elaeagnus pungens
'Variegata'

Thorny Elaeagnus
Plant height: 15 ft.
Zones 7–9

Extremely drought
tolerant
p. 300

Berberis thunbergii
'Atropurpurea'

Japanese Barberry
Plant height: 4–6 ft.
Zones 4–8

Moderately drought
tolerant
Tolerates shade
p. 264

Euonymus alata

Winged Euonymus
Plant height: 8–12 ft.
Fruits: ½ in. wide
Fruits midsummer to frost
Attractive fall color
Zones 4–7

Fairly drought tolerant
Tolerates shade
p. 308

Cotoneaster horizontalis

Rockspray Cotoneaster
Plant height: 2–3 ft.
Fruits: 1/4 in. wide
Fruits in fall
Zones 5–9

Moderately drought tolerant
p. 291

Aronia arbutifolia

Red Chokeberry
Plant height: 4 ft.
Fruits: 1/2 in. wide
Fruits in fall
Attractive fall color
Zones 4–9

Fairly drought tolerant
p. 256

Ilex cornuta
'Burfordii'

Burford Chinese Holly
Plant height: 10 ft.
Zones 7–9

Moderately drought
tolerant
p. 331

Viburnum lantana
'Mohican'

Wayfaring-tree
Viburnum
Plant height: 6 ft.
Fruits: ½ in. wide
Fruits in fall
Zones 4–8

Very drought tolerant
Tolerates partial shade
p. 403

Rhus glabra

Smooth Sumac
Plant height: 8–20 ft.
Flowers: 4- to 8-in.
clusters
Blooms in summer
Attractive fall color
Zones 3–10

Very drought tolerant
p. 380

Rhus trilobata

Threeleaf Sumac
Plant height: 4–6 ft.
Attractive fall color
Zones 4–10

Extremely drought
tolerant
p. 381

Rhus glabra   Smooth Sumac   p. 380
                       Fruits: 4- to 8-in.
                       clusters
                       Fruits in fall

Cotoneaster   Willowleaf Cotoneaster   Moderately drought
salicifolius   Plant height: 7–12 ft.   tolerant
                       Fruits: ¼ in. wide   p. 291
                       Fruits in fall
                       Attractive fall color
                       Zones 6–9

Hippophae rhamnoides

Sea Buckthorn
Plant height: 10–25 ft.
Zones 4–7

Extremely drought tolerant
p. 327

Lindera benzoin

Spicebush
Plant height: 6–12 ft.
Fruits: ½ in. wide
Fruits in fall
Attractive fall color
Zones 4–9

Slightly drought tolerant
Tolerates partial shade
p. 342

Hippophae rhamnoides   Sea Buckthorn   p. 327
                                Fruits: ¼ in. long
                                Fruits fall to winter

Pyracantha coccinea   Scarlet Fire Thorn   Moderately drought
                               Plant height: 10–15 ft.   tolerant
                               Fruits: ⅓ in. wide   p. 376
                               Fruits fall through
                               winter
                               Zones 6–10

Amelanchier alnifolia

Western Serviceberry
Plant height: 10–12 ft.
Fruits: ¼ in. wide
Fruits in summer
Attractive fall color
Zones 3–8

Moderately drought
tolerant
Tolerates partial shade
p. 248

Symphoricarpos orbiculatus

Coralberry
Plant height: 3–5 ft.
Fruits: ¼ in. wide
Fruits in fall
Attractive fall color
Zones 3–10

Moderately drought
tolerant
Tolerates partial shade
p. 394

Symphoricarpos × *chenaultii*

Chenault Coralberry
Plant height: 3–6 ft.
Fruits: ¼–⅓ in. wide
Fruits fall to winter

Extremely drought tolerant
Tolerates partial shade
p. 394

Prunus besseyi

Sand Cherry
Plant height: 4–6 ft.
Fruits: ½ in. wide
Fruits in fall
Zones 3–7

Very drought tolerant
p. 374

Taxus cuspidata   Japanese Yew   Slightly drought tolerant
                    Plant height: 1–12 ft.   Tolerates partial shade
                    Zones 5–8   p. 397

Taxus baccata   Spreading English Yew   Slightly drought tolerant
'Repandens'   Plant height: 2 ft.   Tolerates partial shade
              Zones 6–8   p. 397

Taxus cuspidata   Japanese Yew   p. 397
                     Fruits: ¼ in. wide
                     Fruits in summer and
                     fall

Taxus baccata   English Yew   p. 397
                    Fruits: ¼–⅜ in. wide
                    Fruits in summer and
                    fall

Trees

Robinia pseudoacacia   *Black Locust*   *Moderately drought*
                            Plant height: to 75 ft. *tolerant*
                            Zones 3–10   *p. 383*

Robinia neomexicana   *New Mexico Locust*   *Very drought tolerant*
                           Plant height: 10–25 ft. *p. 382*
                           Zones 5–10

Robinia pseudoacacia   Black Locust   p. 383
                              Flowers: 3- to 8-in.
                              clusters
                              Blooms in early summer

Cercis ᵃ

Robinia neomexicana   New Mexico Locust   p. 382
                              Flowers: 2- to 3-in.
                              clusters
                              Blooms in summer

Mel

Grevillea robusta

Silk Oak
Plant height: to 150 ft.
Zone 10

Very drought tolerant
p. 320

Albizia julibrissin
'Rosea'

Hardy Silk Tree
Plant height: 20–40 ft.
Zones 6–9

Extremely drought
tolerant
p. 247

Grevillea robusta   *Silk Oak*   *p. 320*
Flowers: 4- to 12-in.
clusters
Blooms in early spring

Albizia julibrissin   *Hardy Silk Tree*   *p. 247*
Flowers: 1 in. long
Blooms in summer

Prunus padus   European Bird Cherry   Moderately drought
                          Plant height: to 40 ft.   tolerant
                          Zones 4–7   p. 374

Crataegus crus-galli   Cockspur Hawthorn   Moderately drought
                           Plant height: to 30 ft.   tolerant
                           Zones 5–9   p. 292

Prunus padus *European Bird Cherry* *p. 374*
Flowers: ¹/₂ in. wide
Blooms in mid-spring

Crataegus crus-galli *Cockspur Hawthorn* *p. 292*
Flowers: ¹/₂ in. wide
Blooms in spring

Catalpa speciosa
Northern Catalpa
Plant height: to 60 ft.
Zones 4–8

Moderately drought
tolerant
p. 272

**Koelreuteria
paniculata**
Golden-Rain Tree
Plant height: 30–40 ft.
Flowers: 15-in. clusters
Blooms in summer
Zones 5–8

Very drought tolerant
p. 336

Catalpa speciosa Northern Catalpa p. 272
Flowers: 2 in. wide
Blooms in late spring

Koelreuteria Golden-Rain Tree p. 336
paniculata

Alnus cordata Italian Alder *Slightly drought tolerant*
Plant height: 30–75 ft. *p. 247*
Zones 5–10

Populus tremuloides Quaking Aspen *Slightly drought tolerant*
Plant height: 40–90 ft. *p. 371*
Attractive fall color
Zones 1–5

Alnus cordata   *Italian Alder*   p. 247

Populus tremuloides   *Quaking Aspen*   p. 371

Eucalyptus polyanthemos   *Silver Dollar Gum*   *Very drought tolerant*
                               Plant height: 50–60 ft.   *p. 307*
                               Zones 8–10

Celtis occidentalis   *Common Hackberry*   *Fairly drought tolerant*
                           Plant height: to 100 ft.   *p. 276*
                           Attractive fall color
                           Zones 4–8

*Eucalyptus
polyanthemos*   *Silver Dollar Gum*   p. 307

Celtis occidentalis   *Common Hackberry*   p. 276

Ceratonia siliqua Carob
Plant height: 20–50 ft.
Zones 9–10

Moderately drought tolerant
p. 279

Gingko biloba Gingko
Plant height: 50 ft.
Attractive fall color
Zones 5–9

Fairly drought tolerant
p. 318

Quercus gambelii   *Scrub Oak*   *Very drought tolerant*
                           Plant height: 15–25 ft.   *p. 377*
                           Zones 5–8

Quercus macrocarpa   *Bur Oak*   *Moderately drought*
                          Plant height: 60–   *tolerant*
                          100 ft.   *p. 377*
                          Attractive fall color
                          Zones 2–8

Quercus gambelii　　　Scrub Oak　　　　　p. 377
　　　　　　　　　　　　Fruits: ¹/₂–³/₄ in. long
　　　　　　　　　　　　Fruits in fall

Quercus macrocarpa　　Bur Oak　　　　　p. 377

Ptelea trifoliata   *Common Hop-Tree*   *Very drought tolerant*
Plant height: to 25 ft.   *Tolerates partial shade*
Zones 5–8   *p. 375*

Ulmus pumila   *Siberian Elm*   *Fairly drought tolerant*
Plant height: to 75 ft.   *p. 402*
Zones 2–9

Ptelea trifoliata   *Common Hop-Tree*   *p. 375*

Ulmus pumila   *Siberian Elm*   *p. 402*
'Coolshade'   *Fruits: ½ in. wide*
      Fruits in early summer

Acer campestre

Hedge Maple
Plant height: to 35 ft.
Attractive fall color
Zones 5–8

Slightly drought tolerant
Tolerates partial shade
p. 244

Acer rubrum

Red Maple
Plant height: 40–70 ft.
Attractive fall color
Zones 4–9

Slightly drought tolerant
p. 244

Acer campestre   Hedge Maple   p. 244

Acer rubrum   Red Maple   p. 244

Prunus virginiana 'Schubert'

Schubert Chokecherry
Plant height: 25–30 ft.
Attractive fall color
Zones 3–5

Fairly drought tolerant
p. 375

Pistacia chinensis

Chinese Pistache
Plant height: 30–60 ft.
Fruits: 1/4 in. long
Fruits in fall
Attractive fall color
Zones 7–9

Moderately drought
tolerant
p. 370

Prunus virginiana
'Schubert'

Schubert Chokecherry

p. 375

Pistacia chinensis

Chinese Pistache

p. 370

Gymnocladus dioica
Kentucky Coffee Tree
Plant height: 50–75 ft.
Zones 5–8

Very drought tolerant
Tolerates partial shade
p. 321

Brachychiton populneus
Bottle Tree
Plant height: 30–50 ft.
Flowers: ½ in. wide
Blooms in late spring
Zones 8–10

Extremely drought tolerant
Tolerates partial shade
p. 265

Gymnocladus dioica   Kentucky Coffee Tree   p. 321
                         Pods: 5–10 in. long

Brachychiton   Bottle Tree   p. 265
populneus   Pods: 2–3 in. long
                         Fruits in fall

Morus alba
'Fruitless'

Fruitless White
Mulberry
Plant height: to 60 ft.
Zones 5–9

Moderately drought
tolerant
Tolerates partial shade
p. 352

Prunus americana

Wild Plum
Plant height: 20–30 ft.
Flowers: 1 in. wide
Blooms in mid-spring
Attractive fall color
Zones 4–8

Very drought tolerant
p. 374

Morus alba   *White Mulberry*   *p. 352*
                     Fruits: ³/₈–³/₄ in. long
                     Fruits in late spring

Prunus americana   *Wild Plum*   *p. 374*
                      Fruits: ³/₄ in. wide
                      Fruits in fall

***Elaeagnus
angustifolia***

*Russian Olive
Plant height: 15–20 ft.
Zones 3–9*

*Extremely drought
tolerant
p. 300*

***Gleditsia triacanthos*
var. *inermis***

*Thornless Honey Locust
Plant height: 25–90 ft.
Attractive fall color
Zones 5–9*

*Fairly drought tolerant
p. 319*

Elaeagnus
angustifolia   Russian Olive   p. 300
                         Fruits: ½ in. long
                         Fruits in fall

Gleditsia triacanthos   Thornless Honey Locust   p. 319
var. inermis   Flowers: ⅜ in. wide
                           Blooms in mid-spring

Phellodendron amurense

Amur Corktree
Plant height: 40–50 ft.
Attractive fall color
Zones 4–7

Moderately drought tolerant
p. 364

Nyssa sylvatica

Sour Gum
Plant height: 25–85 ft.
Attractive fall color
Zones 4–9

Slightly drought tolerant
Tolerates partial shade
p. 356

Phellodendron
amurense

Amur Corktree   *p. 364*
Fruits: ½ in. wide
Fruits in fall and winter

Nyssa sylvatica

Sour Gum   *p. 356*
Fruits: ½ in. wide
Fruits in fall

Arbutus unedo

Strawberry Tree
Plant height: 10–35 ft.
Flowers: 2-in. clusters
Blooms in fall
Zones 6–9

Fairly drought tolerant
p. 253

Schinus terebinthifolius

Brazilian Pepper Tree
Plant height: to 30 ft.
Zones 9–10

Extremely drought tolerant
p. 389

Arbutus unedo   Strawberry Tree   *p. 253*
                          Fruits: ¾ in. wide
                          Fruits in fall

Schinus   Brazilian Pepper Tree   *p. 389*
terebinthifolius   Fruits: ¼ in. wide
                          Fruits fall through
                          winter

Juniperus scopulorum   Rocky Mountain Juniper   Extremely drought
                         Plant height: 30–40 ft.   tolerant
                         Zones 4–9   p. 333

Juniperus virginiana   Eastern Red Cedar   Very drought tolerant
                         Plant height: 40 ft.   p. 333
                         Zones 3–9

Juniperus scopulorum   *Rocky Mountain Juniper*   *p. 333*
                         Fruits: ⅓ in. wide
                         Fruits in fall

Juniperus virginiana   *Eastern Red Cedar*   *p. 333*
                         Fruits: ⅓ in. long
                         Fruits in fall

Juniperus monosperma

Cherrystone Juniper
Plant height: to 50 ft.
Zones 7–9

Very drought tolerant
p. 333

Cedrus atlantica 'Glauca'

Blue Atlas Cedar
Plant height: 40–60 ft.
Zones 6–9

Slightly drought tolerant
Tolerates partial shade
p. 276

Juniperus monosperma | *Cherrystone Juniper* | *p. 333*

Cedrus atlantica 'Glauca' | *Blue Atlas Cedar*
Cones: 2–3 in. long | *p. 276*

Pinus mugo
Mugo Pine
Plant height: to 30 ft.
Zones 2–7

Moderately drought tolerant
Tolerates light shade
p. 369

Picea pungens
Colorado Spruce
Plant height: 30–100 ft.
Zones 3–7

Slightly drought tolerant
Tolerates light shade
p. 368

Pinus mugo mugo   *Mugo Pine*   *p. 369*
                         Plant height: 2–6 ft.
                         Cones: ³⁄₄–1¹⁄₂ in. long

Picea pungens   *Hoops' Blue Colorado*   *p. 368*
'Hoopsii'   *Spruce*

Picea glauca White Spruce Slightly drought toleran*
Plant height: 60–70 ft. Tolerates light shade
Zones 3–6 p. 367

Pinus flexilis Limber Pine Moderately drought
Plant height: to 75 ft. tolerant
Zones 4–7 p. 369

Picea glauca   White Spruce   *p. 367*
Cones: 1½–2 in. long

Pinus flexilis   Limber Pine   *p. 369*
Cones: 4–6 in. long

Pinus ponderosa   *Ponderosa Pine*   *Very drought tolerant*
         Plant height: 50–60 ft. *p. 369*
         Zones 6–8

Pinus nigra   *Austrian Pine*   *Moderately drought*
         Plant height: 60 ft.   *tolerant*
         Zones 4–8   *p. 369*

Pinus ponderosa   *Ponderosa Pine*   *p. 369*
                        Cones: 3–6 in. long

Pinus nigra   *Austrian Pine*   *p. 369*
                    Cones: 3 in. long

Encyclopedia of Plants

Abronia
Four O'Clock family
Nyctaginaceae

A-bro'ni-a. Sand Verbena. This genus
contains about 30 species of annuals and
perennials, most from western North
America. Plants may be upright or trailing.
The round to oval leaves are sticky and hairy.
Fragrant tubular flowers bloom in loose
clusters up to 2 inches across.

How to Grow
Sand verbenas grow best in areas where the
growing season is long and cool. They prefer
full sun and light, sandy soil. Like most
plants with thick fleshy leaves, they need
only occasional watering. Start seeds indoors
in mid-spring or outdoors after all danger of
frost has passed. Remove the papery seed
husks before planting to speed germination.
Move plants started indoors into the garden
after the last frost, spacing them 1–2 feet
apart.

Uses
Sand verbenas make good ground covers and
border or rock garden plants. Plant them
along the beach to prevent erosion of sand.

umbellata p. 121

Prostrate Sand Verbena. This trailing plant
sometimes reddish stems grow 6–24 inches
long and 1–2 inches high to form a leafy mat.
They root easily as they creep along the
ground. The ½-inch-long flowers are pink
and appear in clusters of 10–15 blooms off
and on throughout the growing season.
'Grandiflora' has larger flowers; 'Rosea' has
pale rose flowers. Prostrate Sand Verbena is
perennial to zone 8 and may be grown as a
tender annual in other areas.

Acacia
Pea family
Leguminosae

A-ka'si-a, also a-ka'sha. An enormous genus
of fast-growing, free-flowering shrubs and
trees found all over the tropical world, with
few growing in subtropical regions. About
20 species are cultivated, most of them
originating in Australia. The leaves are
compound and sometimes feathery; the

leaflets very numerous and small. The flowers, while small, are crowded into dense finger-shaped or rounded clusters and are primarily yellow. The seedpod, which looks like a pea pod, is sometimes woody or twisted.

How to Grow
Although acacias are easy to grow in sunny locations, they may not live for more than 20 years, so take this into account when planning your garden. Most acacias require dry, sandy soil that is well drained. Water plants freely when they are young but less frequently (although deeply) as they become established. When mature they are drought tolerant. Infrequent watering encourages low growth. Prune plants after they have flowered and pinch back new growth to encourage bushiness. Propagate from seeds; nick the hard seed coat before sowing.

Uses
The acacia described below is best used as a ground cover on dry banks in full sun. Acacias also grow well in seashore gardens.

redolens* var. *prostrata *p. 151*
This dense evergreen acacia grows 1–2 feet high. Its spreading stems are covered with bright green foliage. The clusters of yellow flowers are 2 inches across and bloom in spring. Zones 9–10.

Acer
Maple family
Aceraceae

A'sir. Maple. About 150 species of mostly deciduous trees and large shrubs native to the north temperate zones. Plants vary in height from 15 to 75 feet or more and in habit from rounded to narrow and upright. Depending on the species, leaves are simple, lobed, or compound. The flowers bloom in small panicles in early spring and are often inconspicuous. The seeds are winged.

How to Grow
Grow maples in full sun to partial shade in any good, well-drained soil. Some maples require moist soil, but the species listed below tolerate dry soil. Fertilize maples annually with a high-nitrogen fertilizer.

Prune to provide central leaders and wide
branch angles; remove small internal
branches that don't receive adequate
sunlight.

Uses
There are maples suitable for almost every
kind of ornamental planting in every section
of the country. Many maples make splendid
shade trees and street trees and are valued for
their attractive foliage, which often assumes
brilliant hues in the fall. Hedge Maple is best
used in a screen or hedge.

campestre pp. 216, 217
Hedge Maple. This round-headed tree grows
to 35 feet high. Its branches are slightly
corky. The 2- to 4-inch leaves have 3–5
lobes. They are dull green on the top, soft
and hairy on the bottom, and turn yellow in
the fall. The flowers are greenish and bloom
in erect, flat-topped clusters. The seedpods
are hairy and soft, the wings spreading
horizontally. Hedge Maple tolerates heat and
dry, compacted soil, and withstands heavy
pruning. Zones 5–8.

rubrum pp. 216, 217

Red Maple. This large tree grows 40–70 feet
high. The lobed leaves grow 2–4 inches
across. They are shiny green above, with a
bloom beneath, and turn brilliant scarlet,
sometimes yellow, in fall. The flowers are red
and bloom in showy 1-inch clusters before
the leaves open. The seeds are bright red
when young, the wings spreading at a narrow
angle. Because Red Maples have shallow
roots, grass does not grow well underneath
them. Zones 4–9.

Achillea
Daisy family
Compositae

A-kil-lee'a. Yarrow. A large genus of
perennials, most from the north temperate
zone. Their gray or green leaves are aromatic
and parted, divided, or finely dissected.
Small flowers bloom in summer and often
again in fall in flat-topped clusters.

How to Grow
Yarrow thrives in ordinary, well-drained
garden soil and grows well in poor and dry
soil also. Plant it in full sun, setting plants

12–24 inches apart. Propagate from seeds or
by dividing the roots in spring or fall.
Yarrow is a rapid grower and may need
dividing or thinning every year. Cut the
plants back after the flowers fade to prevent
self-sowing and to encourage a second bloom.
The taller yarrows will need staking.

Uses
Grow yarrow in mixed borders or massed
plantings and use it for cut and dried flowers.
Woolly Yarrow is most effective as a ground
cover or a rock garden plant.

filipendulina p. 73
Fernleaf Yarrow. Plants grow 3–4 feet high
and have dark green, deeply divided leaves
up to 10 inches long. The flowers are yellow
and bloom in clusters 5 inches wide. The
variety 'Coronation Gold' grows 3 feet tall
and has mustard-yellow flowers. It is very
heat tolerant. 'Gold Plate' grows 4½ feet
high and has hairy stems. Zones 4–10.

millefolium p. 90
Common Yarrow; Milfoil. These 2½-foot-
tall plants have green or gray-green leaves
that are hairy and finely dissected. The
species has white flowers; varieties, such as
'Fire King', with 2- to 3-inch clusters of rose-
red to magenta flowers, are more commonly
grown. Common Yarrow flowers best in hot
and dry climates and can become very weedy.
Zones 3–10.

tomentosa p. 110
Woolly Yarrow. These plants form a flat
spreading mat of fernlike dark green leaves
with woolly gray hairs. They grow only 2
inches high and spread to 2 feet wide. The
leaves are semievergreen or evergreen in mild
climates. Gold flowers bloom in 1-inch
clusters on 6- to 10-inch stems. Woolly
Yarrow can be mowed in the spring. Zones
3–10.

Aegopodium
Carrot family
Umbelliferae

Ee-go-po'di-um. This is a small genus of
Eurasian perennials, one of which,
Goutweed, is used as a deciduous edging
plant or ground cover.

How to Grow

Goutweed is an easy-to-grow plant that prefers partial shade but will tolerate full sun. It grows in a wide range of soils and tolerates adverse, dry, wet, and infertile conditions. The plants can become weedy if not controlled; remove flowers before they drop seeds and, if necessary, install an underground barrier. Divide if needed in spring or fall. Goutweed can be mowed.

Uses

Goutweed is an excellent ground cover for large areas, especially those that receive some shade, where it can be left to grow unchecked. In smaller areas it will need constant cutting back.

podagraria p. 133

Goutweed; Bishop's Weed. This coarse, fast-growing plant grows 6 inches high when not in bloom; flowering stems grow about 12 inches tall. The leaves are deeply cut and toothed. The white flower clusters are flat topped and measure 2–3 inches wide. They bloom in early summer. The most popular and least aggressive variety is 'Variegatum', which has white-margined leaflets. Zones 4–9.

Albizia
Pea family
Leguminosae

Al-bizz'ee-a. This genus, which closely resembles and is related to *Acacia,* contains more than 100 species of deciduous trees and shrubs from central Asia. Hardy Silk Tree, the species described below, is hardier than most members of the genus. Albizias have compound leaves with small, numerous leaflets. The flowers are small, bloom in rounded heads, and have showy stamens. After the flowers fade, a long seedpod forms.

How to Grow

Albizias prefer full sun and will tolerate either acid or alkaline soil, as long as it is dry, poor, and sandy, with good drainage. Albizias also tolerate wind, drought, and salt spray. Prune away dead or overcrowded branches in the early spring. Propagate plants from root cuttings or from seeds. Albizias are prone to a wilt disease, which may make them unusable in some areas.

Uses
Hardy Silk Tree will grow at the seashore and in other spots with heavy winds. It is one of the few tropical-looking trees that will grow in the temperate regions; use it as an ornamental or accent plant. It tolerates heat and drought and resists air pollution.

julibrissin pp. 200, 201
Hardy Silk Tree; sometimes incorrectly called Mimosa. This medium-size tree grows 20–40 feet high and has a broad, spreading, low-branched crown. At maturity, it is often wider than it is high. The compound leaves contain up to 60 leaflets, each only ¼ inch long; they are light sensitive and fold up at night. The flowers are bright pink, 1 inch long, and bloom in 3-inch heads in summer. The stamens, also bright pink, are up to 1¼ inches long and give the tree a soft, fluffy appearance. The flat seedpod is 5–7 inches long. 'Rosea' is the most widely grown cultivar; its flowers are richer pink and it is somewhat hardier than the species. Zones 6–9.

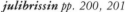

Alnus
Birch family
Betulaceae

Al′nus. Alder. About 30 species of deciduous shrubs and trees. The flowers, which are catkins, and the small, scaly woody cones persist on the bare twigs in fall and winter, creating interesting patterns against the sky. The leaves are handsome and are often burnished or sticky.

How to Grow
Most alders prefer moist soil; Italian Alder, the species listed below, will grow in moist soil but is also drought tolerant. Plant Italian Alder in full sun or very light shade. The roots can become invasive; deep watering will help to prevent this. Propagate from seeds, cuttings, or suckers.

Uses
Plant Italian Alder standing alone as a specimen or use it in a screen; the dried catkins and cones are attractive in winter bouquets or arrangements.

cordata pp. 206, 207
Italian Alder. This handsome tree grows 30–75 feet high in a pyramidal to rounded form.

The shiny dark green leaves are 2–4 inches long, heart shaped at the base, and finely toothed. The catkins grow to 3 inches long, and the cones to 1¼ inches long. The flower open in spring before the leaves unfurl. Twigs are reddish brown. Zones 5–10.

Amelanchier
Rose family
Rosaceae

Am-e-lang'ki-er. Serviceberry; Shadbush; Juneberry. About 25 species of deciduous shrubs or trees found in the north temperate zones. Their profuse white bloom is sometimes called shadblow in the East because it coincides with the onset of shad spawning runs up major Eastern rivers. The leaves are toothed; the flower buds prominently pointed. The flowers are small and white and bloom in terminal clusters. Tiny, applelike purplish-blue fruits form in summer; they can be used in jellies. The smooth bark is gray streaked with red.

How to Grow
Plant serviceberry in full sun or partial shade. Most serviceberries need to be watered during dry spells; Western Serviceberry, the species listed below, is the most drought tolerant and likes rocky, well-drained soil. Serviceberries need little pruning.

Uses
Serviceberry is attractive in all four seasons. Use it in a hedge, at the back of a border, or standing alone as a specimen plant.

alnifolia pp. 168, 190
Western Serviceberry. This shrubby plant usually grows 10–12 feet high. The leaves are toothed and grow 1–2 inches long. They are bronzy red when they open, green in summer, and yellow to orange in the fall. The white flowers bloom 6–8 to a cluster in spring. Zones 3–8.

Anaphalis
Daisy family
Compositae

A-naff'a-lis. A large genus of everlasting perennials. The stalkless, lance-shaped leaves

are white and woolly at first and ultimately
dull green on the upper surfaces. Small white
flowers that are excellent for drying bloom in
tight clusters.

How to Grow
Pearly Everlasting, the most drought-
tolerant species of the genus, prefers full sun
and dry, sandy, well-drained soil of average
fertility. Grow new plants from seeds or by
dividing existing plants in spring or fall.
Replant divisions 12 inches apart. Pick
flowers for drying before they are fully open,
and hang them upside down in a dark, cool
spot to dry. They can be dyed in various
colors.

Uses
Pearly Everlasting, valued for its flowers,
both fresh and dried, is attractive in borders,
rock gardens, and wildflower gardens.

margaritacea p. 104
Pearly Everlasting. These erect plants grow
20 inches high. The slender, pointed leaves
are dull green on the upper surfaces when
mature and gray and hairy on the undersides.
The tiny pearly-white flowers are crowded in
small, flat, fluffy heads at the tops of the
stems during the summer. Zones 4–9.

Anemone
Buttercup family
Ranunculaceae

Correctly, a-nee-moe′nee; usually, a-nem′o-
nee. Windflower; Anemone; Pasque Flower.
A large genus of perennials from the north
temperate zone that range from 3 inches to
5 feet tall, depending on the species. The
leaves are compound, divided, or dissected,
and appear mostly at the base of the plant.
The flowers are usually showy, without
petals, but with petal-like sepals.

How to Grow
Pasque Flower, the species listed below,
grows best in rich, dry, well-drained soil that
is neutral to alkaline. Wet soil during the
winter is very detrimental and may kill these
plants. Plant Pasque Flower in full sun in
cool climates and in partial shade in hot
climates. Propagate from seeds or by
dividing established plants in spring every 5
or 6 years; space new plants 12 inches apart.

Uses
Pasque Flower works well as a border plant, an edging, or in a rock garden.

pulsatilla *p. 97*
Pasque Flower. Plants grow 9–12 inches high and have silky fernlike leaves, 4–6 inches long. The bell-shaped 2-inch flowers are blue or reddish purple and may appear before the leaves in early spring. There are varieties with lilac and red flowers and with variegated leaves. After the flowers fade, seed clusters that resemble feathery smoke-gray pompons appear. Zones 5–8.

Antennaria
Daisy family
Compositae

An-ten-ar´i-a. A genus of woolly white or gray perennials native to the north temperate zone, commonly grown in wildflower gardens. The leaves grow in basal rosettes, above which slender, almost leafless stems bearing tight tufted clusters of small flowers appear in early summer.

How to Grow
Pussytoes, a popular and drought-tolerant species, is very easy to grow in full sun and dry, sandy soil with good drainage. It grows best in soil that is slightly acid. Plants drop seeds and easily self-sow and spread so rapidly that they may become a weedy nuisance. Propagate from seeds or by division, spacing plants 1½ feet apart.

Uses
Pussytoes, often grown as a source of dried flowers, is an attractive addition to a low border, rock garden, or wildflower garden. It also makes an excellent ground cover, especially where growing conditions are less than ideal.

dioica *var.* rosea *p. 134*
Pussytoes. These ground-hugging plants grow 4–12 inches high and spread by underground stolons. The 1½-inch basal leaves are spoon shaped and are green on top, white on the bottom. Even when the plant is not in bloom, the leaves are attractive. The species has white flowers; the variety *rosea* has pink flowers. Zones 4–8.

Anthemis
Daisy family
Compositae

An'them-is. A large genus of Eurasian perennials, some cultivated for ornament, others for their fragrant foliage. The leaves are usually basal and often dissected or cut and in some species they are evergreen. The flowers are daisylike, with yellow centers and yellow or white petals.

How to Grow
Golden Marguerite is a popular drought-tolerant species that is also very tolerant of heat. It is easy to grow in full sun and dry, infertile, well-drained soil. Grow new plants from seeds or by dividing existing plants in spring or fall. Space new plants 12–16 inches apart. Golden Marguerite may need dividing every year, because the plants die out and become bare in the middle. Remove flowers as soon as they fade to extend the blooming period and prevent self-seeding.

Uses
Plant Golden Marguerite in a mixed flower border or wildflower garden; it is a good choice for a cutting garden.

tinctoria p. 74
Golden Marguerite; Yellow Chamomile. Plants grow 2–3 feet tall in an erect shrubby habit. Two-inch-wide golden-yellow flowers bloom during summer and fall amidst the aromatic, finely divided leaves. 'Kelwayi' and 'Moonlight' are favorite varieties. Zones 4–8.

Arabis
Mustard family
Cruciferae

Ar'a-bis. Rock Cress. A large genus of annuals, biennials, and perennials native to the north temperate zone. Flowers are white, pink, or purple, and bloom in loose clusters or spikes. The leaves are basal, usually hairy, and are evergreen in mild climates.

How to Grow
Rock cresses are easy to grow in full sun, although they tolerate partial shade. They thrive in warm, rich, sandy soil and grow well in both moist and dry soils; excellent

drainage is critical. Although they tolerate heat, plants may rot during humid summers. Grow new plants from seeds or cuttings or by dividing plants in spring or fall. Space new plants 12 inches apart. Cut plants back after they flower to encourage compact growth.

Uses
Rock cress is a perfect choice for a ground cover, rock garden, or in the front of a border. Combine plants with spring bulbs for a pretty picture. Wall Cress is very effective when planted on or in a rock wall where it can cascade down.

caucasica p. 127
Wall Cress. The flowering stems of this species grow to 12 inches high over 4- to 6-inch-high mats of white or gray foliage. The ½-inch flowers are white, fragrant, and very plentiful. There are double-flowered forms and varieties with pink flowers and variegated leaves. This species is sometimes sold as *A. albida*. Zones 4–8.

Arbutus
Heath family
Ericaceae

Ar-bew'tus. A genus of 14 species of broadleaf evergreen trees grown in temperate and warm climates for their ornamental flowers and striking bark. The urn-shaped flowers are white or pink and bloom in loose terminal clusters. The bark is usually reddish and is rough and shedding. The fleshy fruit is red or orange.

How to Grow
Strawberry Tree, the species listed below, needs watering only during periods of drought but should be protected from drying winds. It will not grow well in humid climates. Plant Strawberry Tree in full sun and dry, sandy, acid soil that is well drained. It will grow in a shrubby habit unless it is trained into a tree with a central leader.

Uses
Strawberry Tree's shredding bark and dropped fruit can involve a lot of cleanup, so you may not want to plant it over a walkway or patio. Use it in a hedge or screen or standing alone.

unedo *pp. 228, 229*
Strawberry Tree. These trees grow slowly, reaching 10–35 feet high. The sticky, hairy branches become gnarled when they are mature. The toothed 3½-inch leaves are dark green with red stems. The drooping 2-inch-long flower clusters appear in the fall at the same time as the small round fruits, which are edible but flavorless. Zones 6–9.

Arctostaphylos
Heath family
Ericaceae

Ark-to-staff′i-los. About 50 species of woody evergreen plants, mostly North American, ranging from prostrate ground covers to small trees. All have smooth crooked stems and handsome smooth-margined leaves. In spring, small urn- or bell-shaped flowers appear; they are followed by fleshy berries that are showy in some species.

How to Grow
Plant Bearberry, the species listed below, in full sun or partial shade in dry, sandy or rocky, acid soil. Excellent drainage is critical. Bearberry plants will not grow well unless they have freezing temperatures during winter. Prune plants in early spring if they grow out of bounds. Grow new plants from stem cuttings, by layering, or from seeds.

Uses
Bearberry is an excellent ground cover for dry slopes, large areas, or sprawling over rocks so the outline of its branches can be seen. It tolerates salt spray and is therefore a good choice for a coastal garden.

uva-ursi *p. 130*
Bearberry; Kinnikinick. Although these plants grow only 2–8 inches high, they can spread to more than 12 feet across. The reddish or brown branches root as they grow along the ground. The glossy 1-inch leaves are dark green and turn bronze in the winter. The pink flowers are bell shaped and waxy and are followed by tiny, long-lasting red berries. Zones 3–7. A close relative, Little Sur Manzanita, *A. edmundsii,* tolerates heat and poor, dry soil but is hardy only in zones 8–10.

Arctotheca
Daisy family
Compositae

Arc-to-thee′ca. Only one species of this
native South African genus, Cape Weed, is
grown in the garden. It usually acts as a
ground cover and under proper conditions i[s]
a rapid-growing plant.

How to Grow
Cape Weed prefers full sun and dry,
moderately fertile, well-drained soil. It
grows best in cool climates and will die in
hot, humid conditions. Increase the plantin[g]
by division or from seeds, spacing new plan[ts]
12–18 inches apart. Plants will self-sow
easily if faded flowers are not removed.

Uses
Plant Cape Weed in a wildflower garden or
on a hillside or use it as a ground cover in
large areas.

calendula p. 115
Cape Weed; Cape-Dandelion. This spring-
blooming evergreen grows less than 12
inches high but spreads to cover a wide are[a.]
Its gray-green leaves are lobed or deeply
divided. The showy 1- to 2-inch flowers are
yellow and daisylike. Zones 9–10.

Arctotis
Daisy family
Compositae

Ark-toe′tis. African Daisy. A genus of abou[t]
30 species of annuals and perennials native t[o]
South Africa. The whitish woolly leaves are
toothed or deeply cut and grow in a mound a[t]
the base of the plants. Blue, yellow, or
orange flowers bloom on long thick stems.

How to Grow
African daisies prefer a long, cool growing
season. Plant them in full sun and poor,
sandy soil with good drainage. Hairy-leave[d]
plants such as these require little watering.
Fertilize them little, if at all. You can start
seeds outdoors in early spring, but for bett[er]
results, start them indoors 6–8 weeks befor[e]
the last frost. Germination takes 21–35 day[s.]
Set the plants outdoors, 6–12 inches apart,
after night temperatures are above 50° F.
Remove faded flowers to prolong bloom.

Uses
African daisies can be planted in beds or
borders or used as a splashy ground cover.

stoechadifolia p. 81
Blue-eyed African Daisy. This species is a
stout plant with 4-inch leaves that grows
2½–4 feet high. Flowers are 3 inches across
and have blue-violet centers; the petals are
creamy white above and red on the
undersides. The flowers close up at night.
The widely available hybrids grow 10–12
inches high and have yellow, white, pink,
bronze, red, purple, brown, or orange
flowers. The plants bloom off and on all year
in mild climates; in hot areas, use Blue-eyed
African Daisy as a spring or fall annual. It
is a tender perennial usually grown as a
tender annual.

Armeria
Plumbago family
Plumbaginaceae

Ar-meer′i-a. Thrift; Sea Pink. Small genus of
low-growing, spring- and summer-blooming
perennials native to mountains and
shorelines. Tufts of grassy evergreen leaves
grow at the bases of these plants. Stiff,
leafless flowering stalks grow from the center
of the leaves.

How to Grow
Plant Common Thrift, described below, in
full sun in dry, sandy, fast-draining soil. If
the soil is too rich, plants will produce lots of
foliage but few flowers. If the soil is too
moist or too fertile, the dense mat of leaves
will rot in the middle. Shear plants back after
the flowers fade to keep them compact and
attractive. Thrift is easy to propagate from
seeds or by dividing plants in spring or fall;
space new plants 9–12 inches apart.

Uses
Common Thrift is perfect for a rock garden,
set alongside paving stones, as an edging
plant, or as a ground cover. Since it tolerates
salt spray, it is a good plant for a seashore
garden, where its grassy appearance fits in
well.

maritima p. 91
Common Thrift. Foliage is blue-green and
grows in mats 6 inches high and 12 inches

wide. Flowers start appearing in mid-spring
and bloom off and on throughout the
summer on 6- to 10-inch stems. The dense,
globe-shaped ¾-inch flower clusters may be
white, pink, or purple. In mild climates,
Common Thrift blooms all year. Zones 4–9.

Aronia
Rose family
Rosaceae

A-rone′i-a. Chokeberry. A small genus of
North American deciduous shrubs grown for
their showy white flowers, which bloom in
clusters in mid-spring, and their persistent
brightly colored berries, whose bitter taste
explains the common name. The leaves are
toothed. The white flowers are contrasted by
black stamens.

How to Grow
Chokeberries grow well in a variety of soils
and can adapt to wet or dry conditions. Plant
them in full sun or light shade in well-
drained acid soil. They are easy to propagate
from seeds, from cuttings, or by layering.
Thin out branches in winter or early spring.

Uses
Informal borders and the edges of woodland
gardens are good locations for chokeberries.

arbutifolia pp. 171, 184
Red Chokeberry. Plants can reach heights of
8 feet but rarely grow more than 4 feet tall.
They spread by underground suckers. The 2-
inch leaves are oblong, with shiny green
surfaces and gray undersides. In fall, they
turn bright red. The 1½-inch flower clusters
are followed in fall by brilliant red berries
that last all winter. Zones 4–9.

Arrhenatherum
Grass family
Gramineae

Ar-re-nath′er-rum. A genus of tall, oatlike
perennial grasses that originated in Europe.
The leaves are coarse, flat, and rough edged,
and grow in erect clumps. Thin stems are
topped with narrow spikes of flowers,
followed by seeds.

How to Grow
Plant Bulbous Oat Grass, a species that is
quite drought tolerant once established, in
full sun or light shade and fertile, well-
drained soil. It does best in a cool climate; in
warm areas, the plants perform best in spring
and fall. Cut foliage back in summer if it
becomes unattractive. Increase plants by
division.

Uses
Bulbous Oat Grass is useful as an edging or
ground cover, especially on dry slopes. Its
colorful seed heads also make it a good accent
plant.

elatius bulbosum p. 142
Bulbous Oat Grass. This garden curiosity has
small bulbils at the base of the stems; the
plants form wide-spreading clumps. The
rough, narrow leaves are 12 inches long. A
purplish-green flower/seed cluster, also 12
inches long, forms on 3½-foot stems in late
spring or fall. 'Variegatum' has attractive,
white-striped leaves and is not as invasive as
the species. Zones 5–8.

Artemisia
Daisy family
Compositae

Ar-te-miz'i-a. Wormwood. The wormwoods
comprise a very large genus of bitter or
aromatic annuals, perennials, and low-
growing shrubs. They are found in most
countries and have been cultivated since
ancient times for their aromatic, savory, and
ornamental qualities. Plants have divided or
finely cut leaves that are usually silvery, gray,
or white. The flowers bloom in small heads
but are inconspicuous; the plants are grown
for their foliage.

How to Grow
Wormwoods need full sun and well-drained
soil. Like most plants with silver or gray
leaves, they are very drought resistant. They
are easy to grow and do better in poor, sandy
soil than in rich soil, which causes loose,
floppy growth. They may rot in high
humidity and in wet soil, especially if it is
wet during the winter. Increase plants by
division in spring or fall, planting the
divisions 12–24 inches apart.

Uses

Depending on the species, wormwood can be used in a rock garden, as an edging, as a ground cover, or as a background plant in a mixed border. All wormwoods are effective in seashore gardens, for fresh or dried arrangements, and as a contrast to bright colors in the garden.

absinthium p. 136

Common Wormwood. This white to silvery-gray woody perennial or small shrub grows 2½–4 feet tall. The divided leaves have a bitter taste and a pungent odor. The flowers are only ⅛ inch across and are greenish yellow. Zones 4–9.

ludoviciana p. 134

Western Sage. This perennial grows 2–3 feet high and has narrow gray leaves that grow to 4 inches long. The ⅛-inch flowers are grayish white. Most common varieties are 'Silver King', which has small silver leaves, and 'Silver Queen', with larger and downier leaves. Zones 5–9.

schmidtiana 'Silver Mound' p. 135

Silver Mound Artemisia. Woolly, finely cut silvery leaves grow in mounds 4–12 inches high and 12–24 inches across. The very small flowers are white or yellow. To prevent the clumps from opening in the center, prune the plants before they flower. Zones 4–9.

stellerana p. 137

Beach Wormwood; Dusty Miller. This plant's lobed 1- to 4-inch leaves are densely covered with woolly white hairs. Plants grow 2½ feet tall and have small yellow flowers. This wormwood is one of the least inclined to rot in humid conditions. Zones 3–9.

tridentata p. 137

Big Sagebrush. This evergreen shrub can grow up to 4–8 feet tall, although it may reach only 1½ feet in height. It is multibranched and has small, narrow hairy leaves that are toothed at their tips. The foliage is very aromatic; this is the plant that gives the desert the aroma of sage. Zones 4–10.

Asclepias
Milkweed family
Asclepiadaceae

As-klee′pi-as. Milkweed. A genus of showy
but sometimes weedy perennials whose stems
contain a milky juice. The flowers are small
and bloom in dense, flat, or rounded clusters.
After the flowers fade, seedpods form that are
filled with tufts of silky hairs. The species
listed below, Butterfly Weed, is the showiest
of the native milkweeds.

How to Grow
Butterfly Weed prefers full sun and sandy,
well-drained, average to dry soil. It is fairly
resistant to drought and needs watering only
in the driest summers. Propagate from root
cuttings or seeds (plants readily self-sow);
space plants 12–18 inches apart.

Uses
Plant Butterfly Weed in a wildflower garden
or mixed border. It is especially attractive
combined with blue flowers. Both the
flowers and the seedpods can be used fresh or
dried in arrangements.

tuberosa p. 83
Butterfly Weed. This species grows 1–3 feet
high and may be erect or sprawling. The
4½-inch-long leaves grow along stems that
are topped by 2-inch clusters of small bright
orange flowers in midsummer. Butterfly
Weed was well named, for it attracts all
kinds of butterflies, especially the monarch.
Zones 4–9.

Aster
Daisy family
Compositae

As′ter. Asters are an immense group of
perennials (the annual China Aster,
Callistephus, is another genus). Most asters
are easy-growing plants native to woods and
fields, and many are too aggressive for the
small garden. The flowers are daisylike, with
yellow centers and primarily blue or purple
petals. Most asters bloom in late summer and
fall.

How to Grow
Asters grow best in full sun and well-drained
soil. Some like moist soil during the

summer; Tartarian Aster, described below,
tolerates dry soil. None will survive in soil
that is wet during the winter. Asters self-sow
freely, but the seedlings will not grow true to
type; remove flowers as soon as they fade to
prevent self-sowing. Divide plants every
other year in spring or fall, discard the center
of the plant, and plant the divisions from the
outside of the plant 2–3 feet apart. Fertilize
plants once each year in spring.

Uses
Plant Tartarian Aster at the back of the
border, against walls and fences, or in a
wildflower garden. It is valued for its
flowers, which are long-lasting when cut.

tataricus p. 94
Tartarian Aster. This large perennial is easy
to grow and needs plenty of space; plants can
grow 6–8 feet tall and spread to 4 feet wide.
Lower leaves can reach 2 feet long. The
1-inch flowers are blue or purple and bloom
in profuse clusters. Zones 4–8.

Atriplex
Goosefoot family
Chenopodiaceae

At'ri-plex. Saltbush; Orach. About 100
species of annual and perennial herbs and
evergreen and deciduous shrubs grown
primarily for their attractive gray or silvery
foliage. They bear small flowers in clustered
spikes that are not showy. These plants often
grow naturally in saline soil, thus, the
common name saltbush.

How to Grow
Saltbush, like most plants with gray or silver
foliage, needs dry, well-drained soil and is
extremely drought tolerant. It grows well in
full sun. Start new plants from seeds.

Uses
Four-wing Saltbush, the species described
below, is a good choice for the seashore or for
desert gardens that have highly alkaline soil.
Use it as a hedge or in massed plantings. It is
fire resistant and is a good barrier plant in
areas where potential fire is a threat.

canescens p. 174
Four-wing Saltbush. This shrub grows
3–6 feet tall and 4–8 feet wide. It is covered

with minute gray scales. The leaves are linear or very narrow and grow 2 inches long. Zones 4–10.

Aurinia
Mustard family
Cruciferae

Aw-ri'nee-a. A small genus of mounded low-growing perennials, mostly from the Mediterranean region. The leaves are green to silvery gray and grow in rosettes at the base of the plant. In spring, clusters of tiny single flowers cover the plants. This genus was formerly included in the genus *Alyssum*.

How to Grow
Basket-of-Gold, the most popular species, is easy to grow in full sun and dry, sandy, infertile soil. It needs excellent drainage and may die out in moist soil or hot, humid conditions. Cut plants back by half after they flower to keep them compact. Propagate from seeds; plants have long taproots and are difficult to divide or transplant. Space plants 9–12 inches apart.

Uses
Plant Basket-of-Gold in a rock garden, in a massed planting, or cascading over a wall, or use it as an edging or ground cover.

saxatilis p. 111
Basket-of-Gold. This plant, which grows in a dense 6- to 12-inch-high clump, is named for its profuse clusters of golden-yellow flowers. The grayish leaves are 2–5 inches long. 'Citrina', one of many cultivars, has pale yellow flowers; 'Compacta' is known for its dwarf habit. Zones 4–10.

Baccharis
Daisy family
Compositae

Bak'kar-is. About 350 species of erect or trailing shrubs, some of which are evergreen, that have diverse origins from marshes to deserts. There are separate male and female plants; the female plants produce cottony seed heads after the small tubular flowers fade. Foliage is thick and fleshy.

How to Grow

Dwarf Coyote Brush, the species described below, adapts to various soil conditions. It grows best in rich, moisture-retentive soil but also tolerates drought. Plants grow best in full sun but will tolerate shade. Prune old arching branches to the ground in spring to encourage new dense growth. To avoid the messy and unattractive seeds, plant only male varieties. Grow new plants from cuttings.

Uses

Dwarf Coyote Brush has a strong root system and is therefore a good plant for holding slopes, banks, and sand dunes in place.

pilularis p. 128

Dwarf Coyote Brush. Plants form a dense evergreen mat 1–2 feet high and spread by trailing branches to 6 feet across. The toothed bright green leaves, which are nearly stalkless, are 1 inch long and broadest toward the tip. Inconspicuous off-white flowers bloom in small dense heads in the fall. Although it is a very reliable ground cover, this species is susceptible to spider mites. 'Twin Peaks' is an all-male variety that does not form seeds. Zones 7–10.

Baptisia
Pea family
Leguminosae

Bap-tiz′i-a. False Indigo; Wild Indigo. A genus of about 30 North American perennials. The plants are stout and shrubby, usually growing as wide as they grow high. The dull grayish-green leaves are divided like clover. The flowers bloom in late spring and early summer. Like those of other members of the pea family, these flowers are pealike and bloom in loose, showy clusters. They are followed by seedpods that resemble peas or beans.

How to Grow

False indigo grows best in full sun in soil that is porous, sandy, dry, and well drained. Due to its long taproot, false indigo is drought resistant, but the taproot makes it difficult to transplant or divide. Propagate from seeds or cuttings; space the plants 2–3 feet apart. If plants are cut back after they flower, they may rebloom in the fall.

Uses
Plant false indigo in a wildflower, shrub, or
perennial garden for its showy bloom and
then cut the flowers, foliage, and seedpods
for fresh or dried arrangements.

australis *p. 98*
Blue False Indigo. Plants grow 3–5 feet high
and wide. One-inch blue flowers bloom in 9-
to 12-inch clusters at the ends of the
branches. Zones 4–9.

Berberis
Barberry family
Berberidaceae

Ber'ber-iss. Barberry. This genus includes
almost 500 species of evergreen and
deciduous shrubs scattered throughout the
north temperate zone that are very popular
for their diverse uses. All are more or less
thorny. The leaves appear in small clusters at
the ends of short spurs and turn red, orange,
or yellow in the fall. The flowers are yellow,
blooming in spikes or clusters in mid-spring
to late spring. The berries sometimes shrivel
or lose their color by winter.

How to Grow
Most barberries are easy to grow in full sun to
shade and average, well-drained soil. They
tolerate poor, dry soil. Prune before growth
starts in spring or after the flowers fade;
plants grown as hedges may be sheared as
needed. Start new plants from seeds or
cuttings.

Uses
Plant barberries as hedges, as living fences to
keep out unwanted visitors with their thorns,
or in foundation plantings. Low-growing
varieties make good edgings or ground
covers.

hematocarpa *pp. 148, 149*
Red Barberry. The bluish-green leaves of this
plant are evergreen and hollylike. Plants
grow 3–6 feet high. The flowers are followed
by juicy red berries. Sometimes called
Mahonia haematocarpa. Zones 4–8.

× ***mentorensis*** *p. 182*
Mentor Barberry. This hybrid of *B. thunbergii*
and *B. julianae* is evergreen in zone 8 and

semievergreen in zones 4–7. It is very spiny
and grows 5–7 feet tall. The 1- to 2½-inch
leaves are toothed. The flowers bloom in
small clusters and are followed by dull, dark
red berries. This species is more heat and
drought resistant than other barberries.
Zones 4–8.

thunbergii pp. 181, 183

Japanese Barberry. This deciduous shrub
usually reaches 4–6 feet high. It has purple-
brown branches. The ½- to 1½-inch-long
leaves are variable, usually broader toward
the tip. They turn brilliant scarlet in
autumn. The berries are bright red and last
all winter. The variety 'Aurea' has yellow
leaves; 'Atropurpurea' has dark purple leaves;
'Crimson Pygmy' (also called 'Atropurpurea
Nana') grows 2 feet high and has purple
leaves. Zones 4–8.

Bouteloua
Grass family
Gramineae

Boo-tel-oo'ah. About 50 species of annual
and perennial grasses from North and South
America. They grow in large clumps with
arching mounds of flat smooth blades.

How to Grow
Mosquito Grass, the species listed below,
likes full sun and light, dry, well-drained
soil. To increase the planting, divide existing
clumps in spring or sow seeds.

Uses
Plant Mosquito Grass in a mixed border or a
meadow garden or use it as an accent plant.
The seed heads are attractive in dried flower
arrangements.

gracilis p. 141
Mosquito Grass; Blue Grama. This fine-
textured perennial ornamental grass has
arching 5-inch leaves at the base of the plant.
Thin upright stems 2 feet high bear
numerous 2-inch purplish spikelets that
appear on one side of the stem and resemble
miniature combs. The spikelets form
horizontally to the stems and somewhat
resemble a swarm of insects. Zones 5–8.

Brachychiton
Chocolate family
Sterculiaceae

Brack-ee-ky'ton. The bottle trees are named
for the bottlelike swellings at the base of
their trunks. They comprise a small genus of
mostly deciduous Australian trees. The leaves
are variable and sometimes deeply lobed. The
bell-shaped flowers bloom in showy clusters
of scarlet or yellow. Many species lose their
leaves after flowering; the species listed
below does not.

How to Grow
Bottle trees like partial shade and are not
particular about soil. They are very drought
tolerant and need little pruning. Grow new
plants from seeds or cuttings.

Uses
Bottle trees are useful shade trees and
windbreaks. Use the seedpods in dried flower
arrangements.

populneus pp. 220, 221
Bottle Tree; Kurrajong. This broadleaf
evergreen tree grows 30–50 feet high and 30
feet wide. Its leaves, 3 inches long and
sometimes lobed, shimmer in the breeze like
those of Quaking Aspen. The ½-inch-wide
yellowish-white flowers are reddish inside
and sometimes have dark spots on the
outside. They bloom in 3-inch clusters in late
spring. Woody, canoe-shaped seedpods form
in fall; they are 2–3 inches long and can be
messy. Zones 8–10.

Brachycome
Daisy family
Compositae

Bra-kick'o-me. A genus of about 70 species
of annuals and perennials native to Australia
and New Zealand, one of which, Swan River
Daisy, is a popular annual. Its small leaves
are divided, feather-fashion, into narrow
segments. The flowers are white, blue, red,
violet, or rose; they bloom atop long stems.

How to Grow
Swan River Daisy prefers cool climates. Plant
it in full sun in rich, but dry, well-drained
soil and mulch to keep the soil cool. The
plants may need to be staked. In mild

climates, start seeds outdoors in early spring
in other areas, start seeds indoors 4–6 weeks
before the last frost. Move plants to the
garden after frost danger has passed; space the
plants 6 inches apart. Swan River Daisy has a
short blooming period; for a longer period of
color, add new seeds or plants to the garden
every 3 weeks.

Uses
Swan River Daisy is a good edging plant or
ground cover. It is pretty in a rock garden, in
containers, or mixed with late-spring bulbs
and makes a nice cut flower.

iberidifolia p. 93
Swan River Daisy. These plants grow 8–18
inches high in a mounded form. They are
covered with fragrant 1- to 2-inch flowers
that bloom most abundantly in late spring
and early summer. Half-hardy annual.

Briza
Grass family
Gramineae

Bry′za. A group of slender annual and
perennial ornamental grasses native to the
Mediterranean region. They are known as
quaking grass because of the way they move
in the breeze, or as rattlesnake grass because
the seed heads resemble rattlesnake rattles.
The leaf blades are flat; the seed heads, called
spikelets, are small and flat and often nod in
a delicate graceful manner on threadlike
stems.

How to Grow
The quaking grasses prefer cool weather.
Select a site in full sun, where the soil is
poor, dry, and well drained. Sow seeds
outdoors in early spring, thinning them to
12 inches apart after germination.

Uses
Quaking grass is best used in a naturalistic or
wildflower garden and can be cut for dried
arrangements. It makes a nice accent plant in
a spot where its movement in the breeze can
be enjoyed.

maxima p. 140
Quaking Grass; Quaking Oats. The coarse
leaves of this grass are 6 inches long and
¼ inch wide. Slender 1- to 2-foot stems bear

the ½-inch seed heads, which are reddish
brown to gold when they first appear and
straw colored and papery when dry. Hardy
annual.

Buddleia
Buddleia family
Loganiaceae

Bud'lee-a. Butterfly Bush. A genus of about
100 species of shrubs, primarily from the
tropics, that attract a profusion of butterflies
when they bloom in late summer. The four-
lobed flowers are bell shaped and bloom in
dense spikes. Butterfly bushes are sometimes
called summer lilacs because of their purplish
flowers.

How to Grow
Butterfly bushes need a sunny location. They
tolerate many soils, including poor, dry,
gravelly soil, but grow best in soil that is rich
and fertile. Protect butterfly bushes during
winter in the northern limits of their
hardiness. In areas where plants are not
hardy, the tops will die down, but the roots
may survive. Plants are easy to propagate
from root cuttings.

Uses
Plant butterfly bushes standing alone as
specimens, at the back of a mixed border, or
in a seashore garden.

alternifolia p. 162
Alternate Leaf Butterfly Bush; Fountain
Buddleia. This deciduous butterfly bush is
the only species that does not have opposite
leaves. Its lance-shaped, 1- to 4-inch leaves
are green on the top and gray and rough on
the bottom. The fragrant flowers are lilac-
purple and appear in early summer along
thin, arching branches. Plants grow 10–20
feet tall. Prune them in the fall after they
have flowered. Zones 6–8.

davidii pp. 161, 167
Orange-eye Butterfly Bush. These plants can
reach heights of 6–10 feet if left to grow
unchecked. The 6- to 9-inch-long leaves are
oval to lance shaped. They are green above
and white and felty underneath. Plants are
deciduous in colder climates and
semievergreen in mild areas. The fragrant
flowers are lilac with an orange center. They

bloom in nodding 5- to 12-inch spikes in lat
summer to fall. In early spring, cut back th
branches nearly to the ground to encourage
new growth, a bushy habit, and a multitud
of flowers. Zones 5–9.

Calandrinia
Portulaca family
Portulacaceae

Kal-an-drin'i-a. Rock Purslane. A genus of
150 species of annuals and herbaceous
perennials from the western Americas. Thes
plants have narrow fleshy leaves and short-
lived, single rose-pink or red flowers.

How to Grow
Rock purslanes do best in California, the
Northwest, and cool or high-altitude
gardens. The plants need full sun and poor,
dry soil. They need little, if any, fertilizer.
With their fleshy leaves to store water, rock
purslanes are very drought tolerant. Sow
seeds outdoors in early spring to mid-spring
thinning the plants to 8–10 inches apart.
Seeds can also be started indoors, 4–6 weeks
before moving them outside, but they
require a constant temperature of 55–60° F
during germination, which takes 14–18
days. Plant seedlings in the garden after fros
danger has passed.

Uses
Rock purslane is a good choice for rock
gardens and borders and can be used as an
annual ground cover.

umbellata p. 87
Rock Purslane. This species is a spreading
plant that grows 6 inches high. The ¾-inch
flowers are red to crimson-magenta and
bloom during summer in small clusters.
Tender perennial grown as a half-hardy
annual.

Callirhoe
Mallow family
Malvaceae

Kal-lir'o. A small genus of North American
perennials, well liked for their showy
poppylike flowers, which are deep pink to

purple. The plants grow in clumps from which sprout trailing 1- to 3-foot stems covered with attractive deeply cut or lobed leaves.

How to Grow
Finger Poppy Mallow, the species listed below, is easy to grow in full sun and dry, well-drained soil. Like most plants with deep taproots, it is very drought tolerant but is difficult to transplant or divide. Start new plants from seeds or cuttings; space them 18 inches apart in the garden.

Uses
Plant Finger Poppy Mallow in a rock garden, a wildflower garden, or cascading over walls and raised beds. It grows well by the seashore and makes a good ground cover.

involucrata *p. 86*
Finger Poppy Mallow; Low Poppy Mallow. These 6- to 12-inch-high plants bear numerous purple to pale reddish-purple flowers, 1½–2½ inches wide, during the summer. The blooms are cup shaped and have conical creamy-white centers.
Zones 4–8.

Campanula
Bellflower family
Campanulaceae

Kam-pan'you-la. Bellflowers comprise an important group of annuals, biennials, and perennials that come in a wide variety of shapes and sizes. Their common feature is their handsome bloom, which is typically bell shaped and blue but can also be white, pink, violet, or purple. The leaves at the base of the plant are larger and broader than the stem leaves.

How to Grow
Bellflowers grow best in full sun or light shade and rich, well-drained soil. Although most bellflowers prefer moist soil, Serbian Bellflower, described below, is drought resistant. Propagate Serbian Bellflower from seeds, by division, or from cuttings; space plants 9–12 inches apart. Cut faded flowers off to keep the plants vigorous and tidy. Be on the lookout for slugs, which enjoy devouring the leaves.

Uses
Plant Serbian Bellflower in a rock garden, at the front of a mixed border, or cascading down a rock wall, or use it as a ground cover.

poscharskyana p. 123
Serbian Bellflower. This weak-stemmed, sprawling plant grows 4–6 inches high and can spread as much as 2 feet across. The numerous 1-inch flowers are lilac or light blue. They start to bloom in late spring and continue through the summer. Zones 4–8.

Caragana
Pea family
Leguminosae

Ka-ra-gay'na. Pea Shrub. Decorative shrubs and trees comprising nearly 60 species, most native to central Asia. The leaves are finely divided; the flowers, typically yellow and pealike, bloom in mid-spring to late spring. Seedpods form after the flowers fade; they are shaped like narrow string beans.

How to Grow
Pea shrubs are easy to grow in full sunlight and average to sandy soil with good drainage. They tolerate drought, alkaline soil, salt, and wind. Choose their permanent location carefully; they are difficult to transplant once established. Prune plants after they have flowered; this will eliminate most of the seedpods, which are not ornamental. Propagate from cuttings or from seeds (soak seeds in hot water first).

Uses
Pea shrubs are superior hedge plants in northern climates where they act as windbreaks and snow traps.

arborescens p. 151
Siberian Pea Shrub. These shrubs can grow to 20 feet high but usually reach only 7–9 feet. They have an erect, narrow habit. The leaves are 1–3½ inches long and are composed of 8–12 tiny leaflets. The flowers are ¾ inch long; although they bloom singly, they are close together and therefore showy. The seedpod is 1½–2 inches long. Zones 2–7.

frutex p. 150
Russian Pea Shrub. This smooth, erect shrub grows to 10 feet high. The leaves are divided

into 2–4 oval, dull green 1-inch leaflets that are arranged like fingers on a hand. Bright yellow flowers bloom in small clusters slightly earlier than those of Siberian Pea Shrub. The seedpods are 2½ inches long. Zones 2–7.

Caryopteris
Verbena family
Verbenaceae

Carry-op′ter-is. A genus of attractive Asiatic deciduous shrubs grown for their aromatic leaves and showy bloom. Of the six species, only one, commonly called Bluebeard or Blue Spirea, is well known. The leaves are short-stemmed and toothed; the flowers have five lobes and appear in dense clusters.

How to Grow
Plant Bluebeard in full sun in average to rich, well-drained soil that is neutral to alkaline. Water it deeply but infrequently. Plants may die to the ground in the colder limits of their hardiness, but the roots will survive if they receive winter protection. In winter or very early spring cut the stems back almost to the ground. Propagate from stem cuttings.

Uses
Plant Bluebeard in a mixed border where its color can be appreciated.

× *clandonensis* p. 163
Bluebeard; Blue Spirea. This low mounded plant usually grows 2 feet high. Its lance-shaped grayish leaves are 3 inches long. The blue ½-inch-long flowers bloom in clusters in midsummer to late summer. 'Kew Blue' and 'Blue Mist' are popular cultivars. Zones 5–10.

Cassia
Pea family
Leguminosae

Cash′i-a. Senna. An immense genus of about 500 perennials, shrubs, and trees grown for their usually showy bloom. The leaves are finely divided; the flowers have five petals, one of which is clawed. Flat or roundish seedpods follow the flowers.

How to Grow

Feathery Cassia, the species listed below, is very drought-resistant shrub that grows well in full sun and dry, well-drained, infertile soil. Be careful not to over-water it. Prune plants after the flowers fade to prevent the seedpods, which are not attractive, from forming. Propagate from seeds or cuttings.

Uses

Plant Feathery Cassia in a shrub border, in a hedge, or standing alone.

artemisioides p. 153

Feathery Cassia; Wormwood Senna. This compact evergreen shrub grows to 4 feet tall. The leaves are silky gray; each leaf has 6–8 needlelike 1-inch leaflets. The flowers are yellow and bloom in 2- to 6-inch clusters that arise from the leaf axils in early spring to summer. Zones 9–10.

Catalpa
Trumpet-creeper family
Bignoniaceae

Ka-tal'pa. A genus of attractive deciduous trees from North America and Asia that are valued for their rapid growth and their spectacular late-spring flowers. They can, however, be messy trees as they drop their large leaves, flowers, and seedpods.

How to Grow

Catalpas grow easily in full sun and ordinary soil and tolerate both moist and dry growing conditions. They thrive in hot, dry summers. They are soft-wooded trees that reach maturity quickly and then soon begin to fail. For this reason, combine them with other, more permanent, trees. Catalpa leaves can be damaged by wind, so do not plant them in windy spots. Prune trees when they are young to train an umbrella-shaped crown.

Uses

Because of their size, catalpas are suited only to large properties where they look magnificent standing alone.

speciosa pp. 204, 205

Northern Catalpa; Hardy Catalpa; Western Catalpa. These trees often reach 60 feet tall. They have long trunks and deep reddish-

brown bark. The leaves are oval to oblong or heart shaped. They grow 8–12 inches long and are densely hairy on the undersides. The trumpet-shaped flowers are white with yellow stripes inside; each is 2 inches wide and grows in a cluster 7 inches long. Beanlike seedpods form in fall; they are 10–16 inches long. Zones 4–8.

Catananche
Daisy family
Compositae

Kat-a-nann'ke. A small genus of biennials and perennials native to the Mediterranean region, one of which, Cupid's Dart, is grown in the garden.

How to Grow
This hardy deep-rooted perennial will bloom the first year and can be grown as an annual if seeds are started indoors 6–8 weeks before outdoor planting time. Germination takes 21–25 days. Transplant the seedlings to the garden in early spring to mid-spring, as soon as the soil can be worked, setting them 10–12 inches apart. In mild climates, sow seeds outdoors in late summer or fall. Plant Cupid's Dart in full sun in dry, well-drained soil. It is essential that the soil be dry over the winter, or the plants will not live long. Because it has a deep root, Cupid's Dart is quite drought resistant. It needs little if any fertilizer. Remove faded flowers to prolong bloom. If you are growing Cupid's Dart as a perennial, divide the plants in fall when necessary. Cupid's Dart grows best in warm climates.

Uses
Cupid's Dart is excellent in a mixed flower bed or border; it is a good cut or dried flower.

caerulea p. 95
Cupid's Dart; Blue Succory. This plant grows 2 feet high, with grasslike, woolly gray-green leaves, 8–12 inches long, growing at the base. The showy 2-inch flowers have flat lacy petals of blue, white, lavender-blue, or blue and white, with dark blue centers. They bloom all summer on wiry, 8- to 12-inch stems. Cupid's Dart is a perennial hardy in zones 5–9 but is often grown as a hardy annual.

Catharanthus
Dogbane family
Apocynaceae

Kath-ar-an'thus. A small genus of five
species of annual and perennial herbs native
to the Old World tropics. The species listed
below, Madagascar Periwinkle, is a popular
garden plant.

How to Grow
Madagascar Periwinkle grows best in warm
to hot climates; it is very drought resistant
and will grow in pure sand. Plant it in full
sun or partial shade, in soil that is dry and
well drained. Start seeds indoors 12 weeks
before the last spring frost; keep the seeds in
darkness during the 15- to 20-day
germination period. Move plants to the
garden after all frost danger has passed,
spacing them 6–24 inches apart, depending
on plant habit. Fertilize at planting time; no
further feeding is necessary. In areas where
Madagascar Periwinkle is perennial, fertilize
once a year and prune it to keep it compact.

Uses
Madagascar Periwinkle's versatility makes it
useful in beds, borders, and seashore gardens,
and as a ground cover.

roseus p. 107
Madagascar Periwinkle. Depending on the
variety, these plants are spreading and grow
only 3–5 inches high and 24 inches across, or
upright and grow 10–24 inches tall. The
leaves are shiny, leathery, and waxy. The
showy, 1- to 1½-inch flowers are pink, rose,
or white, and often have a red or pink eye.
They bloom all summer and fall until frost
and will bloom all year in frost-free areas.
Flowers fall cleanly as they fade, and dropped
seeds may easily self-sow. Madagascar
Periwinkle plants tolerate heat, drought,
humidity, and pollution. Sometimes sold as
Vinca rosea. Tender perennial usually grown
as a tender annual.

Ceanothus
Buckthorn family
Rhamnaceae

See-a-no'thus. Wild Lilac. About 55 species
of fast-growing deciduous or evergreen
shrubs or small trees, most native to

California. Their small white or blue flowers
are borne in showy clusters and resemble
lilacs.

How to Grow
Wild lilacs like open sunlight and porous,
well-drained, acid to neutral soil. Too much
water can cause root rot and death of the
plant; water deeply but infrequently. Prune
plants as soon as the flowers fade to shape
them and control their size. Mature plants
become rangy with age and are best replaced.
Wild lilacs grow best where summers are
cool. Propagate the species from seeds, the
named varieties from cuttings or by layering.

Uses
The species listed below, with their different
habits, have different uses in the garden. San
Diego Ceanothus is attractive as an accent
plant or in a hedge and can be trained to
grow against a wall. Carmel Creeper is an
excellent ground cover for a massed planting
on a slope, along the roadside, or at the
seashore.

cyaneus 'Sierra Blue' *p. 163*
San Diego Ceanothus. This evergreen shrub
grows 10–12 feet high and almost as wide.
Its toothed oval leaves are 1–2 inches long.
The blue flowers bloom in showy, 2- to 5-
inch clusters in early spring. Zones 8–10.

griseus **var.** *horizontalis p. 162*
Carmel Creeper. This low-growing evergreen
shrub reaches 1½–3 feet high and spreads 5–
15 feet wide. The oval 1¾-inch leaves are
leathery and bright glossy green. Deep blue
flowers bloom in 2-inch clusters in early
spring. The named varieties have more
predictable growth habits than the species.
'Yankee Point' has profuse bright blue
flowers. Zones 8–10.

Cedrus
Pine family
Pinaceae

See'drus. Cedar. A genus of four species of
handsome coniferous evergreens, three of
which are widely cultivated. The needles are
stiff and are arranged along the branches in
small, dense, tufted clusters. The flowers are
inconspicuous; the cones are tightly scaly and
upright.

How to Grow
Atlas Cedar, the species listed below, needs average, preferably dry, well-drained soil. It performs best if not exposed to drying winds at any time of year. It grows best in full sun but will tolerate some shade.

Uses
Atlas Cedar is a spectacular lawn specimen; give it plenty of space to show it off to its best. It can also be used as a screen.

atlantica pp. 232, 233
Atlas Cedar. These upright trees grow 40–60 feet high and 30–45 feet wide. The branches are stiff and angular, especially when the tree is young. The needles are just under 1 inch long. The light brown cones are 2–3 inches long. 'Glauca', Blue Atlas Cedar, has blue needles. Zones 6–9.

Celtis
Elm family
Ulmaceae

Sell'tis. Hackberry. Only a few of the 70 widely distributed species of the elmlike, usually medium-size, round-headed trees in this genus are in cultivation. Their leaves are three-veined; the flowers are inconspicuous and are followed by green to black, egg-shaped to round, berrylike fruits that are somewhat tasty.

How to Grow
Hackberries are remarkably tolerant of soil variations—acid or alkaline, slightly wet or very dry—and are highly resistant to heat, wind, and city air pollution. Grow new plants from seeds, from cuttings, by layering, or by grafting.

Uses
Hackberries are useful shade, street, and background trees. They are not highly ornamental but, due to their deep roots and resistance to the elements, are valuable trees for difficult sites.

occidentalis pp. 208, 209
Common Hackberry. Although this round-headed tree can grow up to 100 feet tall, it is usually lower-growing. The finely toothed leaves are 3–5 inches long, oval to oblong, tapered at the tip, and rounded at the base.

They turn yellow in fall. The ⅓-inch-long fruit is greenish orange at first, darkening to black. It is somewhat pear shaped and the pulp is thin but tasty. At maturity, Common Hackberry resembles the American Elm. It has deep roots, which make it drought resistant and a good street tree. Zones 4–8.

Centaurea
Daisy family
Compositae

Sen-tor′ree-a. A genus of chiefly Eurasian annuals and perennials comprising more than 400 species. They have long thin leaves that are sometimes divided or lobed and appear on wiry stems. The flowers are double and frilled, ruffled, or tufted; they are usually blue but sometimes white, pink, rose, lavender, or yellow.

How to Grow
Centaureas grow well in full sun and dry, light, neutral soil (adjust your soil's pH if necessary). They are drought tolerant and should not be over-watered. Sow seeds of both annual and perennial centaureas in the garden in early spring where growing seasons are short, and in late summer through fall where winters are mild. Seeds can also be sown indoors, 4 weeks before outdoor planting time in mid-spring; keep seeds in darkness until they germinate. Space or thin the plants to 6–24 inches apart, depending on their ultimate size. Tall plants may have to be staked. Perennial centaureas can be increased from cuttings or by division.

Uses
Plant centaureas in beds, borders, or wildflower gardens. They are good cut flowers, fresh or dried.

cyanus p. 94
Bachelor's Button; Cornflower. This sprawling or bushy annual prefers cool climates. It grows 1–2 feet high and bears 1½-inch flowers and 2- to 3-inch gray-green leaves. The flowers are usually blue but may also be purple, pink, or white. The blooming period is short; for a long period of color, make successive plantings every 2 weeks. Hardy annual.

montana p. 95
Mountain Bluet. This spreading perennial plant grows 18–24 inches high and has lobed oblong leaves that are white and hairy when young. The 3-inch flowers are usually deep blue but are sometimes pink. Plants bloom in late spring and off and on throughout the summer. Cut them back after they flower to encourage further bloom. Zones 3–8.

Cerastium
Pink family
Caryophyllaceae

See-ras'tee-um. Chickweed. Although this genus contains some toxic weeds, it also contains a few perennials, such as Snow-in-Summer, attractive enough for the garden. The leaves are often gray and hairy; the individual flowers are small but they bloom in profuse showy clusters.

How to Grow
Snow-in-Summer grows well in full sun, although it prefers light shade in areas with very hot summers. It can be planted in any well-drained soil, including poor soil (it will even grow in pure sand), and like most plants with gray foliage, it is drought resistant. It also withstands extremes of heat and cold. Shear faded flowers to keep plants compact and neat and to prevent them from becoming invasive; plants can also be mowed in the spring. Grow new plants from seeds or by dividing existing plants in spring or fall. Set plants 12–18 inches apart.

Uses
Snow-in-Summer serves a wide range of landscape needs: It does well in rock gardens on banks, rock walls, and along the sides of stepping stones and can be used for ground covers, edgings, and fillers.

tomentosum p. 131
Snow-in-Summer. This popular, rapid-growing garden plant grows less than 6 inches high but can spread up to 3 feet across. The pointed inch-long leaves are white and woolly. The dense tufts of white flowers with notched petals appear in early summer. Zones 4–10.

Ceratonia
Pea family
Leguminosae

See-ra-tone'ee-a. Carob. This genus has just one species, a broadleaf evergreen tree from the eastern Mediterranean, cultivated since antiquity for its long leathery pods, which contain a sweet edible pulp surrounding the seeds. These pods are known as St. John's bread.

How to Grow
Carob grows in full sun in any well-drained soil and tolerates drought. Water deeply but infrequently to avoid root rot. Remove lower branches when the plant is young to train it as a tree instead of a shrub. Carob needs room; its width may equal its height. There are separate male and female plants and both must be planted to ensure fruit.

Uses
Carob, which can be planted as a shade tree or hedge, is desirable for its attractive flowers and its fruit, a popular substitute for chocolate.

siliqua *pp. 210, 211*
Carob. This rounded tree grows 20–50 feet high. The wavy compound leaves have 4–8 broad leathery leaflets, each 2–4 inches long. The ¼-inch flowers are red and bloom in narrow 6-inch clusters. Unlike the flowers of most members of the pea family, they are not pealike. The dark brown pods are 4–12 inches long and slightly flattened; they form in fall. Zones 9–10.

Cercis
Pea family
Leguminosae

Sir'sis. Redbud; Judas Tree. Four of the seven known species of these very attractive shrubs or small deciduous trees are grown for their showy flowers. Their very early spring bloom, which appears before the leaves open, makes them useful landscape accents while many plants are still dormant. The leaves are round to heart shaped, not compound like those of most members of the pea family. The tiny but numerous flowers are rose-pink, rose-purple, or white. The seedpod is flat, thin, and narrowly winged.

How to Grow

Redbuds are easy to grow in full sun or partial shade and open, dry, sandy, well-drained soil. Select their location carefully as they do not like to be transplanted. In some parts of the country, a vascular wilt disease or a canker disease can be troublesome. Drought may increase the chance of disease; deep irrigation and mulching during periods of drought is beneficial in disease-prone areas.

Uses

Western Redbud, the species listed below, is an attractive specimen plant and will grow on a dry, seldom watered bank.

occidentalis pp. 198, 199

Western Redbud. This shrub or small tree grows 10–15 feet high and wide. It usually grows several trunks from the base. In early spring, the ½-inch magenta flowers bloom, and the plants become a mass of color. The leaves are 3 inches long and notched or rounded at the tip; they are bluish green and turn light yellow or red in the fall. Magenta seedpods start to form in summer; they turn reddish brown and remain on the branches all winter. Zones 5–9.

Cercocarpus
Rose family
Rosaceae

Sir-ko-kar'pus. Mountain Mahogany. A small genus of evergreen or partly deciduous large shrubs or low-growing trees native to dry western North American mountain slopes. The leathery leaves clothe an attractive, open branching pattern. The flowers are small and inconspicuous; they have no petals but their sepals form an elongated tube that opens into five lobes. All species have attractive fruits that look like feather-tailed plumes. The hard heavy wood is mahoganylike, which is how the genus got its common name.

How to Grow

Plant mountain mahogany in full sun and dry, well-drained soil. It will tolerate heavy pruning; old overgrown plants can be cut to the ground to force new growth. Propagate from seeds or cuttings.

Uses
Mountain mahogany grows well on dry
slopes; if pruned to grow densely it can be
used as a screen or hedge.

intricatus p. 175
This intricately branched species grows to
10 feet high. The leaves are narrow and ½
inch long; their margins roll under almost to
the midrib. The long twisted fruits have very
showy plumes. Zones 5–10.

ledifolius p. 175

Curl-leaf Mountain Mahogany. This species
grows 20–30 feet high and has a spreading
open crown of thick twisted branches with
furrowed reddish-brown bark. The leathery,
½- to 1-inch leaves are dark green on the
top, white and hairy on the bottom; their
edges roll under. The fruits have tail-like
plumes. Zones 4–10.

montanus p. 174
This erect open species grows 5–10 feet high.
Its bark is brown and fissured or scaly. The
leaves are prominently veined and coarsely
toothed; they are white and fuzzy on the
undersides. The fruit, which forms in the
fall, has a silky plume that is 2–5 inches
long. Zones 6–10.

Chaenomeles
Rose family
Rosaceae

Kee-nom'e-lees. Flowering Quince. All of
the known species of this plant are from
eastern Asia and are popular garden shrubs
because of their beautiful early-spring bloom.
They also bear hard, aromatic quincelike
fruits that can be made into preserves. True
quince is in the genus *Cydonia*. The flowers of
flowering quince bloom singly or in small,
close clusters; they have five petals and
numerous stamens.

How to Grow
Flowering quince is easy to grow in full sun
and any well-drained soil. It will tolerate
slightly alkaline soil. Plants will not survive
heavy pruning but branches can be clipped
into interesting Oriental-style patterns in
early spring before growth starts. Do not

shear plants, because this will ruin their natural shape. Propagate from semi-hardwood cuttings or by layering.

Uses
Plant flowering quince in hedges, the shrub border, or a rock garden, use it as an accent plant, or train it to grow against a wall.

speciosa p. 155
Common Flowering Quince. These spiny shrubs grow 6–10 feet high and have oval to oblong, 2- to 3-inch leaves that are shiny, dark green, and finely toothed. The 1- to 2-inch flowers are scarlet-red; there are varieties with pink or white flowers. The fruits are yellowish green. The plant is hardy in zones 5–10, but bloom is sparse in zones 9–10.

Chamaebatiaria
Rose family
Rosaceae

Kam-ee-bah'tee-ar-ia. This genus has only one species, Fernbush, a semideciduous shrub native to western North America.

How to Grow
Fernbush grows best in full sun and dry, well-drained soil. It is extremely drought tolerant. Propagate from cuttings or seeds.

Uses
Plant Fernbush in a massed planting or use it as a specimen plant.

millefolium p. 173
Fernbush; Desertsweet Tansybush. This shrub grows 5 feet high and has erect downy stems that are sticky when young. The elegant leaves are finely divided, resembling fern leaves. The fragrant white flowers are single and bloom in panicles in midsummer. Zones 6–10.

Chrysothamnus
Daisy family
Compositae

Chry-so-thame'nus. Rabbitbrush. Thirteen species of shrubs native to the western U.S. and Mexico that have erect multibranched stems. The flowers have yellow or white buttonlike disks but no petals.

How to Grow
Place rabbitbrush in full sun where the soil is dry and well drained. It is extremely drought resistant. Propagate from seeds or cuttings or by division.

Uses
Rabbitbrush is a good plant for a desert garden. Use it as a specimen, on a dry slope, or in a hedge.

nauseosus p. 149
This shrub grows 2–7 feet tall. Its multibranched stems are covered with felty, gray or white, often strongly and unpleasantly scented hairs. The hairy leaves are densely produced; they are 3 inches long and narrow, almost needlelike. The flowers are yellow and bloom in dense clusters in late summer. Zones 3–10.

Cistus
Rockrose family
Cistaceae

Sis'tus. A genus of Mediterranean shrubs, usually called rockroses, long known in Old World gardens. The leaves are evergreen, or nearly so, and soft and hairy. The flowers are large and resemble a single rose, with five petals and numerous stamens.

How to Grow
Rockroses must have open sunlight and dry, slightly alkaline, well-drained soil. They will tolerate drought, heat, and poor soil but not wet, cold winters. Propagate from seeds or cuttings. Once plants are in place, they will not transplant easily. Prune back lightly after flowering if necessary.

Uses
Because rockroses are flame retardant, they are valuable in dry areas of California. They are also useful as edgings and in rock gardens and are tolerant of salt spray.

× *hybridus* p. 169
White Rockrose. This hybrid shrub grows 2–4 feet high and wide and is more or less bushy. Both the twigs and the oval 2-inch leaves are downy. On warm days, the leaves are fragrant. The 1½-inch flowers are white with a yellow eye and bloom in late spring and early summer. Zones 8–10.

Clematis
Buttercup family
Ranunculaceae

Klem′a-tis. About 270 species of perennial herbs and shrubby or woody vines, widely distributed but mostly from eastern Asia, th Himalayas, and North America. The leaves are usually compound, with three, five, or more leaflets; the leafstalk often curls like a tendril. The flowers are often very showy and come in a variety of colors.

How to Grow
Most clematis prefer rich, moist soil, but Western Virgin's Bower, the species listed below, prefers dry growing conditions. Plant it in full sun or partial shade and dry, well-drained soil. It is important to keep the roots cool and shaded, so apply a mulch around them. Provide a strong support for the vine at planting time; its stems are brittle and can break in the wind. Prune Western Virgin's Bower in early spring when growth starts. Overgrown plants may be pruned to within a few inches of the ground. Grow new plants from seeds, from cuttings, or by layering.

Uses
Try Western Virgin's Bower as a ground cover on dry slopes or on a trellis or wall.

ligusticifolia p. 104
Western Virgin's Bower; Hill Clematis. This vining plant climbs to 10–20 feet high. Its leaves have 5–7 thick, firm leaflets that turn yellow in the fall. Numerous clusters of tiny, fragrant white flowers bloom in summer. In fall, there is a distinctive display of showy fruits with feathery tail-like appendages. Zones 4–10.

Cleome
Caper family
Capparaceae

Klee-o′me. This genus contains about 200 species of shrubby plants, most of tropical origin, but only one, Spider Flower, has importance for the gardener. The plants of this genus have a strong and unpleasant odor. The lower leaves are divided finger-fashion; the upper leaves are not divided. The flowers have four long-clawed petals and long prominent stamens.

How to Grow
Plant Spider Flower in full sun and dry, well-drained soil. It is very tolerant of heat and drought. Avoid over-watering it, which causes rank growth, and fertilize little, if at all. Where summers are long and warm, sow seeds outdoors in early spring. Elsewhere, start seeds indoors 4–6 weeks before planting time. Move the plants to the garden after frost danger has passed, spacing them 2–3 feet apart. Spider Flower will reseed in warm areas. Although the plants are tall, they do not need to be staked.

Uses
Plant Spider Flower in a hedge, as a background to lower plants, against a wall or fence, or in a wildflower garden. Use dried flowers and seed heads in arrangements.

hasslerana *p. 92*
Spider Flower. These branching bushy plants grow 4–5 feet high and almost as wide. Stems are spiny; the pink, rose-purple, or white flowers are 6–7 inches across and bloom all summer until frost. The 2- to 3-inch stamens and the slender seed capsules that follow the flowers inspired Spider Flower's common name. Half-hardy annual.

Colutea
Pea family
Leguminosae

Ko-lew′tee-a. A genus of 10 species of Eurasian shrubs of the pea family; the species described below, Common Bladder Senna, is often grown for ornament. The leaves are divided; the flowers are pealike, blooming in clusters in the leaf axils. The bladder in the plant's common name refers to the inflated beanlike seedpods that form.

How to Grow
Common Bladder Senna is easy to grow in full sun and average to dry, well-drained soil. These plants fix nitrogen in the soil and should not be fertilized. To keep them looking neat, cut the stems back to old wood after plants flower. Propagate new plants from seeds or cuttings or by grafting.

Uses
Plant Common Bladder Senna in a shrub border or standing alone.

arborescens *pp. 146, 147*

Common Bladder Senna. This deciduous shrub with erect stems grows 5–8 feet high. The leaves have 9–13 leaflets, each 2 inches long. The inch-long flowers are bright yellow and bloom in long-stalked clusters in spring and summer. The papery, inflated seedpod is 2½ inches long; it stays on the plant into winter. Zones 6–9.

Coreopsis
Daisy family
Compositae

Ko-ree-op′sis. A genus of more than 100 species of annuals and perennials from the Americas and Africa, many of which are called tickseed. About a dozen are commonly grown for their yellow, orange, or maroon, single or double flowers. The leaves vary from whole to finely divided.

How to Grow
Coreopsis need full sun and dry, light, sandy soil with good drainage. They grow best in warm or hot climates and need little or no fertilizer. Sow seeds of both annual and perennial species outdoors in early spring. In warm areas, seeds may be sown in late summer or fall. Seeds can also be started indoors 6–8 weeks before outdoor planting in mid-spring. Do not cover the seeds; they need light during the germination period (5–10 days for annuals and 20–25 days for perennials). Transplant the seedlings carefully, so as not to disturb the roots, spacing them 6–12 inches apart—they bloom best when somewhat crowded. Remove faded flowers to prolong bloom and prevent self-sowing. Divide perennial coreopsis in spring or fall.

Uses
Plant coreopsis in flower beds and borders or standing alone as accent plants. They are good cutting flowers.

tinctoria *p. 75*

Golden Coreopsis; Calliopsis. These slender plants with wiry stems grow 1½–3 feet tall. The 1¼-inch flowers are yellow, orange, brown, purple-red, or yellow with a brown base, and have dark red or purple-brown centers. There are double and dwarf varieties. Hardy annual.

verticillata p. 75

Threadleaf Coreopsis. These perennial plants grow 1–3 feet high and have finely cut needlelike leaves. The yellow flowers are 2 inches across. This species is the most drought tolerant of the perennial coreopsis. Zones 4–10.

Coronilla
Pea family
Leguminosae

Kor-ro-nil'la. A small genus of shrubs or herbaceous perennials scattered from the Canary Islands to western Asia. A few are of interest to the gardener, including Crown Vetch, listed below. The leaves are compound; the leaflets arranged in a feathery fashion. Clusters of pealike flowers grow up from the leaf axils, followed by slender seedpods.

How to Grow
Crown Vetch grows best in full sun but tolerates light shade. Plant it in dry, well-drained soil and apply no fertilizer. Crown Vetch seeds are often sold mixed with seeds of annual ryegrass. The ryegrass anchors the Crown Vetch in place until it becomes established, then the ryegrass dies out. Crown Vetch plants can be purchased and planted in the same manner as turfgrass plugs. Mow and water the planting in spring to encourage growth; little care is needed after that.

Uses
Crown Vetch is not a plant for a small garden but is perfect to cover bare areas and slopes that are difficult to mow. It is especially useful in areas needing soil erosion control.

varia p. 93

Crown Vetch. This sprawling plant grows 18–24 inches high and creeps by rhizomes to 4 feet across. The ½-inch-long flowers bloom in dense, showy clusters of pink and white in summer. The leaves are divided into as many as 25 oval leaflets, each ¾ inch long. 'Penngift' is a particularly drought-resistant variety. Zones 4–8.

Cortaderia
Grass family
Gramineae

Kor-ta-deer′i-a. Pampas Grass. Two dozen
species of tall reedlike grasses from southern
South America and New Zealand. They grow
in large clumps, with leaves clustered at the
bases of stems that bear large bushy plumes
in the fall.

How to Grow
Pampas grass likes full sun and fertile soil
with excellent drainage, especially in winter.
Select its location carefully; it may crowd out
smaller plantings. Water only in the spring
when growth starts; the soil should be dry
the rest of the growing season. Divide the
roots when the clumps become crowded.
Occasionally remove dead leaves from the
center of the clumps to improve the
appearance of the plant. Plants can be cut to
the ground in late winter, but handle them
carefully—the leaf edges are razor sharp.
Pampas grass may survive winters in zone 7 if
the clumps are tied up in fall and the ground
mulched.

Uses
Pampas grass is a dramatic accent plant for
the garden year-round. It can be used at the
back of a border or as a screen and will help
control erosion on slopes. Cut the plumes for
indoor decoration in winter.

selloana p. 140
Pampas Grass. The stems of this striking
perennial species reach heights of 8–12 feet.
There are separate male and female plants;
the female plants produce the graceful,
feathery, plumed spikes. The spikes, which
grow 1–3 feet long, are silvery to pale pink.
The leaves at the base of the plant are long
and narrow. Zones 8–10.

Cosmos
Daisy family
Compositae

Kos′mus. A genus of showy summer- and
fall-flowering annuals and perennials from
the Americas, primarily Mexico. The plants
are open, bushy, and branching, with bright
green, usually finely divided leaves. The
daisylike flowers are single, double, or

crested and often have frilled or notched petals. They bloom in loose open clusters on slender stems.

How to Grow
Plant cosmos in full sun in poor, dry soil. Rich soil encourages lush foliage at the expense of flowers, so give plants little or no fertilizer. Cosmos are quite drought resistant. Start seeds outdoors after the last frost or indoors 5–7 weeks earlier. Space the plants 1–3 feet apart depending on their ultimate height. Stake the tall varieties if necessary and plant them out of the wind. Cut off faded flowers to prolong bloom. Cosmos self-sow easily.

Uses
Plant cosmos at the front or back of the border, depending on its height, or in large massed plantings. It makes an excellent cutting flower.

bipinnatus p. 89
Garden Cosmos. Plants can grow up to 8 feet tall but usually reach 3–4 feet. The foliage is lacy. The 3- to 6-inch-wide flowers bloom in light, airy clusters. They have white, pink, crimson, or lavender petals and yellow centers. Tender annual.

Cotinus
Cashew family
Anacardiaceae

Ko-ty′nus. Smoke Tree. Three species of deciduous shrubs or small trees, the one below, Common Smoke Tree, cultivated for ornament. The small yellowish flowers are not very showy; they bloom in large-branching terminal clusters. The common name refers to the soft cloudlike masses of pink, gray, or purple fruiting panicles that appear in summer with and after the flowers. The fruiting cluster consists mostly of the lengthened stalks of the numerous sterile flowers, which are plumed and silky. The small, slightly lopsided fruit is fleshy but somewhat dry.

How to Grow
Grow Common Smoke Tree in full sun and any well-drained soil that is not too rich or too moist. Water young plants well, but cut down on watering as plants mature because

they will tolerate drought once established. I
necessary, prune plants lightly when they are
dormant. Common Smoke Tree is easy to
propagate from seeds or cuttings but difficult
to transplant.

Uses
Plant Common Smoke Tree in a screen or
hedge or at the back of the shrub border, or
use it as an accent plant.

coggygria *pp. 176, 177*
Common Smoke Tree; Smokebush. This
multibranched shrub grows 10–15 feet tall.
It has 2- to 3-inch oval leaves that are
abruptly narrowed at the base and turn red in
the fall. The leaves have a strong aroma when
crushed. The multibranched fruiting cluster
is 7–10 inches long and is covered with long
spreading purplish-green hairs. The actual
fruits are few; they are ¼ inch wide and
kidney shaped. 'Purpureus' has purple leaves
and dark hairs. The species is sometimes sold
as *Rhus cotinus*. Zones 5–9.

Cotoneaster
Rose family
Rosaceae

Ko-to′nee-as-ter. About 50 species of
deciduous or evergreen shrubs or small trees
native to the Old World temperate zone.
They are an important group of plants for the
garden because of their growth habit and
showy fruit. Most species have stiff,
spreading branches. The leaves are usually
small, as are the flowers, which are pink or
white and bloom in mid-spring. Bright red
or black berries form in fall and last well into
the winter.

How to Grow
Cotoneasters prefer full sun but will tolerate
partial shade, especially in the afternoon.
They prefer neutral to slightly acid soil that
is well drained. Once established, they
tolerate drought and wind but are prone to
spider mite and lace bug in dry summers.
The little pruning they need, to shape plants
and control their size, can be done any time
of year. Grow new plants from cuttings or by
layering. Large plants are difficult to
transplant.

Uses
Cotoneasters have diverse uses, depending on their habits, that include edgings, ground covers, and rock garden and foundation plantings. They are effective spilling over walls or growing over rocks so the outline of their branches can be seen.

adpressus p. 179
Creeping Cotoneaster. This ground-hugging deciduous shrub grows 12–18 inches high. Its stems grow in a herringbone pattern and root as they creep along the ground. Plants spread 3–4 feet across. The ½-inch-long leaves have wavy margins and turn red in fall; the ¼-inch flowers are pinkish. Red berries form in the fall. The variety *praecox* grows 3 feet tall. It is more vigorous and has pinker flowers and larger fruit than the species. Zones 5–9.

divaricatus p. 179
Spreading Cotoneaster. This upright deciduous shrub grows 3–7 feet tall and has wide-spreading branches. The ¾-inch leaves are pale green on the underside and turn orange and red in autumn. The pinkish flowers are ¼ inch wide. The profuse and showy berries are bright red, ultimately turning plum-red. This is one of the handsomest and easiest-to-grow cotoneasters. Zones 5–9.

horizontalis p. 184
Rockspray Cotoneaster. This low-growing cotoneaster can reach 2–3 feet high and has fan-shaped or herringbone-shaped, almost trailing branches that spread to 6 feet across. Plants are semievergreen in warm climates and deciduous in the colder limits of their hardiness. The ½-inch leaves are nearly round; they turn orange-red in autumn. The pinkish flowers are ¼ inch wide; the berries are red. Zones 5–9.

salicifolius p. 187
Willowleaf Cotoneaster. This upright shrub grows 7–12 feet high and wide. It is evergreen in mild climates and deciduous in the North; foliage turns purple to red-purple in the fall. The narrow leaves are 1½–3 inches long. They appear on supple branches that make this the most graceful of the cotoneasters. The flowers are white, the berries red. 'Repens' is a prostrate variety that grows only 12 inches high. Zones 6–9.

Crataegus
Rose family
Rosaceae

Kra-tee'gus. Hawthorn; Thornapple. An enormous genus of perhaps 1,000 species of thorny deciduous shrubs and trees found in the north temperate zone but most common in eastern North America. Fewer than 20 are landscape worthy; they are grown for their spring flowers and bright fall fruit. The leaves are toothed or lobed. Mature specimens develop round tops and attractive horizontal branches. The bark on twigs and younger branches is usually light gray and is attractive in winter. The single flowers are white, red, or pink. The brightly colored fruits resemble crabapples.

How to Grow
Hawthorns prefer open, sandy, alkaline, well-drained soil; they tolerate poor soil and drought. Although they are used as barrier plants because of their thorns, they do not tolerate being clipped into hedges.
Hawthorns suffer from a number of problems including insects, fireblight, and cedar apple rust, and therefore need frequent spraying.

Uses
Hawthorn is effective as a barrier plant and in an informal massed planting. Its berries attract birds. Cockspur Hawthorn tolerates city growing conditions.

crus-galli pp. 202, 203
Cockspur Hawthorn. This species is a large shrub or small tree that grows up to 30 feet high. The 4-inch-long thorns are numerous, slender, and sharp. The shiny 3-inch leaves are wedge shaped at the base, toothed in the upper part; they turn bronze-red in the fall. The flowers are ½-inch wide and bloom in 2- to 3-inch, flat-topped clusters. The rounded fruits last into winter; they are bright red. *C. c. inermis* is a thornless variety. Zones 5–9.

Cynoglossum
Borage family
Boraginaceae

Sin-o-gloss'um. A genus of 90 species of widely distributed biennials and perennials, most of them weedy. The leaves are often

rough and hairy. The flowers are small and
funnel shaped, with five rounded lobes; they
bloom in arching, one-sided clusters.

How to Grow

Chinese Forget-Me-Not, described below, is
a drought-tolerant species. Plant it in full
sun or light shade in average to dry soil that
is well drained. Mulch to keep the soil cool
and retain moisture. Where winters are mild,
sow seeds in the fall; elsewhere, sow seeds
outdoors in early spring as soon as the soil can
be worked. Seeds can also be started indoors,
6–8 weeks before outdoor planting time;
they need darkness during germination.
Space plants 9–12 inches apart. Fertilize at
planting time; no further feeding is
necessary. Chinese Forget-Me-Not prefers
cool weather but will tolerate warm climates.

Uses

Plant Chinese Forget-Me-Not in beds,
borders, or wildflower gardens, or combine it
with late spring bulbs. It is a good flower for
cutting.

amabile *p. 102*

Chinese Forget-Me-Not. These plants grow
18–24 inches high. Their gray-green leaves
are hairy and lance shaped. The tiny flowers
bloom in loose, showy clusters in spring (and
summer in cool climates). The flowers are
usually blue but may be pink or white; they
resemble those of True Forget-Me-Nots but
are larger. Chinese Forget-Me-Not is a
biennial but it blooms the first year and is
usually grown as a hardy annual.

Cytisus
Pea family
Leguminosae

Sigh'ti-sus. Broom. Fifty species of mostly
southern European shrubs, many grown for
their spreading, multistemmed habits and
their profuse pealike flowers. The graceful
and slender stems remain green all winter,
making even the deciduous species look as if
they are evergreen. The leaves are often
compound and are sometimes so small they
are barely discernible. The irregular two-
lipped flowers are yellow, red, purple, or
white. After the flowers fade, flat beanlike
seedpods form.

How to Grow

Brooms are easy to grow in full sun and dry, poor soil with good drainage. The species listed below prefer slightly acid to neutral soil. Plants will tolerate average moisture but also grow well in drought conditions. Once established, brooms do not like to be transplanted. Prune plants after they have flowered to keep them compact. Propagate from seeds or cuttings.

Uses

Use brooms in shrub borders, to cover slopes, or as specimens.

× *praecox* p. 152

Warminster Broom. This dense handsome plant grows 6–10 feet high in an arching habit. The pale yellow or yellowish-white flowers bloom in mid-spring. They are very attractive but have an unpleasant odor. The ¾-inch-long leaves are silky. The cultivar 'Allgold' has a dense mounded habit and bright yellow flowers. 'Hollandia' has pale cream and purple-red flowers. Zones 7–10.

scoparius pp. 146, 147

Scotch Broom. The green branches of this 4- to 9-foot-high shrub make it look evergreen through the winter even after all its leaves have fallen off. The leaflets are ⅓–½ inch long and cling closely to the branches. The 1-inch flowers are bright yellow and bloom in mid-spring. There are cultivars with red or red and yellow blooms. This species is a rampant grower. Zones 6–10.

Delosperma
Carpetweed family
Aizoaceae

Dell-o-sperm'a. Ice Plant. About 140 species of small, dense succulent perennials or small shrubs from South Africa. The leaves may be cylindrical, triangular, or flat. The spring-blooming flowers are daisylike.

How to Grow

Plant ice plants in full sun and sandy, rich, well-drained soil. They tolerate drought once established but look better if they receive water during summer heat. Dry soil and temperatures below 50° F are critical during the winter. Propagate from seeds or cuttings. Fertilize lightly when flower buds form.

Uses
Ice plants are at home in rock gardens, as edgings, and as ground covers on slopes, especially those needing soil erosion control.

cooperi p. 119
Hardy Ice Plant. The ground-hugging spreading branches of this species reach 6 inches high and 24 inches wide. Their thick evergreen leaves are covered with gray-green blisters that glisten like ice in the sun. The leaves are 2½ inches long, ¼ inch wide, and nearly cylindrical but flattened on the upper side. Foliage is brilliant red during fall and winter. The flowers are 2 inches across and have purple petals. Zones 7–10.

nubigenum p. 114
The hardiest of all ice plants, this species grows only 1–2 inches high but spreads to 3 feet across. Its fleshy leaves turn red in fall. The large clear yellow flowers bloom profusely in spring. Zones 5–10.

Dianthus
Pink family
Caryophyllaceae

Dy-an'thus. A large genus of annuals, biennials, and perennials, mostly Eurasian, that are important garden plants. The leaves are usually narrow, tinged blue or gray, and grow in grassy clumps or tufted mats. In mild climates, the foliage is evergreen. The single or double flowers are red, white, or pink, and have a spicy fragrance. Most members of the genus are called pinks because the petals look like they have been cut with pinking shears.

How to Grow
Pinks grow best in full sun but they like afternoon shade in very hot climates. They also like dry soil that is extremely well drained, so be careful not to over-water. Some species, such as *D. plumarius,* below, prefer soil that is slightly alkaline; most thrive in climates with cool summers and mild winters. Plants are inclined to die out in 2 or 3 years. To keep your planting healthy, propagate new plants by division or by layering, or from cuttings or seeds; set them 12–18 inches apart. Remove flowers as they fade and cut the flowering stalks to the ground in fall. Apply a light mulch of evergreen branches to reduce winter damage.

Uses
Plant pinks in the front of a border, in a rock garden, or along a path. Use the flowers for cutting.

plumarius p. 91
Grass Pink; Border Pink; Cottage Pink. This mat-forming pink has smooth blue-gray leaves and grows 9–18 inches high. The 1½-inch flowers are white or rose-pink to purple and have dark centers; they may be single or double. They bloom heavily in late spring to early summer and continue to flower sporadically through the rest of the summer. Zones 4–10.

Dimorphotheca
Daisy family
Compositae

Dy-more-fo-thee′ka. Cape Marigold. A small genus of annuals and perennials from South Africa. Leaves are slightly toothed and grow at the base of the plants. The flowers are cheerful and free blooming, they appear singly on long stems. The long strap-shaped petals are yellow, orange, or white, with blue or lavender undersides.

How to Grow
Plant Cape marigolds in full sun and light, sandy, well-drained soil. They tolerate drought and heat, but their blooms are larger in cool temperatures. In areas with mild winters, sow seeds in late summer for fall to winter bloom and again in late spring. Elsewhere, start seeds indoors 4–6 weeks before the last spring frost. Transplant outdoors after frost danger has passed, spacing plants 4–8 inches apart. Fertilize every other month. Cape marigold seeds do not store well.

Uses
Plant Cape marigolds in borders or massed plantings, or use them as filler plants or ground covers.

sinuata p. 107
Cape Marigold. These plants grow 4–12 inches high and have lobed gray-green leaves. The 1½-inch flowers have creamy white, orange, or yellow petals, with yellow centers. There are hybrids with white, yellow, orange, apricot, or salmon flowers, some

with a dark center. Flowers bloom in winter
and spring in mild climates and in summer
elsewhere. They close at night and on cloudy
days. Tender annual.

Duchesnea
Rose family
Rosaceae

Doo-shay′nee-a. Two species of Asiatic
perennials related to the strawberry; Mock
Strawberry, described below, is a drought-
tolerant species. The leaves, which resemble
those of the strawberry, are divided into three
toothed oval leaflets. They remain on the
plant well into winter. The small yellow
flowers have five petals.

How to Grow
Mock Strawberry is very easy to grow; plant
it in full sun to partial shade in any well-
drained soil. It likes moist soil but tolerates
drought. Add organic matter to the soil to
increase flowering and fruiting. Plants are
rapid-growing and may become invasive;
divide them or thin them out as needed.

Uses
Mock Strawberry is an effective ground cover
in large areas.

indica p. 131
Mock Strawberry; Barren Strawberry. Plants
grow 2–3 inches high and spread to 2 feet
across by runners that produce new plants at
their ends. The ½-inch flowers appear in
summer; they are followed by red
strawberrylike fruits that have little flavor.
The fruits stand above the leaves, not under
them as they do in the strawberry plant.
Zones 4–10.

Dyssodia
Daisy family
Compositae

Diss-o′di-a. A genus of strongly scented
annuals and perennials native to Mexico and
the southwestern U.S. The leaves of some
species are divided. The daisylike flowers
bloom one to a stem or in slender, one-sided
clusters.

How to Grow

Dahlberg Daisy, the species described below
tolerates drought especially well. It prefers
cool weather but will withstand heat. Sow
seeds indoors 6–8 weeks before the last frost
and move the plants outside when frost
danger has passed. Plant them in full sun and
dry, sandy soil with good drainage, spacing
them 4–6 inches apart. Fertilize sparingly, if
at all.

Uses

Use Dahlberg Daisy in massed plantings,
beds, borders, or rock gardens, or as an
edging, ground cover, or accent plant.

tenuiloba p. 74

Dahlberg Daisy. Plants grow 6–12 inches
high. Dark green finely divided leaves clothe
the slender stems. The bright 1-inch flowers
are yellow or yellow-orange and bloom from
early summer to frost; they will bloom in the
winter in mild climates. Dahlberg Daisies act
as short-lived perennials in frost-free areas.
Half-hardy annual.

Echinacea
Daisy family
Compositae

Ek-in-a'see-a. A genus of North American
perennials commonly called coneflowers
because the centers of the daisylike flowers
are conical. Plants are coarse, with large
clumps of stiff, erect hairy stems. The flowers
have drooping petals and bloom in
midsummer to late summer.

How to Grow

Plant coneflowers in full sun or light shade
and sandy, well-drained soil. If the soil is too
fertile, the stems become floppy. Like many
plants with hairy stems and leaves,
coneflowers are very drought tolerant; they
also tolerate wind. Coneflowers self-sow
easily. If necessary, divide in spring or fall.

Uses

Plant coneflowers in a wildflower garden, in
the middle or back of the perennial border, or
in a cutting garden.

purpurea p. 89

Purple Coneflower. Plants grow 2–4 feet
high. The oblong, 3- to 8-inch leaves are

coarsely toothed. The flowers are 3–6 inches wide and have white, pink, violet, or purple petals. Zones 4–10.

Echium
Borage family
Boraginaceae

Ek'i-um. A genus of more than 35 species of Eurasian biennials and perennials that are often grown as annuals. Leaves are rough and broad; both stems and leaves are hairy. The funnel-shaped flowers are primarily blue; they bloom in erect, one-sided spikes.

How to Grow
Viper's Bugloss, the species described below, is a good choice for drought conditions. It requires full sun and poor, dry, well-drained soil. If the soil is too rich, the plant produces lush foliage but few flowers. It needs little or no fertilizer. Sow Viper's Bugloss seeds outdoors in fall where winters are mild and in early spring elsewhere. (Seeds can be started indoors, 4–6 weeks before planting time in mid-spring, but they must have a constant temperature of 60° F during germination.) Space the plants 12–15 inches apart. They grow best in a cool climate.

Uses
Viper's Bugloss grows best in borders or rock gardens and is also an excellent plant for a seashore garden.

lycopsis p. 101
Viper's Bugloss. This 2-foot-tall plant has small blue, lavender, purple, rose, or white flowers. It is a biennial grown as a hardy annual.

Elaeagnus
Oleaster family
Elaeagnaceae

Eel-ee-ag'nus. A genus of about 40 species of handsome shrubs and trees from the north temperate zone. Several are cultivated for their ornamental foliage, which is covered with silvery scales, and their decorative berrylike fruits, which are edible in some species. The tubular or bell-shaped flowers are small and not very showy.

How to Grow

Elaeagnus is easy to grow in full sun and sandy, well-drained soil. It will tolerate adverse growing conditions as well as drought and wind. Leave plants to grow naturally or shear them into formal hedges. Cut back side shoots in spring to encourag colorful new growth. Propagate from cuttings, by layering, or from seeds.

Uses

Elaeagnus can serve as a windbreak, hedge and screen, and grows well in seashore gardens. It also tolerates city conditions.

angustifolia pp. 224, 225

Russian Olive. This sometimes spiny Eurasian deciduous shrub or small tree grow 15–20 feet high and wide in a rounded habi Its twigs are silver; the mature bark is brow and flaking. The narrow leaves, which grow 2–3 inches long, are silvery underneath. Th fragrant flowers are silvery or white outside and yellow inside; they appear in spring. Th ½-inch fruits are yellow with silver scales; they are sweet but mealy. Zones 3–9.

pungens p. 182

Thorny Elaeagnus. This usually spiny, spreading shrub grows 15 feet high. The 5 inch-long evergreen leaves have wavy margins and are silvery underneath. The drooping silvery-white flowers are very fragrant and bloom in fall. The fruit is brow at first, then red. Zones 7–9.

Ephedra
Ephedra family
Ephedraceae

Eff-ee′dra. Joint-Fir. Perhaps 40 species from the deserts of the Northern Hemisphere and South America of scraggly, multibranched coniferous shrubs with slender green stems. The tiny leaves are dry and scaly, two or thre growing at each node. The cones also appea in the stem nodes. This is one of the few genera of cone-producing plants that has significant flowers.

How to Grow

Plant joint-firs in full sun and dry, well-drained soil. They are extremely drought resistant. Increase plants by dividing the clumps, by layering, or from seeds.

Uses
Joint-fir is a good choice for dry slopes and large bare areas. Mormons used to make tea from the stems of Green Mormon Tea, the species listed below.

viridis p. 139
Green Mormon Tea. This species grows 4 feet tall and has evergreen stems and insignificant leaves. Bright yellow flowers appear in spring; they are showier on the male plants. Zones 5–10.

Epimedium
Barberry family
Berberidaceae

Ep-i-mee′di-um. Sometimes called Barrenwort. All of the 20 known species of these rather woody perennials are from the north temperate zone. They have clumps of finely toothed, heart-shaped 1- to 3-inch leaves that are light green and often tinged with red in the fall. The flowers bloom in clusters in spring, sometimes hidden under the leaves. Because of their squarish shape, they are sometimes called Bishop's Hats. Both the flowers and the leaves appear on thin wiry stems. The plants spread slowly by underground stems.

How to Grow
Epimediums grow best in partial shade but will tolerate full sun in cool climates. If the leaves burn, they are receiving too much sun. They prefer soil that is rich, moist, and slightly acid, but they tolerate drought. Cut plants back in early spring to encourage compact growth. Propagate by division; space plants 8–12 inches apart.

Uses
Plant epimedium under trees and shrubs, in a rock garden, or in the front of a perennial or shrub border, or use it as a ground cover.

alpinum p. 132
Alpine Epimedium. These low-growing plants reach 10 inches high and are usually evergreen. The small flowers are red and yellow. Zones 4–10.

grandiflorum p. 120
Longspur Epimedium. Plants grow 12 inches tall and are semievergreen, the old leaves

falling when the new leaves emerge in
spring. The spurred, 1- to 2-inch flowers,
which are the largest of the epimediums, are
white with violet and red sepals. There are
varieties with yellow, pink, and violet
flowers. Sometimes sold as *E. macranthum*.
Zones 5–10.

Eragrostis
Grass family
Gramineae

E-ra-gros′tis. About 250 species of annual
and perennial grasses, a few, such as Sand
Love Grass, described below, grown for their
delicate flower spikes. The dark green leaf
blades are arching, fine textured, and very
narrow, tapering to a point. The flower
spikes are borne in loose, open, branching
clusters.

How to Grow
Sand Love Grass grows best in full sun and
light, sandy, fertile soil. Plants are native to
the western plains states and will survive
without much water in summer. Increase
plants by division or from seeds.

Uses
Plant Sand Love Grass in a mixed border, in
naturalistic garden, or alone as a specimen
plant. The dried seed heads are ornamental.

trichodes p. 142
Sand Love Grass. This slow-spreading, tufted
ornamental perennial has 3-foot-long, erect
or arching leaves. The flower and seed heads
are borne on 4-foot stems; they are narrow
when they first form and later spread to 12
inches wide. They are purplish in early
summer and dry to a buff-brown in fall.
Zones 5–9.

Erigeron
Daisy family
Compositae

E-rij′er-on. Fleabane. A genus of more than
200 species of annuals and perennials of
widely spread origins. Most have pointed soft
green leaves at the base of the plant from
which the flower stems emerge. The blooms
are freely produced in summer, appearing
singly in some species, in clusters in others.

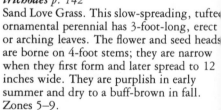

The daisylike flowers have white, pink, lavender, blue, or purple petals in two or more rows around yellow centers.

How to Grow
Plant fleabane in sun or light shade and sandy soil with excellent drainage. It needs watering only during periods of drought. These easy-to-grow plants need only to be cut back after they have flowered, and to be divided in spring or fall when they become crowded. Plants self-sow readily.

Uses
Plant fleabane in a rock garden, mixed border, wildflower garden, or meadow. It is a good plant for the seashore, as it tolerates salt spray and sandy soil.

compositus p. 126
Fleabane. A native of the western U.S., this plant grows in a cushion of soft green, hairy, finely divided leaves. The white or purple flowers are ¾ inch wide and bloom singly on 4- to 8-inch stems from early to late summer. Zones 4–10.

Eriogonum
Buckwheat family
Polygonaceae

E-ri-og'o-num. Wild Buckwheat. Genus of annuals, perennials, and shrubs that are native to the western U.S. The leaves grow in rosettes at the base of the plant; large branched clusters of small flowers appear in summer on almost leafless stalks.

How to Grow
Plant wild buckwheat in full sun and loose, gravelly, well-drained soil. Once established, it requires little watering and withstands wind well. If the flower clusters are not removed from the plants as they fade, the seeds drop and easily self-sow. Grow new plants from seeds or by division.

Uses
Plant wild buckwheat on dry banks or in rock gardens or use it as a ground cover. The dried flower clusters are attractive in bouquets.

umbellatum p. 111
Sulphur-Flower. This woody perennial with spreading branches grows in a loose mat no

more than 12 inches high and up to 3 feet wide. The leaves have woolly undersides; the flowers are cream to bright yellow and bloom in showy, dome-shaped clusters. Zones 9–10.

Eryngium
Carrot family
Umbelliferae

Er-rin'ji-um. Sea Holly; Eryngo. Very striking perennials widely cultivated for borders. The plants are tall, bold, and unlike most members of the carrot family, do not have finely divided leaves. The leaves are cut or lobed and usually spiny. The flowers are unusual looking; their dense, conical blue or green central clusters are surrounded by spiny blue-gray to silvery-gray bracts.

How to Grow
Sea hollies thrive in full sun and well-drained, sandy soil of moderate to low fertility. They are difficult to transplant because of their long taproot, but thanks to this root, are drought resistant. Root cuttings are the best means of propagation since not all plants come true from seed. Plants self-sow easily and may need to be thinned out each spring. Space new plants 12–18 inches apart.

Uses
Sea holly is such an unusual-looking plant that it is most effective as an accent plant in the garden. It contrasts well with bright colors and makes a unique cut flower.

bourgatii p. 138
Mediterranean Eryngo. This perennial has stiff stems and grows 24 inches high. The toothed leaves are silvery gray, marked in white. The flowers bloom in late summer; they are blue with long, spiny silvery-white bracts. Zones 5–7.

Erysimum
Mustard family
Cruciferae

E-riss'i-mum. Blister-Cress. A large genus of annuals and perennials from the north temperate zone, closely related to the wallflower *(Cheiranthus).* The four-petaled flowers are orange, yellow, lilac, or blue; they bloom in terminal clusters. The fruits are long, four-sided, usually beaked pods.

How to Grow
Grow blister-cress in full sun in average to dry, well-drained soil. The plants are remarkable in their ability to withstand unfavorable conditions. They flower profusely in cool weather; they are less satisfactory in excessive heat. The species described below withstands moderate heat if the humidity is not too high. Where winters are mild, sow seeds in the fall; elsewhere, sow seeds as early in the spring as the soil can be worked.

Uses
Plant blister-cresses in a mixed flower border; they are especially attractive when planted with blue flowers.

perofskianum p. 82
This species, often sold as *Cheiranthus allionii,* grows to 2 feet high. It has ½-inch yellow or orange flowers that bloom in dense clusters in late spring and early summer. Hardy annual. A related plant, *E. hieraciifolium,* is also sold as *Cheiranthus allionii.* This plant is a 3½-foot perennial that has narrow bright green leaves and spikes of fragrant yellow, orange, or red flowers. Zones 3–8.

Eschscholzia
Poppy family
Papaveraceae

Esh-sholt'zi-a. Genus of annuals and perennials native to the western U.S. The blue-green leaves are smooth and finely divided. The yellow to orange flowers are cup shaped and have four petals.

How to Grow
The species described below, California Poppy, requires full sun and poor, dry, sandy soil with good drainage. It needs no fertilizer. In areas with mild winters, sow seeds in fall. Elsewhere, sow seeds outdoors in spring as soon as the soil can be worked. (Seeds can be started indoors 4–6 weeks before outdoor planting in mid-spring, but California Poppies do not transplant well.)

Space the plants 6–12 inches apart. Remove faded flowers immediately or the plants will turn brown.

Uses
California Poppy can be planted formally in borders or informally in massed plantings, wildflower gardens, and meadows.

californica p. 76
California Poppy. This plant, the state flower of California, grows 8–24 inches high. The 2- to 4-inch flowers bloom on long stems; their silky, crinkled pale yellow to orange flowers open in the sunshine. Each petal has a deep orange spot at the base. Cultivars are available in different colors and with double blooms. Flowers are most abundant during spring and early summer and will bloom in fall and winter in mild climates. California Poppy self-sows easily if the faded flowers are not removed. Tender perennial grown as a hardy annual.

Eucalyptus
Myrtle family
Myrtaceae

You-ka-lip′tus. Gum Tree; Stringy-bark. An enormous genus of more than 500 species of chiefly Australian, sometimes gigantic, mostly aromatic, fast-growing evergreen trees, widely planted in zones 9 and 10 for their striking flowers and foliage. More than 70 species are grown in California, where they are very popular. The leaves of eucalyptus are often variable on the same plant. The red, white, or yellow flowers usually bloom in the leaf axils, often in small clusters.

How to Grow
Eucalyptus are easy to grow in California and similar climates and do well in a variety of soils. They withstand both flood and drought. Be sure to choose a site with ample space to accommodate the ultimate size of the species. Select eucalyptus carefully as some species are messy, brittle, and can pose a danger during storms. Prune from spring to late summer to shape and to maintain strong crotch angles. The easiest way to grow eucalyptus is from seeds.

Uses
Eucalyptus are popular street and shade trees
and are often used as windbreaks. Their fruits
and leafy branches can be dried, even colored,
and used in flower arrangements.

polyanthemos pp. 208, 209

Silver Dollar Gum; Red Box; Australian
Beech. This slender upright tree grows 50–
60 feet tall and has persistent mottled bark.
The gray-green leaves are round or oval when
young and lance shaped when mature. The
off-white flowers are small and appear in
profuse branched clusters in spring and
summer but are not ornamental. This species
grows poorly in wet soil but tolerates
drought. Zones 8–10. In addition to Silver
Dollar Gum, *E. camaldulensis* (Red Gum) is
particularly well suited to a water-saving
garden. It is a large slender tree that grows
80–125 feet tall and often has weeping
branches. It has smooth tan and gray mottled
bark. The thin leaves are lance shaped and
taper to a point. The white to pale yellow
flowers appear in groups of 5–10 in summer
but are insignificant. They are followed by
numerous long clusters of round pea-sized
seed capsules. The species grows best in
alkaline soil and tolerates wet and dry
conditions. Formerly called *E. rostrata*. Zones
9–10; semihardy in zone 8.

Euonymus

Spindle tree family
Celastraceae

You-on'i-mus. A genus of shrubs, vines, and
trees, some deciduous, some evergreen, often
called spindle trees. Of the 170 known
species, more than a dozen are of great garden
importance and are grown for their showy
fruits, foliage, or both. All flower in spring
and bear fruits from midsummer to frost.
The leaves are nearly always smooth; the
flowers are greenish, white, or yellowish, and
bloom in small clusters in the leaf axils.

How to Grow
Euonymus grow well in full sun to full shade
and in any well-drained soil. They tolerate a
wide range of moisture conditions, from wet
to dry. Plant several shrubs together to
encourage maximum berry production.

Prune in early spring to remove twiggy
growth and enhance the outline of the
branches. Propagate from seeds or cuttings.

Uses
Winged Euonymus, the species listed below,
is attractive standing alone or planted in a
hedge or a shrub border. The bare branches
are often used in flower arrangements.

alata p. 183
Winged Euonymus; Burning Bush. This
stiff, neat, flat-topped shrub grows 8–12 feet
high and wide and has corky, winged
branches. The 2-inch-long leaves are finely
toothed, elliptic to oval, and turn brilliant
red in the fall. The yellowish flowers are
insignificant. The ½-inch fruits have an
orange covering that splits open to reveal the
red to purplish berry inside. 'Compactus' is a
smaller, globe-shaped cultivar. Zones 4–7.

Euphorbia
Spurge family
Euphorbiaceae

You-for'bi-a. A very large genus of annuals,
biennials, perennials, and shrubs, with wide
distribution and great diversity of habit. A
popular member is the Poinsettia. All have a
milky sap in the leaves and stems that is not
toxic but can irritate the skin. Some have
very small flowers with no petals or sepals
that are nonetheless showy because of their
brightly colored petal-like bracts. Some
species are cactuslike succulents.

How to Grow
Euphorbias are easy to grow in full sun and
dry, well-drained soil. The succulent species,
including those listed below, require very
little watering. They need excellent drainage;
dry soil is especially critical during the
winter. They tolerate heat but do not like
the combination of heat and humidity.
Euphorbia plants reseed easily. They can also
be increased from cuttings.

Uses
Either of the euphorbias listed below can be
planted in a rock garden. Cushion Spurge
makes a good edging plant and combines
nicely with spring bulbs. Myrtle Euphorbia
looks best spilling over walls and the sides of
raised beds.

epithymoides p. 72
Cushion Spurge. These neat plants grow
12 inches tall in a cushion shape or roundish
mound or clump. The flowers are greenish
and are surrounded by showy inch-long
yellow-green bracts. They bloom in late
spring. The foliage turns bright red in fall.
Also sold as *E. polychroma*. Zones 5–10.

myrsinites p. 112
Myrtle Euphorbia. These foliage plants are
3–6 inches high and sprawl to 18 inches
across. They have numerous round, fleshy
blue-green or gray leaves that are closely set
around the stems. Small flowers with
greenish bracts appear in early spring.
Zones 5–10.

Fallugia
Rose family
Rosaceae

Fahl-oo′gia. A genus containing one small
deciduous or semievergreen shrub, Apache-
Plume, that is native to the western U.S.

How to Grow
Plant Apache-Plume in full sun or partial
shade and dry, sandy, well-drained soil.
Prune as needed to enhance the outline of the
rigid branching pattern. Propagate from
seeds or cuttings.

Uses
Apache-Plume is most beneficial as a ground
cover in an area needing erosion control.

paradoxa p. 176
Apache-Plume. This shrub grows 3–7 feet
high and has whitish stems and shredding
bark. Its hairy rust-colored leaves are divided
into 3–7 lobes, each ½ inch long. The leaf
margins roll under. The 1½-inch flowers are
white and single and bloom one to a long
stem in mid-spring. They are followed in fall
by fruits with purplish feathery plumes
1½ inches long. Zones 5–10.

Feijoa
Myrtle family
Myrtaceae

Fa-jo′a. A small genus of evergreen South
American shrubs or small trees. The species

listed below, Pineapple Guava, is grown mainly for its delicious white-fleshed fruit, which ripens in late summer, but its flowers and foliage are also attractive. This genus is considered the hardiest of the subtropical fruits.

How to Grow

Pineapple Guava grows well in sandy, well-drained soil. If you plant more than one, space them 15–20 feet apart. Two plants may be necessary to ensure cross-pollination and fruit production. Plants grown in cool areas (especially coastal California) yield the best-tasting fruits, but plants will also produce well in areas with hot, dry summers. Plants can be pruned to almost any shape in late spring. Propagate from seeds or cuttings.

Uses

Pineapple Guava can be trained as a hedge, screen, small tree, or espalier. It also makes a good background for other plants. Both the flowers and the fruits are edible.

sellowiana p. 156

Pineapple Guava. This large shrub with many stems grows to 20 feet high and wide. The oval to oblong, 2- to 3-inch-long leaves are shiny on the top and white and felty on the bottom. The ¾- to 1½-inch-long flowers are white and felty on the outside and purple inside, blooming on long stems in spring. They have 4 petals and prominent, showy red stamens. The fruits are 1–4 inches long, oval, and grayish green. Their pulp tastes slightly like pineapple. Zones 8–10.

Fendlera
Saxifrage family
Saxifragaceae

Fend'ler-a. A small genus of deciduous, intricately branched shrubs native to the southwestern U.S. They are grown for their large, showy white or rose-tinted flowers, which bloom in mid-spring at the same time as the true mock-oranges *(Philadelphus)*.

How to Grow

False Mock-Orange, the species listed below, does not grow well in rich, moist soil and is best used in hot, dry areas where other plants will not do well. Plant it in full sun or light shade and sandy, well-drained soil. Once

established, it is difficult to transplant.
Propagate new plants from seeds or cuttings.
Prune as needed to enhance the structure of
the branches.

Uses
Plant False Mock-Orange standing alone as a
specimen or in a shrub border in the hottest
part of the garden.

rupicola *p. 169*
False Mock-Orange. This shrub grows 5–6
feet high. Its twisted 1¼-inch-long leaves
are elliptic to oblong. The flowers are
1½ inches wide. Zones 6–10.

Festuca
Grass family
Gramineae

Fess-too′ka. Fescue. A genus of almost 100
annual and perennial grasses from the
temperate regions, some used as lawn grasses
and others as ornamentals. The leaf blades are
usually flat; those of some species are very
fine and threadlike. The flowers and seeds
usually appear in a narrow cluster.

How to Grow
The fescues, including those grown as lawn
grasses, are among the most drought-tolerant
grasses. Ornamental fescues prefer full sun
and light, well-drained soil. They tolerate a
little shade but have better color in full sun.
Cut plants back in early spring as new
growth starts. Propagate plants by dividing
them every few years or when they die out in
the center.

Uses
Plant ornamental fescue in the front of a
border or in a rock garden or use it as an
accent plant.

ovina *p. 143*
Sheep's Fescue. These plants produce an
abundance of very fine, slender, tufted
blades. The variety *glauca* (also sold as
F. caesia), Blue Fescue, which has silvery-
blue foliage and grows 12 inches high, is very
widely grown. Zones 4–9.

Filipendula
Rose family
Rosaceae

Fill-i-pen′dew-la. A genus of perennials related to the rose, all from the north temperate zone, that are grown as ornamentals in the flower garden. They are sometimes listed under the genus *Spiraea*. The leaves are compound, with finely cut, feathery leaflets. The individual flowers, which are pink or white, are small but they blossom in large clusters at the tops of the stems in early summer to midsummer.

How to Grow
Dropwort *(F. vulgaris)* is the one species in this genus that grows in average to dry soil; the other species prefer moist soil. Plant Dropwort in sun or shade, spacing plants 18–24 inches apart. Plants self-sow easily; they can also be increased by division of the clumps in early spring.

Uses
Plant Dropwort in a mixed border or woodland or wildflower garden and use its flowers for cutting.

vulgaris p. 105
Dropwort. Plants grow 2–3 feet high. They have tuberous roots and finely dissected fernlike leaves. The flowers are white, ½–¾ inch wide, and bloom in loose clusters. Dropwort does not grow as densely as other species in the genus. 'Flore Pleno' is a double-flowered form that is shorter than the species. Zones 4–9.

Forestiera
Olive family
Oleaceae

Fo-res-ti-ee′ra. About 20 species of deciduous, and occasionally evergreen, trees or shrubs from North America, the West Indies, and South America. Small greenish-yellow flowers bloom in clusters in the leaf axils but are inconspicuous. The fruits, which are the size of an olive, are black or dark purple and covered with bloom. They are not edible.

How to Grow
Desert Olive, the species described below, thrives in full sun and sandy, dry, well-

drained soil. Other members of the genus are native to swamps and wet-soil areas. Propagate Desert Olive from cuttings or by layering. Prune as needed each spring to shape the plant and control its size.

Uses

Desert Olive has little ornamental value but makes a good hedge or screening plant in an area where soil is dry and fast results are needed.

neomexicana p. 178

Desert Olive; New Mexico Privet. This weedy and rapid-growing shrub reaches 10 feet high and wide. Its leaves are 1½ inches long and open after the flowers bloom in spring. Zones 5–10.

Gaillardia
Daisy family
Compositae

Gay-lar′di-a. A small genus of showy North American annuals and perennials, some very popular in the flower garden. They have brightly colored daisylike flowers up to 4 inches across that bloom profusely in summer above mounds of hairy leaves.

How to Grow

Plant gaillardia in full sun and light, average to poor soil with good drainage. Plants are quite heat and drought resistant and will not survive if the roots are wet during the winter. They are short-lived in fertile soil. Cut the plants back after they flower to increase their vigor. Grow new plants from seeds or cuttings or by division of existing plants.

Uses

Plant gaillardia in a flower border, on banks, in a wildflower garden, at the seashore, or in a cutting garden.

aristata p. 80

Blanketflower. This native of western North America grows 2–3 feet tall and has 3- to 4-inch yellow flowers that are dark red to purple at the bases of the petals. The tips of the petals are toothed or fringed. This species is the parent of *G.* × *grandiflora*, the popular perennial blanketflower found in many gardens today. *G.* × *grandiflora* also performs well in poor, dry soil. Zones 3–8.

Gaura
Evening primrose family
Onagraceae

Gau'ra. About 20 species of rather coarse,
primarily perennial plants native to North
and South America, one of which, White
Gaura, is grown for ornament. The plants
bear small, delicate tubular flowers with
prominent stamens. They bloom in
branching spikes along slender stems.

How to Grow
Plant White Gaura in full sun and dry, well
drained soil. It has a long taproot and needs
water only in the driest part of the summer.
It prefers warm weather and needs no
fertilizing. Sow seeds outdoors after frost
danger has passed or start them indoors 4–6
weeks earlier. Move the plants to the garden
after the last spring frost and space them
2 feet apart.

Uses
White Gaura is best used in an informal
border or a wildflower garden.

lindheimeri p. 106
White Gaura. Plants grow 4 feet tall and
have downy 2- to 4-inch leaves. The ½- to
1-inch flowers are white but become rose
colored as they age. They bloom throughout
the summer. The flowers fall cleanly as they
fade, but the seed-bearing spikes should be
cut off to prevent self-sowing. White Gaura
is a perennial in zones 6–9 but is often grown
as a half-hardy annual.

Gazania
Daisy family
Compositae

Ga-zay'ni-a. Genus of annuals and perennials
from South Africa. The leaves grow at the
base of the plant and are often lobed. The
single daisylike flowers are white, golden, or
yellow, and often have a dark spot at the base
of the petals. They bloom on long stems and
close at night and in cloudy weather.

How to Grow
Plant gazanias in full sun and dry, sandy,
well-drained soil. They are best adapted to
dry desert gardens; excellent drainage is
critical in humid areas. Sow seeds outdoors

after the last spring frost or start them inside
4–6 weeks earlier. Seeds need darkness
during the germination period. Space plants
8–10 inches apart and fertilize at planting
time. Cut the flowers as soon as they fade to
prolong the blooming period. Take cuttings
in late summer to grow plants indoors during
the winter. In areas where these plants are
perennial, fertilize them once a year and
divide them every 3 or 4 years.

Uses
Treasure Flower, the species listed below,
makes a good ground cover, edging plant, or
filler in beds and borders.

rigens p. 78
Treasure Flower. The 2- to 5-inch-wide
flowers have orange, yellow, gold, cream,
white, pink, or bronze-red petals with a
black spot near the base. Some are striped or
ringed. The stems grow 8–10 inches high
over mounds of foliage. Individual leaves
grow 6–9 inches long and are dark green on
the upper surface and gray and woolly on the
underside. Plants bloom from late spring
through summer; in mild climates, they may
bloom all year. Tender perennial grown as a
tender annual.

Genista
Pea family
Leguminosae

Je-niss′ta. Broom. The brooms in this genus
comprise more than 75 species of low,
handsome, often evergreen or nearly leafless
shrubs, all from temperate or mild regions of
the Old World. These shrubs usually have
green bark and are sometimes spiny. The
leaves are compound but are sometimes so
small they are barely discernible. The yellow
or white flowers are typically pealike and are
usually borne at the ends of the stems in late
spring and early summer. The seedpod is
long and flat.

How to Grow
Brooms are easy to grow in alkaline or acid
soil that is dry, infertile, and well drained.
Plant them in full sun. Prune them back after
they flower to promote sporadic bloom later
in the season. Once they are established, do
not transplant them. Propagate from seeds or
by layering.

Uses
Brooms are effective in hedges, massed plantings, on slopes, and in shrub borders.

tinctoria p. 150
Woadwaxen; Dyer's Greenweed. This upright shrub grows 3 feet high and has small leaves only ½–1 inch long. The leaf margins are fringed with hairs. The flowers are yellow and bloom in profuse 1- to 3-inch clusters. The seedpod is narrow, oblong, often slightly hairy. The cultiver 'Plena' has double flowers. Zones 5–10.

Geranium
Geranium family
Geraniaceae

Ger-ray'ni-um. Cranesbill. A genus containing about 300 species of biennials and perennials, and rarely annuals, commonly called cranesbills after the shape of the seeds. This genus does not include the common garden geranium, which is in the genus *Pelargonium* and is not a plant for a low-water garden. Generally low-growing, cranesbills have thin stems and toothed, lobed, or dissected leaves. The flowers have five petals.

How to Grow
Some cranesbills grow best in light shade, especially in hot and dry weather, but *G. sanguineum,* described below, will tolerate full sun. Cranesbills dislike high humidity, and most prefer moist soil; the one listed below is the most drought tolerant. Cranesbills are easy to grow in rich, well-drained soil. Divide plants in spring or fall. New plants can also be grown from seed.

Uses
Plant cranesbills at the front of the border or in a rock garden.

sanguineum p. 87
Blood-red Cranesbill. Plants grow 12–18 inches high and spread to 2 feet across. The 1-inch reddish-purple to pale pink flowers bloom most abundantly in late spring and early summer and off and on the rest of the growing season. The leaves are deeply lobed and turn red in the fall. The variety *lancastriense* is lower-growing and has light pink flowers veined in red. There is also a white-flowered variety. Zones 4–10.

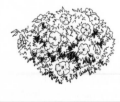

Geum
Rose family
Rosaceae

Jee'um. Avens. Most of the 50 known
species are from the cooler parts of the north
temperate region. They have downy basal
leaves that are compound, deeply cut, or
lobed. In mild climates, the foliage is
evergreen. The 1- to 1½-inch flowers are
red, yellow, orange, or white, and have
ruffled petals. The seed heads are covered
with silky hairs and are almost as attractive as
the flowers.

How to Grow
Avens are easy to grow in full sun or, in hot
climates, partial shade. The soil must have
excellent drainage; dry, poor, gravelly soil is
perfect, although addition of organic matter
is beneficial in hot climates. Grow new
plants from seeds or by dividing established
plants every 2–3 years; set new plants 12–18
inches apart. Remove faded flowers to extend
the blooming period.

Uses
Plant avens in a rock garden or at the front of
a flower border. It makes a good cut flower
and the dried seed heads are attractive in
bouquets.

reptans *p. 80*
Avens. Mounds of basal foliage grow 6–8
inches high and are topped in late spring by
1½-inch yellow or orange flowers on 12-inch
stems. Plants spread by runners to 2 feet
across; leaves are lobed and toothed.
Zones 5–9.

Ginkgo
Ginkgo family
Ginkgoaceae

Gink'o; jin'ko. The single species in this
genus is the only surviving member of a
mostly extinct family of once widely
distributed plants that lived far back in
geological time. All the cultivated specimens
of this remarkable deciduous Chinese native
have been grown from trees that were
preserved around Chinese temples. Young
trees are often unattractive, with somewhat
awkward branches, but mature trees have a
dignified appearance. The leaves are

distinctive and fan shaped. There are separate male and female plants; the female plants produce messy fruits that have an unpleasant odor but are edible nonetheless.

How to Grow
Plant only male plants to avoid the strong odor of the female fruit. Ginkgos require full sun; otherwise they are very tolerant of soil conditions and air pollution. They like well-drained soil and are fairly drought tolerant. Prune young trees when they are dormant to control unruly branches. Propagate from seeds, by layering, or from cuttings.

Uses
Ginkgo is one of the finest street trees available for temperate climates and is very tolerant of city conditions.

biloba pp. 210, 211
Ginkgo; Maidenhair Tree. This smooth tree can grow up to 125 feet tall but usually does not exceed 50 feet. The 2½- to 3½-inch leaves are fan shaped and lobed at the tip, similar to those of the Maidenhair Fern. They turn soft yellow in fall; most leaves drop simultaneously from the tree, as if by command. The cultivar 'Autumn Yellow' is more spreading than the species and has rich yellow fall foliage. There are also several upright cultivars that make excellent street trees. Zones 5–9; semihardy in zone 4.

Gleditsia
Pea family
Leguminosae

Gle-dit'see-a. Honey Locust. A genus of 12 species of thorny deciduous trees, most Asiatic but one from South America and two from North America. Honey locusts are handsome open-branched trees that cast light dappled shade, but do not compare with the common locust *(Robinia)* in the beauty of their flowers. They are usually tall, their trunks and branches armed with often-branched thorns. The leaves are compound, the leaflets arranged feather-fashion and often irregularly toothed. The flowers are greenish and fragrant and bloom in narrow clusters in mid-spring. The large, usually flat seedpod is sometimes sickle shaped and twisted. Mesquite *(Prosopis juliflora)* is often mistakenly called honey locust.

How to Grow
Honey locusts transplant easily and perform
well in a variety of soils, including alkaline,
dry, wet, and salty soils. Plant them in full
sun. Because the ferny foliage casts a light
shade, grass grows beneath the trees, but the
trees grow more vigorously if mulched
instead. Prune anytime to remove low and
crossing branches.

Uses
Honey locusts are excellent lawn specimens
and street trees.

***triacanthos* var. *inermis** pp. 224, 225*
Thornless Honey Locust. Although the
species has perilously sharp thorns and
flattened, twisted brown pods, var. *inermis* is
usually thornless and fruitless. It grows
25–90 feet tall and has 6- to 8-inch
compound leaves, each divided into 20–30
inch-long leaflets. The airy, lacy leaves
appear late in spring and drop early in fall
after turning a pleasant yellow. The form of
the tree is conical when young and broad and
rounded with age. The trunk is short; the
branches are spreading and sometimes
drooping. Zones 5–9.

Gomphrena
Amaranth family
Amaranthaceae

Gom-free′na. A genus of about 100 annuals
and perennials native to the tropics. The
leaves are oblong, 2–4 inches long, and have
slightly hairy margins. The flowers bloom in
dense cloverlike heads.

How to Grow
Plant amaranths in full sun and light, sandy,
well-drained soil. They are truly resistant to
heat, drought, and humidity. Start seeds
indoors 6–8 weeks before the last frost or sow
them outdoors after frost danger has passed.
Germination takes 15–20 days; cover the
seeds, as they need darkness to germinate.
Space the plants 10–15 inches apart. Fertilize
once a month.

Uses
Usually grown as a source of dried flowers,
Globe Amaranth, the species listed below, is
also a good plant for edging and massed
plantings.

320

globosa p. 90

Globe Amaranth. These stiff branching
plants grow 8–20 inches high and bear rou
to mounded flowers with a papery texture.
The 1-inch flowers are red, pink, white,
purple, or orange, and bloom all summer
until frost. To harvest flowers for drying, c
them before they elongate. Tender annual.

Grevillea
Australian oak family
Proteaceae

Gre-vil′lee-a. About 250 species of
Australasian broadleaf evergreen trees and
shrubs, a few species grown as shade or scre
trees in warmer regions. The leaves are sma
and heathlike in some species and large an
divided or deeply parted into five segments
in others. The flowers have no petals but
appear in dense clusters.

How to Grow
Grevilleas grow well in sandy soil, whether
is rich or poor, and tolerate drought quite
well. They will also grow well in deep, ric
soil if they are planted in full sun. Because
their wood is brittle, plant grevilleas away
from heavily used areas.

Uses
Silk Oak, the species described below, is a
popular street tree but is always dropping
parts and littering the ground.

robusta pp. 200, 201

Silk Oak. This tall narrow tree can grow to
150 feet in height outdoors; as a potted
houseplant it will grow no taller than 3–10
feet. The leaves are twice divided into
graceful, feathery, fernlike segments that a
silvery beneath. The flowers are orange and
bloom in narrow, one-sided, 4- to 12-inch
clusters on leafless branches in early spring.
Zone 10; semihardy in zone 9.

Gymnocladus
Pea family
Leguminosae

Jim-nock′lay-dus. A genus of three species
deciduous trees, two from east Asia and one
from eastern North America. This last

species, the Kentucky Coffee Tree, is grown for the striking appearance in winter of its thick, conspicuous twigs on strong, asymmetrical branches. The leaves are large and divided; flowers are either male or female, present on the same tree or on separate trees; fruit is a large thick-walled pod.

How to Grow
Plant Kentucky Coffee Tree in full sun or partial shade in deep, rich, well-drained soil. Adequate moisture and fertile soil bring best results, but these trees will endure dry soil, acid or alkaline pH, and city conditions. The leaves and seedpods of the female trees are messy in fall, but the trees are tidy the rest of the year.

Uses
Kentucky Coffee Tree is a good lawn specimen or street tree. Plant male trees if possible, as they produce no litter.

dioica pp. 220, 221
Kentucky Coffee Tree. Although this tree can grow up to 90 feet tall, it usually reaches 50–75 feet. The individual leaves are up to 3 feet long and 2 feet wide but have a delicate texture because the leaflets are moderately spaced. Each leaf has 3–7 pairs of feathery 2- to 4-inch leaflets. The greenish-white flowers bloom in terminal clusters but are not ornamental. The thick, flat, pulpy seedpod is 5–10 inches long. The dark gray to black bark is scaly and ridged. Zones 5–8; semihardy in zone 4.

Gypsophila
Pink family
Caryophyllaceae

Jip-sof'fill-a. Baby's-Breath. A genus of 125 handsome annuals and perennials, chiefly Eurasian, that bear a profusion of small flowers in large, delicate, airy clusters. The small bluish-green leaves appear on thin stems with slightly swollen joints. Plants bloom during the summer.

How to Grow
Plant baby's-breath in full sun; in areas where summer sun is intense, give it afternoon shade. It needs dry, loose, neutral to alkaline soil that is well drained. Plants will produce

few flowers in very rich soil. Sow seeds in fall where winters are mild; elsewhere sow in early spring as soon as the soil can be worked. Seeds of Annual Baby's-Breath can be started indoors 4–6 weeks before planting time in mid-spring. Set plants 12–18 inches apart. Annual Baby's-Breath is not long-lived; make successive plantings for a continual supply of flowers. Cut perennial baby's-breath back as soon as the flowers fade to encourage a second bloom. Pick flowers when they are fully open and hang them upside down in a cool, dark place to dry.

Uses

Use baby's-breath as a contrast to coarser plants, in beds, borders, or rock gardens, or on top of walls. It is an excellent flower for cutting and drying. Creeping Baby's-Breath is a good ground cover.

elegans p. 102

Annual Baby's-Breath. These upright, branching plants reach 10–18 inches in height. The ¼- to 1-inch flowers are white or pinkish; the petals are slightly notched. Leaves are lance shaped and 3 inches long. Hardy annual.

repens p. 92

Creeping Baby's-Breath. These perennial plants grow 6–8 inches high and spread to 24 inches across. The ¼-inch flowers are white or pink; leaves are 1 inch long. Zones 4–8.

Helianthemum
Rock rose family
Cistaceae

He-li-an'thee-mum. Sun-rose; Frostweed. A genus of usually low-growing, sprawling woody perennials or shrubs, a few of which are cultivated for their roselike flowers. Branches root as they crawl along the ground; they are covered with narrow 1-inch leaves that are shiny green or silver-gray. Leaves are evergreen in mild areas. The plants have single flowers that last only one day; those that bloom early in the season are larger and showier.

How to Grow

Sun-roses grow best in full sun and sandy, well-drained soil that is neutral to alkaline. They grow well in moist or dry soil but must have excellent drainage. Cut plants back in early spring to keep them compact and after the first bloom to encourage a second flowering in the fall. They benefit from winter protection in the colder limits of their hardiness, as well as protection from winter wind. Sun-roses do not like to be transplanted and are best propagated from cuttings or seeds. Set new plants 18 inches apart.

Uses
Plant sun-roses on slopes, in front of low borders, or spilling over walls. They make a good ground cover and are very useful in Western gardens, as they are fire resistant.

nummularium p. 116
Rock Rose. Plants grow 6–12 inches tall and spread to 3 feet across; they have hairy oval leaves. The round 1-inch flowers have a soft crepe-papery texture and bloom in clusters in late spring and early summer. Cut plants back after the first bloom to promote a fall bloom. The species has yellow flowers; cultivars may have yellow, pink, red, orange, or white blooms. Those of 'Fire Dragon' are bright red. Zones 6–10.

Helianthus
Daisy family
Compositae

He-li-an'thus. Sunflower. A genus of 150 species of coarse, sturdy annuals and perennials, most from North America. They are very diverse in size and character since they hybridize readily in their natural surroundings; some are spreading, invasive plants. The leaves are hairy, sticky, and coarsely toothed. The daisylike flowers are mostly yellow or gold and range in size from 3 to 12 inches.

How to Grow
Plant sunflowers in full sun in light, dry, well-drained soil. They are drought resistant and grow best in warm to hot weather. Sow seeds outdoors after all danger of frost has passed. (Seeds started indoors will germinate in 10–14 days, but this is an unnecessary step since the seedlings sown outdoors grow so quickly.) Depending on the variety, space the plants 1–4 feet apart. Tall varieties may need to be staked. Fertilize little, if at all.

Uses
Dwarf sunflowers may be used in beds,
borders, or massed plantings, or grown for
cut flowers. Tall sunflowers can be planted at
the back of the border or against walls and
fences. All have edible seeds, which attract
birds, and are a favorite for children's gardens
because they are so easy to grow.

annuus p. 79
Common Sunflower. Depending on the
variety, these plants grow from 15 inches to
12 feet tall. The flowers may be single or
double, and white, yellow, orange,
brownish, or maroon, with yellow or brown
centers. Tender annual.

Helichrysum
Daisy family
Compositae

Hell-i-kry'zum. A well-known group of
annual and perennial everlastings comprising
over 300 species from the Old World. They
have smooth-margined leaves and their
flowers have no petals, but surrounding the
scaly yellow centers are stiff, papery petal-
like bracts that maintain their color long
after they have dried.

How to Grow
Strawflower, the species listed below, thrives
in heat and drought. Plant it in full sun and
dry, porous, well-drained soil. In climates
with long summers, sow seeds outdoors after
the last frost. Elsewhere, start seeds indoors
6–8 weeks before the last frost. Do not cover
the seeds during the germination period.
Move plants to the garden after frost danger
has passed, spacing them 9–15 inches apart.
Fertilize them monthly. In sandy soil, plants
will self-seed.

Uses
Strawflowers are popular fresh and dried cut
flowers, and the plants are attractive in beds,
naturalistic gardens, and on hillsides.

bracteatum p. 78
Strawflower; Everlasting. Plants grow
2–3 feet high and have wiry stems and
narrow leaves. The 1- to 2½-inch flowers are
red, yellow, orange, white, pink, purple, or
rose, and bloom all summer until frost. Cut
flowers for drying just before the centers are

fully open and hang them upside down to dry
in a dark, cool spot. Half-hardy annual. The
'Bikini' cultivars are dwarf forms.

Helipterum
Daisy family
Compositae

Hell-lip′ter-rum. Everlasting. More than 60
species of annual and perennial everlastings
from South Africa and Australia, widely
grown for dried bouquets. The leaves have
smooth margins and are often white and
felty. The flowers have no petals; their scaly,
generally yellow centers are surrounded by
papery bracts of white, yellow, or rose-pink.

How to Grow
Grow everlastings in full sun and dry, sandy,
well-drained soil. They grow best in warm
climates but are not as heat resistant as those
of the genus *Helichrysum*. Sow seeds outdoors
after frost danger has passed. Seeds started
indoors 6–8 weeks before the last frost will
germinate in 14–21 days. Grow them in
individual pots to make transplanting easier.
Space plants in the garden 6–12 inches apart.
Fertilize them every 2 months.

Uses
Everlastings are usually grown for their cut
flowers but are also good plants for beds,
borders, and massed plantings.

roseum p. 84
Everlasting; Strawflower. The branching
stems of these 2-foot-tall plants are clothed in
narrow, felty whitish leaves. The 1- to 2-inch
flowers are single or double and white, rose,
or salmon, with brown or green at the base of
the bracts. Blooms appear all summer until
frost. Cut flowers for drying when they are
fully open and hang them upside down to dry
in a dark, cool area. Everlasting is sometimes
sold as *Acroclinium roseum*. Tender annual.

Hemerocallis
Lily family
Liliaceae

Hem-mer-o-kal′lis. Daylily. A small genus
of perennials found naturally from central
Europe to Japan that have been widely

hybridized. Narrow, sword-shaped, arching leaves grow from the base of the plant. Flowers bloom at the top of thick leafless stems from spring through fall, depending on the variety. The flowers may be single or double, are funnel to trumpet shaped, and are sometimes ruffled. Colors include off-white, yellow, gold, orange, pink, and red.

How to Grow
Daylilies grow best in full sun but appreciate partial shade in hot climates. Plant them in soil that is well drained and water them only when they are in flower. Divide plants when they become crowded (every 2–6 years). The roots are tough, but pulling them apart or dividing them with a spade will not damage them. Set new plants 12–36 inches apart.

Uses
Plant daylilies in a mixed border, in a massed planting, or on slopes needing erosion control, or use them as accent plants or to make an informal hedge.

hybrids *p. 114*
Daylily. Although some species daylilies are still grown in the garden, they have given way to new and improved hybrids. Depending on the variety, plants grow from 1–6 feet tall, but are usually around 3½ feet, and have flowers from 2–6 or even 8 inches across. Blooms last only one day but are quickly replaced by others in the cluster. 'Admiral Nelson' grows 3 feet high and has red flowers. 'Bonanza' reaches 15 inches high, and its flowers are light orange with a maroon to brown center. 'Hyperion' has greenish-yellow flowers and grows 4 feet tall. 'Stella D'Oro' grows 2 feet tall and bears rich gold flowers; it has the longest blooming period of any daylily. Zones 4–10.

Hippophae
Oleaster family
Elaeagnaceae

Hip-po'fee. A genus of spiny Eurasian shrubs or small trees with narrow willowlike leaves covered with silvery scalelike hairs. The male and female flowers are borne on separate plants; they bloom in early spring before the leaves open but are inconspicuous. The fruit is fleshy and appears in large clusters on the female plants in the fall.

How to Grow
Sea Buckthorn, the species listed below, is
easy to grow in full sun and any well-drained
soil. It tolerates infertile, dry, and sandy or
gravelly soil. Plant male plants and female
plants in close proximity to ensure fruit, one
of the attractive features of this species.
Prune in early spring if needed. Propagate
from seeds, from root cuttings, or by division
or layering. Mature plants are difficult to
transplant.

Uses
Sea buckthorn is effective in massed
plantings and as a windbreak or barrier plant.
It tolerates salt spray and will help control
erosion on sand dunes.

rhamnoides pp. 188, 189

Sea Buckthorn; Swallow Thorn. This shrub
or small tree grows 10–25 feet high and wide
and spreads by underground stems. The
leaves are 1–3 inches long, silvery when
young, and green on the upper surface when
mature. The yellowish flowers have no petals
and are therefore inconspicuous. The
¼-inch, nearly egg-shaped fruit is orange-
yellow and is edible but somewhat hard; it
remains on the plant for most of the winter.
Zones 4–7.

Holodiscus
Rose family
Rosaceae

Ho-lo-dis′kus. A genus of American shrubs,
mostly hairy, that are planted as
ornamentals. They have long-stalked, usually
toothed, sometimes slightly lobed leaves.
The flowers are white, very small but
numerous, and bloom in branching clusters
on arching stems. Numerous stamens
protrude slightly from the center of the
flowers.

How to Grow
Plant Rock Spirea, the species described
below, in full sun and open, dry, sandy soil.
Propagate from seeds or by layering. Prune
plants if necessary after they have flowered.
Mature plants are difficult to transplant.

Uses
Plant Rock Spirea in a mixed shrub border or
in a rock garden.

dumosus p. 171

Rock Spirea. This shrub grows 3–4 feet high in an upright habit. Its ¾- to 1-inch leaves are coarsely toothed. Foliage turns orange in the fall and has a spicy odor when crushed. Flowers appear in 7-inch clusters in summer. Flowers left on the plant after they have bloomed will dry to an attractive orange. Zones 6–10.

Hypericum
St. Johnswort family
Hypericaceae

Hy-per′i-cum. St. Johnswort. About 300 species of perennials and shrubs, nearly all from the north temperate zone. Plants are primarily low-growing and have shiny, light to medium green leaves. The cup-shaped golden-yellow flowers have prominent stamens that give the center of the flower a tufted appearance.

How to Grow
St. Johnsworts like full sun or partial shade and will grow in any well-drained soil. They are drought resistant. Most species prefer acid soil but Aaronsbeard grows well in sandy, alkaline soil. Do not over-fertilize St. Johnsworts; it will result in lush growth but few flowers. Shear plants back in early spring before growth starts to keep them compact. Grow new plants from cuttings, by division, by layering, or from seeds.

Uses
Aaronsbeard and Hidcote Goldencup St. Johnswort, the species listed below, are good ground covers on slopes and under trees. They can also be used as informal hedges and planted in rock gardens and in areas needing erosion control.

calycinum p. 152

Aaronsbeard St. Johnswort. This evergreen shrub grows 12 inches high and spreads by underground stems to 24 inches across. The oblong 3- to 4-inch leaves are pale green to silvery underneath. The flowers are 2 inches across; they bloom in summer. Zones 5–10.

patulum 'Hidcote' p. 153

Hidcote Goldencup St. Johnswort. This 18- to 24-inch-tall shrub has oval to oblong, evergreen leaves, 2½ inches long. The fragrant flowers are 2 inches across; they bloom in summer. In northern areas plants die to the ground each winter but grow again in spring. Zones 7–10.

Hyssopus
Mint family
Labiatae

Hiss-o'pus. Hyssop, a hardy perennial herb from southern Europe to central Asia, is the only species in this genus. It is widely grown for ornament and as an herb for flavoring. Like all members of the mint family, it has squarish stems.

How to Grow
Plant Hyssop in full sun and dry, rocky, alkaline soil with good drainage. In areas where summers are long, plants will bloom the first year. Propagate from seeds, from cuttings, or by division. To harvest the leaves for teas, shear them just before the plants flower when they are most aromatic.

Uses
A common plant in herb gardens, Hyssop is valued for its leaves, which are used fresh or dried in teas. It is also attractive in a mixed flower bed or as a border plant.

officinalis p. 100
Hyssop. This dense, mounded plant is covered with short, chubby spikes of tubular blue flowers. It grows 2–3 feet high. Its willowlike, ¾- to 1½-inch leaves have a heavy musty odor and a strong, almost bitter flavor. Zones 3–10.

Iberis
Mustard family
Cruciferae

Eye-beer'is. A genus of 30 species of annuals and perennials, most from the Mediterranean region. Plants grow in neat, slightly spreading mounds. They have dark green leaves and flat-topped or dome-shaped clusters of single flowers.

How to Grow
Candytuft, the species described below, will thrive in moist or dry soil but may stop

flowering if the soil is too dry. Plant
Candytuft in a spot with full sun and good
drainage. Propagate from seeds or cuttings or
by dividing existing plants in spring. Set
new plants 18–24 inches apart. In cold and
windy northern climates, apply winter
protection to keep the leaves from turning
brown. Shear plants back after they flower to
keep them compact and to prevent the center
of the plant from dying out.

Uses
Plant Candytuft in a rock garden, along
paths, or on rock walls, or use it as an edging
or a filler.

sempervirens p. 125
Candytuft. Plants grow to 12 inches high
and spread 18–36 inches across. The narrow
1½-inch leaves are usually evergreen; they
occur on wiry, branching stems. The white
flowers bloom in mid-spring in 1½-inch
domed clusters. 'Autumn Snow' grows
9 inches high and 3 feet wide and reblooms
in the fall. The variety 'Snowflake' has the
largest flowers and grows 10 inches high and
24 inches across. Zones 4–10.

Ilex
Holly family
Aquifoliaceae

Eye′lecks. Holly. About 400 species of
extremely valuable evergreen and deciduous
shrubs and trees widely scattered in
temperate and tropical regions. They are
grown for their attractive leaves, showy
fruits, and pleasing shapes. The leaves
sometimes have spiny teeth. The white,
yellow, or greenish flowers bloom in clusters
in the leaf axils and are sometimes
inconspicuous. Red or black berries form on
the female plants; they are usually showy.

How to Grow
Evergreen hollies, such as the ones described
below, are more valuable than deciduous
hollies but are slower-growing and more
difficult to establish. They will grow in
partial shade but produce more berries in full
sun. They prefer rich, acid, well-drained soil.
The species described below tolerate heat,
drought, alkaline soil, and salt spray once
established. Keep balled-and-burlapped and

container plants moist until planting, and
water new plants freely the first year or so.
Male and female plants must grow close
together to ensure a crop of berries for most
hollies. Prune as needed in early spring.
Propagate from seeds (they may take
18 months to germinate) or cuttings.

Uses
Hollies are attractive in foundation
plantings, as hedges, and as specimens.

cornuta pp. 181, 185
Chinese Holly. This densely branched
evergreen shrub grows 8–15 feet high. It has
lustrous rectangular leaves with a spine at the
leaf tip that curls under. The flowers are
yellow and showy; the ½-inch berries are
round, red, and long-stalked. Chinese Holly
produces fruit without fertilization, so it is
not necessary to have a male plant to ensure
berry production. The cultivar 'Burfordii'
grows 10 feet high and has bright green
wedge-shaped leaves; it also has a dwarf
form. 'Rotunda' grows 6 feet high and does
not produce berries. Zones 7–9.

vomitoria p. 180
Yaupon; Cassena. This species is a
multistemmed evergreen shrub or small tree
that grows 15–25 feet high. Its 1½-inch
leaves are elliptic to oblong and have wavy-
toothed margins. The berries are red. There
are many different cultivars. Zones 7–10.

Ipomoea
Morning glory family
Convolvulaceae

Ip-po-mee′a. Many of the 500 species of
these annual and perennial twining vines are
of tropical origin. A few are of importance in
the garden, including the Morning Glory,
described below. Leaves are either simple or
compound with several leaflets. The large
showy flowers are funnel shaped, single or
double, and have five pointed lobes.

How to Grow
Plant Morning Glory in full sun in light,
sandy, well-drained soil. Soil too rich will
produce lush foliage and few flowers. These
plants grow best in warm to hot weather and
need watering only in the hottest and driest
days of summer. Sow seeds outdoors after the

last frost or start them indoors 4–6 weeks earlier. Germination takes only 5–7 days if the hard seed coats are nicked or the seeds are soaked in water for 24 hours before sowing. Space plants 12 inches apart and provide a trellis, fence, or other support; they may need to be tied.

Uses
Cover fences and trellises with Morning Glory for privacy and screening. Morning Glory also grows well in hanging baskets.

tricolor p. 97
Morning Glory. The vines grow to 10 feet long and have attractive, heart-shaped leaves. The flowers are blue, red, purple, lavender, or white, and may be solid colored, or striped, starred, or edged in white. Flowers open in the morning and fade by afternoon. Blooms appear all summer until frost. Tender perennial grown as a tender annual.

Juniperus
Cypress family
Cupressaceae

Jew-nip′er-us. Juniper. About 70 species of coniferous evergreens ranging from low prostrate shrubs to tall slender trees. They are found throughout the Northern Hemisphere from the Arctic to the subtropics. Their diverse habits make them valuable ornamental plants. Junipers have two different types of foliage. The juvenile foliage is sharp, needlelike, and borne in groups of three; the mature leaves are small and scalelike and pressed close to the branches. Some plants have both types of foliage; others have one or the other. Juniper foliage ranges from light to dark green to blue-green, blue, silver, and gold-tipped. It often turns purple in the winter. There are separate male and female plants, and the female plants produce small round blue berries used to flavor gin.

How to Grow
Junipers grow best in full sun; the species listed below prefer dry, sandy or rocky, acid to neutral soil with good drainage. Be careful not to over-water them. Propagate from cuttings or seeds or by layering or grafting. Prune junipers to shape them or control their size any time of the year.

Uses
Depending on its size and form, juniper can
be used as a ground cover, especially in areas
needing erosion control, as a specimen,
screen, or background for other plantings, or
in a foundation planting.

horizontalis p. 130
Creeping Juniper. This low-growing shrub
has long, spreading branches. Both juvenile
and mature foliage can be found on the plant
at the same time; it is often gray-blue or
blue-green. The cultivar 'Bar Harbor' forms a
dense mat 8–12 inches high and up to 8 feet
wide. Its leaves are steel blue and turn silvery
purple in winter. 'Plumosa' (Andorra
Juniper) has ascending branches that grow
18 inches high and feathery light green
foliage that is tinged purple in winter. Plants
spread to 10 feet wide. 'Wiltonii' (Blue Rug
Juniper) has ground-hugging branches
forming a 6-inch-high, 8-foot-wide silver-
blue carpet. Zones 3–9.

monosperma pp. 232, 233
Cherrystone Juniper; Oneseed Juniper. This
large, densely branched shrub or tree can
grow to 50 feet high and almost as wide. Its
bark is reddish brown to gray and its foliage
is gray-green and scalelike. It tolerates a wide
variety of adverse conditions but can be slow
to establish. Zones 7–9.

scopulorum pp. 230, 231

Rocky Mountain Juniper; Western Red
Cedar; Colorado Red Cedar. A tree with a
narrow, conical to pyramidal habit, this
species often has several main stems covered
with shredding reddish-brown bark. It grows
30–40 feet high and 3–15 feet wide. The
spreading branches are clothed in scalelike
light green to blue-green leaves. There are
cultivars that range from small rounded
shrubs to narrow columnar trees to shrubs
with weeping branches to prostrate ground
covers. Zones 4–9; semihardy in zone 3.

virginiana pp. 230, 231
Eastern Red Cedar. This juniper is a medium
to large tree, usually 40 feet high, with a
broad, conical habit. The thin branches are
ascending on young trees and horizontal on
mature trees. They are covered with both
scalelike and needlelike leaves that are
medium green in summer and purple to
brown in winter. Zones 3–9.

Kniphofia
Lily family
Liliaceae

Nip-ho'fi-a. Torch Lily; Flame Flower; Poker-Plant. A genus of more than 65 robust South African perennials. The grassy arching leaves, which grow from the base of the plants, are 3 feet long and 1 inch wide. The flowers bloom on tall leafless stems from early summer to fall, depending on the species. The individual flowers are tubular and bloom in long, narrow spikes. This genus is sometimes called *Tritoma*.

How to Grow
Plant torch lilies in full sun and rich, fertile soil with excellent drainage. They like to be watered when blooming but withstand dry soil the rest of the season; they must have dry soil in winter. Propagate from seeds, by dividing established plants in spring, or by removing the offsets that grow at the base of the plants. Space new plants 15–18 inches apart; they are somewhat slow to establish. Cut flower stems back after the blooms fade. In the colder limits of their hardiness, mulch plants heavily and tie the leaves over the crown to keep moisture out of the crown during winter.

Uses
Mix torch lily in a perennial border or use it as a specimen plant. It makes a good cut flower and tolerates seashore conditions.

uvaria p. 82
Red-hot Poker; Torch Lily. Depending on the variety, plants grow 2–4 feet high. Individual flowers are 1½–2 inches long and are borne in spikes 6–12 inches long. Blooms are red and yellow. Zones 5–10.

Kochia
Goosefoot family
Chenopodiaceae

Ko'ki-a. Eighty species, chiefly Eurasian, of herbs and small shrubs; one, Summer Cypress, is widely cultivated and valued for its bushy, brilliantly colored fall foliage.

How to Grow
Plant Summer Cypress in full sun and dry soil with excellent drainage. It is very heat

and drought resistant. Where summers are long, sow seeds outdoors after frost danger has passed. In short-season gardens, start seeds indoors 6–8 weeks before the last frost. Do not cover the seeds; they need light during the germination period. Sow them in individual pots, as seedlings do not transplant well. Space the plants 18–24 inches apart in the garden. Fertilize once each month. Shear plants to shape them.

Uses
Summer Cypress is effective as a hedge or an accent plant.

scoparia var. *tricophylla* p. 129
Summer Cypress; Burning Bush. The plants are bushy and globe or cone shaped. They usually grow 2–3 feet high, although they can reach 5 feet. The numerous narrow, feathery leaves give the plant the appearance of a conifer. Light green during the summer, the leaves turn bright cherry-red to purple-red in fall. The greenish flowers are inconspicuous. Plants self-sow in warm climates. Summer Cypress may cause hay fever. Half-hardy annual.

Koelreuteria
Soapberry family
Sapindaceae

Kel-roo-teer′i-a. Golden-Rain Tree. A small genus of deciduous Asiatic trees often planted for their drooping yellow flower clusters in summer and their seedpods in fall. The trees have deep roots and are not invasive, so grass and flowering plants grow readily beneath them. The leaves are compound and feathery.

How to Grow
Golden-rain trees do well in a variety of soils and are better suited to open sunshine than to shade. Young plants may be injured by cold winter temperatures, but mature trees withstand drought and grow well in acid to slightly alkaline soils. Stake and prune young trees to promote high branching; prune out weak, crowded branches periodically.

Uses
Golden-rain trees are good lawn specimens and street trees. Use one as an accent plant in a flower bed. They tolerate city growing conditions.

336

paniculata pp. 204, 205
Golden-Rain Tree. This dome-shaped tree
usually does not grow more than 30–40 feet
high and wide. The leaves are 9–18 inches
long and are divided into 7–15 coarsely
toothed, oval to oblong leaflets. The showy
flower clusters are 12–15 inches long. The
seedpods are 2 inches long and papery. They
are brilliantly colored—first green, then
yellow, and finally brown—before dropping.
Zones 5–8.

Kolkwitzia
Honeysuckle family
Caprifoliaceae

Kolk-wit'zi-a. This genus contains a single
species of Chinese shrub much grown for its
showy bloom and known as Beauty Bush.

How to Grow
Beauty Bush is easy to grow in full sun or
partial shade in any type of well-drained soil.
Plant it where it will have room to spread
out; if it outgrows its space, transplanting is
not difficult. Prune out old stems every year
to prevent plants from becoming twiggy.
Propagate from softwood cuttings.

Uses
Beauty Bush is attractive planted alone as a
specimen, in a hedge, or in a shrub border.

amabilis p. 158
Beauty Bush. This deciduous shrub grows 6–
12 feet high and has an upright, arching
habit. The ovalish leaves are 2–3 inches long;
they turn dull red in the fall. The bell-shaped
flowers, which are pink with a yellow throat,
appear in late spring. They are ½ inch long,
borne in pairs along the stems. Stems develop
peeling brown bark at maturity. Fruit is dry,
both it and its stalk covered with bristly
hairs. Zones 5–8.

Lantana
Verbena family
Verbenaceae

Lan-ta'na. A genus of 155 species of tropical
or subtropical perennials or shrubs, two of
which are grown for their showy flowers. The
stems are hairy, sometimes prickly, and are

clothed with pungent-smelling leaves. Small flowers are borne in dense rounded heads at the ends of the branches.

How to Grow

Grow lantana in full sun in rich, dry, well-drained soil. Water deeply but infrequently; soil too moist produces lush growth but few flowers. Plants are quite heat tolerant. In warm climates, sow seeds outdoors in early spring; elsewhere, start seeds indoors 12–18 weeks before the last frost and move the plants outside after frost danger has passed. Germination may take as long as 6–8 weeks. Space the plants 2–3 feet apart and fertilize them every 2–3 months. Lantana plants root easily from cuttings and may be grown indoors over the winter. In areas where they are perennial, cut plants back hard each spring to encourage new growth.

Uses

Plant trailing lantana in beds, borders, or hanging baskets. It grows well in a seashore garden and is a good ground cover, especially in areas where soil is eroding.

montevidensis p. 117

Weeping Lantana. This species is a vinelike shrub that trails from 3–6 feet across. The toothed inch-long leaves are dark gray-green and sometimes tinged in red or purple. The flowers are pink to lilac and bloom in dense 1-inch clusters. They bloom all year in mild climates and from early summer to frost elsewhere. Tender perennial grown as a half-hardy annual.

Lavandula
Mint family
Labiatae

La-van′dew-la. Lavender. Old World perennial herbs and shrubs grown for their ornamental value and their aromatic oil. The narrow, slightly textured foliage is gray-green and aromatic; it is evergreen in mild climates. The tiny fragrant flowers are lavender to dark purple and bloom in dense, narrow clusters. Depending on the variety, plants bloom from early to late summer.

How to Grow

Plant lavender in full sun and dry, loose, sandy soil. Soil that is too fertile can adversely affect lavender's winter hardiness. Drainage must be excellent. To keep the roots dry during winter, apply a mulch or cover the plants with a basket. In spring, prune back to old wood; shear the plants back again after they have flowered. Grow new plants from cuttings or divide established plants in spring; set new plants 12–18 inches apart.

Uses
Lavender is often planted in herb gardens but also makes a beautiful hedge, edging, border plant, or rock garden plant. Use its dried flowers in bouquets, sachets, or potpourri.

angustifolia p. 99
English Lavender. Plants grow from 1–3 feet tall in a mounded habit and have narrow, felty white leaves. The blue-violet flowers appear in 3- to 8-inch spikes. 'Hidcote' grows 18 inches high and has purple flowers. This species is sometimes listed as *L. spica, L. officinalis,* or *L. vera.* Zones 5–10.

Leontopodium
Daisy family
Compositae

Lee-on-to-po′di-um. A genus of low-growing tufted alpine perennials; Edelweiss is a popular, drought-tolerant species. Plants grow by creeping stems to form mats 12 inches across. The leaves are gray and woolly on both surfaces. The flowers are very small and tightly clustered; they are surrounded by woolly white bracts, which are showy.

How to Grow
Plant Edelweiss in full sun and gritty alkaline soil with excellent drainage. Wet winters or standing water will kill the crowns of the plants. Edelweiss grows best in climates with low humidity. Grow plants from seeds or divide existing plants in spring, setting new plants 12 inches apart. Edelweiss may be short-lived.

Uses
Edelweiss is typically grown in alpine and rock gardens but also makes a good plant for the front of the border or a rock wall.

alpinum p. 135
Edelweiss. Short erect stems, 4–12 inches high, grow from spreading branches and are covered with woolly gray or white leaves. The tiny yellow flowers are borne in clusters of 7–9 heads; each cluster is 1½ inches across. The surrounding white or gray petal-like bracts, sometimes tipped in black, are in turn surrounded by a circle of leaves. Zones 4–8 in the East; 4–10 in the West.

Leptospermum
Myrtle family
Myrtaceae

Lep-to-sper'mum. Tea Tree. Australasian shrubs and trees comprising more than 40 species, several of which are widely cultivated in mild climates for their long, graceful drooping branches of white, pink, or red flowers, which are bell shaped and quite numerous. The leaves are small, rigid, and often pricklelike.

How to Grow
Tea trees are easy to grow in full sun and well-drained acid soil. Water them generously when newly planted; they are fairly drought tolerant after establishment. Prune back to side branches in early spring to shape the plants. Propagate from seeds or cuttings.

Uses
New Zealand Tea Tree, the species described below, is a valuable specimen, windbreak, tall screen, or hedge.

scoparium p. 157
New Zealand Tea Tree. A tall shrub or small tree, this species grows 10–25 feet high, or occasionally occurs in a dwarf form only 1–2 feet high. It has a soft, informal look. The ½-inch-long leaves, which are very numerous, are almost prickle tipped and are silky when young. The ½-inch flowers are white or pink, with the petals encircling a hard central cone. They bloom in spring or summer. Several varieties are cultivated and are more valuable than the species because they are smaller and more compact. Zones 9–10.

Liatris
Daisy family
Compositae

Ly-a'tris. Button Snakeroot. A genus of showy, but sometimes weedy, North American perennials. The plants are coarse and have stiff, narrow swordlike leaves at the base and along the flowering stems. The flowers are small and thready or fuzzy, blooming in stiff, erect cylindrical spikes in summer or early fall. Unlike most flowers, the blooms on the spikes open from top to bottom. They are mostly rose-purple although there are white varieties.

How to Grow
Plant Dotted Gay-Feather, the species listed below, in full sun or light shade and light, well-drained soil. It is very tolerant of heat, cold, drought, and poor soil. Increase by division or from seeds.

Uses
Plant Dotted Gay-Feather in a mixed border or use it as an accent plant. It also makes a nice cut flower.

punctata p. 99
Dotted Gay-Feather. Plants grow 12–24 inches high and wide. The leaves are 4 inches long at the base of the plants and become smaller toward the top of the stem. The leaves are dotted. The flower spikes are up to 6 inches long. Zones 4–10.

Ligustrum
Olive family
Oleaceae

Ly-gus'trum. Privet. A genus of 50 species of shrubs, or rarely trees, all from the Old World. Privets are popularly used as hedge plants, since most species tolerate pruning, pollution, wind, and drought. The leaves are generally ovalish and may be deciduous or evergreen. The flowers are small, white, and sometimes foul smelling; they bloom in terminal clusters. Blue-black berries follow in the fall. Flowers and fruits often do not form on clipped hedges.

How to Grow
Privets are easy to grow and will adapt to any soil condition except constant wetness. They

adapt well to dry, infertile soil. Plant them in full sun or partial shade. They will grow fast and are not difficult to transplant. Prune to shape at any time; pruning in early spring will eliminate the flowers. Propagate from softwood cuttings, which root easily.

Uses
Privets are mainly used in hedges and screens and can be pruned into formal shapes.

japonicum p. 170
Japanese Privet. This evergreen shrub grows 7–10 feet high. The 3- to 4-inch-long leaves are leathery and smooth. The flower clusters are 4–6 inches long; they bloom in spring. This species is often used for topiary and grown in containers. The cultivar 'Rotundifolium' (sometimes sold as *L. coriaceum*) is a lower, more compact shrub, with lustrous dark green leaves that are more numerous than those on the species and nearly circular in outline. Zones 7–10.

vulgare pp. 167, 172
European Privet; Common Privet. This deciduous privet grows 5–15 feet high and may be semievergreen in the South. The leaves are oblong to oval and grow 1½–2½ inches long. The flower cluster is not more than 3 inches long; bloom is in late spring. This is one of the most widely grown of all hedge privets. Zones 4–10.

Limonium
Plumbago family
Plumbaginaceae

Ly-mo'ni-um. Sea Lavender; Sea Pink. A genus of annuals and perennials widely distributed on all continents. Leathery, oblong deep green leaves grow in a tufted rosette at the base of the plants. The flowers are small, but numerous, and when a plant is in bloom it looks like a delicate cloud of flowers. Blooms appear on wiry many-branched stems during the summer or early autumn. The flower center is surrounded by a papery segment called a calyx, which is usually a different color.

How to Grow
Even though sea lavender is often found in wet soil and salt marshes in the wild, it tolerates heat, full sun, and drought once it is

established. Do not plant it in soil that is too fertile or the stems will become weak, and the plants will need to be staked. Sea lavender plants have deep roots and do not transplant well. Grow new plants from seeds or by carefully dividing existing plants.

Uses
Sea lavender is a good plant for the seashore and is useful as a filler plant in a mixed border. Its flowers are excellent for cutting and drying.

latifolium *p. 100*
Sea Lavender. These hairy plants grow 1½– 2½ feet tall and have flowers of lavender, white, pink, or blue. They are sometimes called statice, but this name is more correctly applied to the annual species, *L. sinuatum.* Zones 4–10.

Lindera
Laurel family
Lauraceae

Lin-der′a. A group of 100 species of aromatic trees and shrubs, most of them tropical. Small yellow flowers bloom along the branches in dome-shaped clusters before the leaves open. Fleshy bright red berries form on the female plants.

How to Grow
Spicebush, the species described below, prefers partial shade and moist, well-drained, neutral to acid soil but is drought resistant. It needs little pruning; cut older branches to the ground in early spring and thin and shape other branches. Propagate from seeds or softwood cuttings or by layering.

Uses
Spicebush is a good plant for massing and for screens.

benzoin *p. 188*
Spicebush; Spicewood; Benjamin-Bush. This shrub grows 6–12 feet high and wide. Its oblong leaves are wedge shaped at the base and grow 3–5 inches long; they turn yellow in the fall. The flowers are crowded in small, nearly stalkless clusters that are only ⅓ inch long. The ½-inch berries are scarlet. Zones 4–9.

Linum
Flax family
Linaceae

Ly'num. Flax. Nearly 200 species of slender
annuals and perennials, most from the
Northern Hemisphere. One species is the
source of linen and linseed oil; the others are
grown for ornament. The plants have narrow
leaves covering erect branching stems. The
single cup-shaped flowers are usually yellow
or blue.

How to Grow
Flax is easy to grow in full sun and dry, well-
drained soil. It is very drought resistant. Wet
soil in winter is detrimental to the plant's
hardiness. Plants are often short-lived, so
divide them frequently or grow new plants
from seeds or cuttings. Space plants 10–15
inches apart.

Uses
Plant flax in a mixed border, in a rock
garden, or in a wildflower garden.

perenne p. 103
Perennial Flax. Plants grow 1–2 feet high
and have narrow blue-green leaves. The 1-
inch flowers are primarily blue, but there are
white and red forms as well. Each flower lasts
only one day, but the plants bloom over a
long period from late spring through
midsummer. The subspecies *alpinum* grows
2–12 inches high and has ¾-inch flowers.
Zones 5–10.

Liriope
Lily family
Liliaceae

Li-ri'o-pe. Lily-turf. A genus of Asiatic
perennials that have clumps of grassy, narrow
dark green leaves. In mild climates, the
leaves are evergreen. The flowers bloom in
late summer to fall in narrow spikes among
the leaves.

How to Grow
Lily-turf prefers partial to full shade and rich,
moist, well-drained soil but tolerates dry soil
once it is established. It is also resistant to
summer heat. Foliage may become tattered
or brown in northern winters; if it does, cut

or mow it to the ground in spring. Lily-turf plants are easily divided; replant divisions 10 inches apart.

Uses
Use Creeping Lily-turf, described below, as a ground cover on flat areas and slopes or in the front of a flower border. It is a good plant for a seashore garden.

spicata p. 141
Creeping Lily-turf. This plant grows 8–10 inches high and spreads to 18 inches across. The flowers, which may be white, purple, or blue, appear in 4- to 8-inch spikes and are often partially hidden by the foliage. There is a variety with striped leaves. Zones 5–10.

Lonicera
Honeysuckle family
Caprifoliaceae

Lon-iss'er-ra. Honeysuckle. The honeysuckles comprise a group of 150 or more species of deciduous or semievergreen shrubs and woody climbers found throughout the Northern Hemisphere. The often showy flowers are abundant and sometimes sweetly scented. They are tubular or bell shaped, five-lobed or two-lipped, and are borne in pairs in the leaf axils or in clusters at the ends of the branches. The berries, which are white, yellow, orange, red, blue, or black, are ornamental but do not last long, as they are a favorite food for birds.

How to Grow
Honeysuckles are easy to grow, thriving in almost any light condition from full sun to full shade. Most prefer moist soil, but the species listed below will tolerate drought. Prune plants just after they flower; they can become very twiggy and need annual thinning. Propagate from seeds or cuttings.

Uses
The two species listed below are of different habits and thus have different uses in the garden. Amur Honeysuckle is an attractive lawn specimen, large screen, or hedge plant. Japanese Honeysuckle makes a good ground or bank cover and can be trained as a screen on a trellis, arbor, or support.

japonica p. 105

Japanese Honeysuckle. This vigorous deciduous or semievergreen climbing vine can grow 20–30 feet high but can be trained to lower heights as well, depending on the height of the support. It has slender hairy branches and pointed oval to oblong leaves, 1–3 inches long, that are usually downy on the undersides. The sweetly scented flowers are white tinged with purple, fading to yellow. They appear in late spring and early summer. The berries are black. The variety 'Halliana' (Hall's Honeysuckle) has all-white flowers that fade to yellow. Zones 5–9.

maackii p. 166

Amur Honeysuckle. A vigorous wide-spreading shrub or small tree, this honeysuckle grows 10–15 feet high and wide. The leaves are oval, with long, slender points, and grow 1½–3 inches long. The ⅔-inch flowers are white, turning yellow with age; they bloom in mid-spring. The berries are red. One of the largest honeysuckles, this species is also among the handsomest, with its conspicuous bloom and its bright red berries in fall. Zones 3–9.

Lychnis
Pink family
Caryophyllaceae

Lick'nis. Catchfly; Campion. A genus of annuals, biennials, and perennials from the north temperate zone, some of which have been garden favorites for centuries. The plants are slender and erect, often covered with sticky hairs. The flowers are single; some bloom one to a stem, others in clusters.

How to Grow
Maltese Cross, the species listed below, grows best in full sun and dry soil. It tolerates moist soil, light shade, and a wide range of adverse growing conditions as long as it has excellent drainage. Plants will not live long in poorly drained soil. Grow new plants from seeds or by dividing existing plants in spring. Set plants 12 inches apart.

Uses
Plant Maltese Cross in a mixed flower border; it combines well with white or blue flowers.

chalcedonica p. 85
Maltese Cross. This perennial grows 18–30 inches tall and has hairy leaves and stems. The 1-inch flowers are bright orange to scarlet and bloom in dense clusters at the tops of the stems. The petals are deeply notched. Zones 4–8.

Mahonia
Barberry family
Berberidaceae

Ma-ho'ni-a. About 100 species of handsome American and Asian evergreen shrubs. The leaves are compound, with spiny, hollylike leaflets that are glossy and dark green, turning purple in the fall. The small flowers are yellow and fragrant; they bloom in clusters at the ends of the branches in early spring to mid-spring. In fall, edible dark blue or purple berries that resemble small grapes appear.

How to Grow
Creeping Mahonia, the species listed below, thrives in rich, moist soil but will tolerate rich, dry soil; it is the most drought-tolerant member of the genus. Plant it in partial to full shade and protect it from winter wind and sun to prevent leaf scorch. Mahonias benefit from winter protection in the northern limits of their hardiness and will survive as far north as Canada if they are protected by a heavy snow cover in winter. Prune plants in early spring or after the flowers fade. Propagate from seeds or suckers or by layering.

Uses
Creeping Mahonia is best used as a ground cover in a woodland garden or planted under trees or shrubs.

repens p. 132
Creeping Mahonia. This shrubby ground cover grows 12–24 inches high and creeps by rooting underground stems to 6 feet across. Each leaf has 3–7 round to oval, 1½- to 2½-inch leaflets. They are dull bluish green and leathery. The berries are black, covered with bloom. Zones 6–10.

Malva
Mallow family
Malvaceae

Mal′va. Mallow. About 30 species of widely
distributed perennials, some weedy, some
ornamental. Plants have finely cut foliage
and bear single flowers with notched petals
and a satiny texture.

How to Grow
Mallows are related to *Hibiscus* but are not as
striking in the garden. They are, however,
easy to grow; plant them in full sun or partial
shade and dry, well-drained soil. In hot
climates, add organic matter to the soil and
prepare it deeply so roots will grow down to
seek moisture. Plants may be short-lived, so
divide them often in spring or fall. Place new
plants 24 inches apart. Mallows self-sow
readily.

Uses
Plant Hollyhock Mallow, the species listed
below, in a mixed border or a naturalistic
garden.

alcea p. 86
Hollyhock Mallow. These 2- to 4-foot-tall
plants bear loose spikes of deep pink or white
flowers in summer over hairy divided leaves.
The blooms are 2 inches across; they are more
delicate than those of true hollyhock.
Zones 4–9.

Matricaria
Daisy family
Compositae

Ma-tri-cay′ri-a. This Old World genus of 35
species of annuals, biennials, and perennials
is closely related to *Chrysanthemum,* with
which it is often confused. The leaves are
finely cut; the flowers are daisylike with
yellow centers but often have no petals.
When petals are present, they are white.
Many species are aromatic.

How to Grow
German Chamomile, the species described
below, will grow in either moist or dry soil
once it is established, and so is a good choice
for areas with unpredictable rainfall. It
grows best in cool climates but is somewhat heat
tolerant. Plant German Chamomile in full

sun and poor, sandy soil with good drainage.
Sow seeds outdoors as soon as the soil can be
worked in early spring. (Seeds can be started
indoors, but the seedlings do not transplant
well.) Space plants 8 inches apart; do not
fertilize them. Pick flowers for drying when
they are in full bloom and dry them on a
screen.

Uses
Plant German Chamomile in beds, borders,
or an herb garden. Use the dried flowers to
make herbal tea.

recutita p. 106
German Chamomile; Sweet False
Chamomile. Plants are multibranched and
grow 1–2½ feet high. The gray-green leaves
are lacy and apple scented. The 1-inch
flowers have yellow centers and may have
white petals. Plants bloom in summer except
where it is very hot. German Chamomile
self-sows easily. Hardy annual.

Melia
Mahogany family
Meliaceae

Mee′lia. A genus of Asian or Australian
deciduous or semievergreen trees. About 20
have been described, but only one is
commonly grown. The Chinaberry has been
in cultivation since the 16th century and is
naturalized in all parts of the warm-
temperate and tropical regions of the world.
It is popular in the South for its fragrant,
lilac-colored spring blossoms.

How to Grow
Chinaberry will grow in almost any type of
soil within its hardiness range with no care.
It tolerates wet and drought, thrives in heat,
withstands poor, alkaline soil, and is pest
free. Plant it in full sun. Propagate from
seeds or cuttings.

Uses
Chinaberry is an attractive lawn specimen or
accent tree.

azedarach pp. 198, 199
Chinaberry; Bead Tree; China Tree. This
mostly deciduous, fast-growing, weak-
wooded tree of spreading habit grows 30–50
feet high. It has furrowed bark and 12- to

36-inch leaves that are divided into toothed leaflets 1½–2 inches long. The flowers are conspicuous and bloom in late spring or early summer in loose 8- to 16-inch-long clusters. Round yellow berries form in fall and last well after the leaves fall; they are somewhat ornamental but are poisonous. The cultivar 'Umbraculiformis', Texas Umbrella Tree, has drooping foliage on erect crowded branches that spread from the trunk like spokes of a wheel or umbrella. Zones 7–10.

Mesembryanthemum
Carpetweed family
Aizoaceae

Me-sem-bri-an'thee-mum. Fig-marigold. Originally, the fig-marigolds made up a huge genus, but over the past 100 years they have been divided into several separate genera. *Mesembryanthemum* contains about 50 species of low-growing annual and biennial succulents that have fleshy stems. The leaves are nearly cylindrical, some flecked with glistening specks. The large, showy flowers are white, red, or yellow.

How to Grow
Although best suited to dry soils and arid western climates, Ice Plant, the species listed below, will give 4–6 weeks of color in cool climates if it is grown in poor soil. Plant it in full sun in poor, sandy, well-drained soil. The plants are drought tolerant and rarely need watering. Start seeds indoors 10–12 weeks before the last frost. The fine seeds need darkness during the 15- to 20-day germination, so cover the seed flats with black plastic until the seeds sprout. Space the plants 8–12 inches apart in the garden. Fertilize every other month.

Uses
Use Ice Plant as a ground cover, in a rock garden, or at the seashore.

crystallinum p. 88
Ice Plant; Sea Fig; Sea Marigold. Plants grow only 8 inches high but spread 1–2 feet across. Lumps or blisters on the 4-inch oval leaves glisten like ice in the sun. The flowers have thin, narrow petals and measure ¾–1¼ inches wide. Blooms are white or pale pink. Ice Plant has become naturalized along the California coast. Tender annual.

Microbiota
Cypress family
Cupressaceae

Mike-roe-by-oh′ta. This genus contains a single species of coniferous evergreen shrub, the Siberian Carpet Cypress. It was first discovered in Siberia in 1921 and has come into general distribution only recently.

How to Grow
Siberian Carpet Cypress grows in sun or shade in any well-drained soil. Once it is established, it is very adaptable and tolerates drought. Prune to shape and control size at any time of year. Propagate from hardwood cuttings or by layering.

Uses
Use Siberian Carpet Cypress as an open-space ground cover, under taller evergreens, as a low hedge, or in a massed planting.

decussata p. 128
Siberian Carpet Cypress; Russian Cypress. This low, flat-topped shrub grows 1½–2 feet high and spreads up to 15 feet wide. The lacy, arching branches have a fanlike appearance. The bright green leaves are scalelike or needlelike and feathery. In winter, the foliage turns bronzy or copper colored in full sun. The female plants have tiny berrylike cones with brown scales covering a glossy oval nut. Zones 3–10.

Mirabilis
Four-O'Clock family
Nyctaginaceae

Mi-ra′bil-is. A genus of tropical annuals and perennials that have thick tuberous roots and brightly colored tubular flowers. The genus name—*Mirabilis* means "wonderful"—refers to the flowers, which may be of several different colors on the same plant. Flowers open late in the day and remain open until mid-morning the following day.

How to Grow
Desert Four-O'Clock is a very drought-tolerant species. Plant it in full sun and dry, sandy soil with excellent drainage. The plants self-sow easily; thin them out each year as necessary. They can be increased by

division, but the roots are quite large and
sometimes hard to handle. Space plants
3–4 feet apart.

Uses
Plant Desert Four-O'Clock in meadow
gardens and wildflower gardens. It grows
well in areas with air pollution.

multiflora p. 88
Desert Four-O'Clock. This relative of the
Four-O'Clock *(M. jalapa)* has brightly
colored purplish-red flowers, 1½–2 inches
across. Plants grow in dense mounds 2 feet
high and 4 feet wide. They spread by
creeping stems that are covered with leathery
oval to triangular leaves. Plants bloom from
midsummer until frost. Zones 6–10.

Monarda
Mint family
Labiatae

Mo-nar′da. Bergamot; Horse Mint. A North
American genus of 12 aromatic annuals and
perennials, some grown for their showy
flowers. The 1½- to 3-inch-wide blooms
have tubular bracts arranged daisy-fashion
around central flowers. The squarish stems
are covered with aromatic leaves.

How to Grow
Wild Bergamot, listed below, is easy to
grow, sometimes too easy, and can become
invasive, especially in rich soil. Plant it in
full sun to partial shade in average, well-
drained soil. It will grow in both moist and
dry soil and is quite drought resistant. In dry
soil, the plants are shorter and are not as
invasive. Plants spread quickly and can be
divided in the spring; replant divisions
18–24 inches apart.

Uses
Plant Wild Bergamot in meadows, woodland
gardens, borders, or herb gardens. It is
attractive to butterflies and hummingbirds.

fistulosa p. 96
Wild Bergamot. This coarse perennial
covered with soft hairs grows 3–4 feet tall.
The 1½-inch-long flowers are lilac to purple
and are surrounded by white or purple bracts.
Zones 4–9.

Morus
Mulberry family
Moraceae

More'us. Mulberry. These fruit-bearing deciduous trees, one of them widely grown in the Far East as food for silkworms, comprise 12 species. All the cultivated species are Asiatic except for White Mulberry, the species described below, which is native American. Varieties of White Mulberry were once widely planted in the U.S. for their edible fruit and for their foliage. Mulberry leaves are often lobed; the small greenish flowers bloom in stalked hanging catkins. The male and female flowers are separate and are often on separate plants. The fruit is edible and resembles a blackberry; it is actually a dry fruit covered with fleshy sepals from several flowers.

How to Grow
Plant White Mulberry in full sun to partial shade in almost any soil except a swampy one. Trees withstand drought, salt, and city conditions and need little pruning except the occasional removal of dead branches. A canker disease may kill the branches; if it occurs, prune below the infected area.

Uses
White Mulberry is a nice specimen tree; all of the fruitless cultivars make good street trees.

alba pp. 222, 223

White Mulberry. The species grows to 60 feet tall and produces messy fruit. Fruitless varieties are generally less vigorous, forming a round-topped tree, 35–40 feet high and wide. Some nonfruiting cultivars are 'Kingan', 'Chaparral', 'Stribling', and 'Fruitless'. The shiny green leaves vary with the cultivar; they are sometimes lobed, grow 2–7 inches long, and have little or no fall color. Mulberries bloom in early spring; the flowers are insignificant. The fissured bark is orange-yellow to brown. Zones 5–9.

Myrica
Bayberry family
Myricaceae

Mir-i'ka. A genus of deciduous and evergreen shrubs or trees, often pleasantly aromatic, comprising about 50 species. The leaves are small and lance shaped; the inconspicuous greenish flowers are usually catkins. The male and female flowers are separate and often on different plants. The fruit is a fleshy or nutlike berry covered with an aromatic wax or resin.

How to Grow
Northern Bayberry, the species listed below, is a useful shrub for dry, sandy, poor soil, its natural habitat. Other bayberries are native to swamps and must have moist soil. Plant Northern Bayberry in full sun to partial shade. Prune old leggy plants to the ground in late winter or early spring. Propagate from seeds, by layering, or by division.

Uses
Plant Northern Bayberry in a shrub border, in a massed planting, or in combination with broadleaf evergreens. It is an excellent plant for a seashore garden and will effectively hold sand dunes in place.

pensylvanica p. 178
Northern Bayberry. This shrub grows 3–10 feet high and wide. Its very aromatic leaves hang on the branches into early winter. They are 3–4 inches long and more or less elliptic or broadest toward the tip. The berries are gray, waxy, and very aromatic; they are used in making bayberry candles. Zones 3–9.

Myrtus
Myrtle family
Myrtaceae

Mir′tus. Myrtle. A genus of tropical or subtropical shrubs or trees comprising about 16 species from the Old and New Worlds, one of them widely grown for its handsome evergreen foliage. The white or pink flowers are saucer shaped; they appear singly or in small clusters and are neither large nor showy. The numerous stamens, which are longer than the petals but not conspicuously protruding, give the flowers a delicate, fluffy look. Berries appear in the fall.

How to Grow
Myrtle grows well in full sun or partial shade in any well-drained soil. It tolerates heat and drought. Shear or prune plants in early spring before growth starts. Propagate from semi-hardwood cuttings or seeds.

Uses
Myrtle is primarily used for hedges because it is easily clipped and trained, but it can also be used in a massed planting. The dwarf varieties are useful for edgings. Myrtles are excellent plants for seashore gardens because they tolerate salt spray and wind.

communis p. 168
True Myrtle. This aromatic evergreen shrub grows 3–15 feet high in a dense rounded habit. The shining green leaves are oval to lance shaped and grow 1–2 inches long. They are thick and almost stalkless. The small fragrant flowers bloom in summer. The ½-inch fruit is bluish black or white.
'Compacta' is a small slower-growing form, reaching 2–3 feet high; 'Microphylla' is a dense dwarf variety. Zones 9–10.

Nemophila
Waterleaf family
Hydrophyllaceae

Nem-off'i-la. A genus of 11 species of annual herbs from North America, only a few of garden interest. Some are climbing or trailing plants, all are hairy. The leaves are usually cut and the flowers are showy, growing in clusters at the tips of the branches.

How to Grow
The nemophilas are cool-weather wildflowers that do well in northern and high-altitude gardens. They grow quickly and easily, especially if given afternoon shade, and will provide a cheerful display of color before heat and humidity sets in and kills them. In mild climates, sow seeds in fall; elsewhere, sow them in early spring. Thin plants to 1 foot apart.

Uses
Nemophilas make pretty covers for bulb gardens and do well in wildflower gardens and in naturalized settings.

maculata p.123
Five Spot. This species trails to 12 inches long. The 1¾-inch flowers are bell shaped; they are white with a blue or purple spot at the tip of each petal. Hardy annual.

menziesii p. 122

Baby Blue-Eyes. These trailing plants grow to 1 foot long. The bright blue flowers are bell shaped and are 1½ inches wide. There are white and blue-and-white forms. Hardy annual.

Nerium
Dogbane family
Apocynaceae

Neer'i-um. Oleander. Oleanders are widely cultivated ornamental shrubs or trees from the tropics. The leaves are lance shaped, thick, and leathery and usually appear in whorls around the branches. The funnel-shaped flowers bloom in showy terminal clusters. All parts of the oleander plant are poisonous and the leaves may cause a skin rash.

How to Grow
Plant oleanders in a sunny location in any well-drained soil. They tolerate strong all-day sun, heat, drought, air pollution, wind, and salt. Spring rains encourage heavier flowering. Prune plants in early spring to shape them. Propagate from softwood cuttings taken in summer.

Uses
Oleander is a magnificent specimen, can be planted as a border, windbreak, or screen, and is very useful at the seashore.

oleander pp. 154, 165

Common Oleander; Rose-Bay. This species is a shrub or small tree that grows 8–20 feet high. Its leaves are narrow and grow 4–10 inches long; they are dark green above and paler with a prominent midrib underneath. The 2½-inch-wide flowers are yellowish, red, white, pink, or purple, blooming 4–5 in a cluster. Plants bloom most abundantly in summer and off and on all year. Some cultivars have double flowers and some are fragrant. Recommended cultivars include 'Calypso', with cherry-red flowers; 'Hardy Pink'; 'Hawaii', salmon-pink with a yellow throat; 'Jannoch', large red flowers; and 'Mrs. Roeding', double, salmon-pink flowers. Zones 8–10.

Nyssa
Tupelo family
Nyssaceae

Nis'sa. Tupelo; Sweet Gum. A small genus of six or seven species of North American and Asiatic deciduous shade trees noted for their fine fall foliage. The Sour Gum of eastern North America, described below, is the only widely planted species.

How to Grow
Plant Sour Gum in full sun to partial shade. Light shade will weaken the fall color somewhat but will not affect growth. Sour Gums are hard to transplant so select their location carefully. Though often found growing naturally in swampy sites, Sour Gum grows in most soil situations and tolerates drought. It will not withstand polluted air and is therefore not a tree for cities.

Uses
Sour Gum is a good specimen or shade tree and can be naturalized in a woodland border.

sylvatica pp. 226, 227
Sour Gum; Pepperidge; Black Gum; Tupelo. A tree, 25–85 feet high, often taller in the wild, with horizontal branches drooping gradually and gracefully at the ends. The leaves are 3–5 inches long and somewhat broader near the tip. The small greenish flowers are not showy; they are followed by inconspicuous black-purple fruits. Older trees have dark furrowed bark. Sour Gum is one of the earliest trees to show fall color, and its brilliant scarlet hue is one of the brightest. Zones 4–9.

Oenothera
Evening primrose family
Onagraceae

Ee-no-thee'ra or ee-noth'er-ra. Genus of 80 species of American biennials and perennials, some of which are grown as annuals. The genus contains the evening primroses and their day-blooming relatives, the sundrops. They have smooth-margined leaves and showy flowers that are primarily yellow but can also be white or rose colored. Tubular flowers bloom in summer.

How to Grow
Plant evening primroses and sundrops in full
sun or partial shade in sandy, poor to average
soil with good drainage. They tolerate
drought but will rot in wet soil. In areas with
mild winters, sow seeds outdoors in fall;
elsewhere, sow seeds in early spring. Seeds
may also be started indoors 8–12 weeks
before the last frost, when they can be moved
into the garden. If the seeds are started early
enough, the plants can be grown as annuals.
Germination takes 21–25 days. Space plants
6–12 inches apart in the garden; do not
fertilize them. In areas where they are
perennial, these plants can become invasive
and should be divided or thinned as needed.

Uses
Plant evening primroses and sundrops in
borders, massed plantings, or rock gardens.

missourensis *p.* 77
Missouri Evening Primrose. Plants grow 12–
15 inches high and spread to 15 inches
across. The 5-inch-long leaves are soft and
velvety. The flowers are yellow and measure
up to 5 inches across. They open in the
evening and remain open until the end of the
next day. Missouri Evening Primrose is a
perennial hardy in zones 5–9 but can be
grown as a hardy annual.

tetragona *p.* 76
Common Sundrop. This day-blooming
perennial grows 18 inches high and has shiny
lance-shaped leaves 1–2 inches long. The
bright yellow saucer-shaped flowers are up to
2 inches wide. They bloom in early summer
to midsummer, opening in the morning and
closing at night. Zones 5–9.

Opuntia
Cactus family
Cactaceae

O-pun′ti-a. Prickly Pear; some species are
called Tuna and Cholla. A large genus of
cacti comprising 300 species, some of which
are upright-growing, others ground-
hugging. There are two general types: those
with flat broad pads, and those with
cylindrical segments. The flowers are large
and showy and are followed by juicy berries
that are edible in some species.

How to Grow

Plant prickly pear in full sun and dry, sandy, well-drained soil. It is very drought tolerant; in moist soil, it will rot. Protect plants from accumulated snow and ice during the winter. To propagate, break apart the pads and root them or grow plants from seeds. Set new plants 12 inches apart. Handle the plants carefully to avoid injury from the spines.

Uses

Plant prickly pear in rock gardens and on dry slopes. Because of the spines, do not plant it in an area with heavy foot traffic.

humifusa p. 112

Prickly Pear. This species (sometimes sold as *O. compressa* or *O. vulgaris*) has flat, oblong to oval, 2- to 6-inch pads that are covered with spines. Plants grow 12 inches high and spread horizontally along the ground. The 2- to 3-inch flowers are bright yellow and bloom in early summer. Green to purple oval fruits develop in fall; they are edible but not tasty. Zones 5–10.

Osteospermum
Daisy family
Compositae

Os-tee-oh-sper′mum. About 70 species of annual and perennial herbs or shrubs, most native to South Africa and a few naturalized in California and the southwestern U.S. Plants are shrubby and spreading and are clothed in 2- to 4-inch-long evergreen leaves. The daisylike flowers bloom on leafless stems in a variety of colors.

How to Grow

Trailing African Daisy, the species listed below, needs deep watering during summer but is drought resistant the rest of the year. Plant Trailing African Daisy in full sun in any good well-drained soil; it will not grow well in clay soil. Cut back old sprawling branches to encourage flowering and keep plants tidy. Increase from seeds, cuttings, or in some types, by layering. North of zone 9, grow Trailing African Daisy as an annual by starting seeds indoors in early spring.

Uses

Plant Trailing African Daisy in borders, on slopes, or cascading over a wall.

fruticosum p. 118

Trailing African Daisy; Freeway Daisy. This
trailing plant grows 12 inches high and
spreads to 3 feet wide. The stems root as they
creep along the ground. The leaves are
variable but are usually oval with a few teeth.
The 2-inch flowers are lilac fading to white
on the upper surfaces and deeper lilac or rose
on the undersides. They appear most
profusely in late winter and early spring and
continue to bloom on and off during the rest
of the year. There are several cultivars
with flowers of purple, pink, or white.
Zones 9–10.

Papaver
Poppy family
Papaveraceae

Pap-a'ver. Poppy. Genus of 50 species of
annuals and perennials from the temperate
regions of the world. They bloom in winter,
spring, or summer, depending on the
climate. The leaves are deeply cut and hairy
and grow at the base of the plant. The cup-
shaped, 1- to 3-inch flowers have a crepe-
papery texture and bloom singly on long
slender stems. They may be red, violet,
yellow, or white, and are sometimes blotched
at the base. If cut or broken, the stems exude
a milky substance.

How to Grow
Grow poppies in full sun and dry, well-
drained soil; they will rot in moist soil. They
prefer cool climates. Where winters are mild,
sow seeds outdoors in fall or very early
spring; elsewhere sow seeds outdoors in early
spring to mid-spring for summer bloom.
Poppy seeds are difficult to start indoors. To
be ready to plant in mid-spring they have to
be sown in midwinter. They need a constant
temperature of 55° to 60° F and must be in
darkness during their germination period.
Sow them in individual pots, because the
seedlings do not transplant well. Space poppy
plants 9–12 inches apart. Give them little or
no fertilizer. Remove flowers as soon as they
fade.

Uses
Plant poppies in beds, borders, or standing
alone as accent plants; use them for cutting
flowers.

nudicaule *p. 81*
Iceland Poppy. Plants grow 12 inches high and have slender hairy stems. The leaves are also hairy and are finely divided. The flowers, which are slightly fragrant, are yellow, orange, red, white, salmon, pink, or cream. Some varieties have double flowers. Perennial grown as a half-hardy annual.

Penstemon
Snapdragon family
Scrophulariaceae

Pen-ste′mon. Beardtongue. Large genus of perennials and a few shrubs, most from the western U.S. The flowers are tubular and bloom in loose spikes in summer. Flower colors range from red to blue to pink, salmon, lilac, purple, and white. There are often fine hairs on the insides of the flowers.

How to Grow
Beardtongues grow best in full sun, although they appreciate partial shade in hot climates. The species described below prefer dry, sandy or gravelly soil that drains rapidly. These plants need little watering once they are established. They are somewhat short-lived, lasting only 3–4 years, less in hot climates. Most need a light mulch in winter. Grow new plants from divisions or seeds; plant them 8–12 inches apart.

Uses
Penstemons are popular additions to alpine gardens and are also useful in rock gardens and mixed flower borders.

pinifolius *p. 84*
Pine-leaved Penstemon. Plants grow 12–15 inches high and bear narrow 1-inch red flowers. The species was named for its short, needlelike dark green foliage. Zones 5–9.

strictus *p. 98*
Rocky Mountain Penstemon. This species grows 1–2½ feet high. It has ¾- to 1¾-inch flowers of royal blue to purple. The deep green foliage is grasslike at the top and broad and lance shaped at the bottom. Zones 4–9.

Perilla
Mint family
Labiatae

Per-rill'a. A small genus of annuals that are
native to eastern Asia. The plants have square
stems and crisp, heart-shaped green or
reddish leaves. Small flowers bloom in
slender spikes in late summer, but the plants
are usually grown for their foliage.

How to Grow
Plant perilla in full sun or light shade in
average to dry soil with excellent drainage. In
areas with long summers, sow seeds outdoors
after frost danger has passed; elsewhere, start
seeds indoors 4–6 weeks before the last frost.
Seeds need light during the 15- to 20-day
germination period. Space plants 12–15
inches apart, pinching them when they are 6
inches high to encourage bushiness. Fertilize
once a month. Plants may self-sow in warm
areas.

Uses
Plant perilla in beds and borders as a foliage
accent. It is most attractive when combined
with yellow flowers. The leaves and flowers
of *P. frutescens,* listed below, are edible and
can be used in salads, fruit dishes, soups, and
stir fry.

frutescens p. 129
Beefsteak Plant. Plants grow 1½–3 feet
high. The green or reddish-brown leaves are
slightly wrinkled and have toothed margins.
The most widely planted varieties are those
with a bronze-metallic sheen. 'Atropurpurea'
has purple leaves; 'Crispa' has wrinkled,
deeply cut leaves. The tiny white flowers,
sometimes tinged pink or red, bloom in 3- to
6-inch spikes. Tender annual.

Perovskia
Mint family
Labiatae

Per-ov'skee-a. Russian Sage. A small central
Asian genus of perennials and small shrubs
that resemble salvias. The small leaves are
toothed or finely cut and are covered with
silver or grayish-white hairs. Individual
flowers are tubular; they bloom in showy,
multibranched spikes in midsummer to late
summer.

How to Grow

Azure Sage, the species listed below, is drought tolerant, as are most plants with silvery leaves. It is easy to grow in full sun and well-drained soil. It tolerates partial shade but tends to sprawl in low light. Each spring, cut the plants to the ground to encourage compact growth and profuse flowering. Propagate from seeds or from cuttings taken in summer. Space plants 1½–3½ feet apart; close spacing helps to keep the plants from sprawling and flopping over. A light mulch is beneficial during winter in the north.

Uses

Because of its size, Azure Sage can be planted at the back of the border, in a hedge, or as a screening plant. The silvery leaves are attractive against bright colors and the flowers are good for cutting. It makes an interesting accent plant.

atriplicifolia p. 101

Azure Sage. Growing like a bushy shrub, this plant reaches heights of 3–5 feet and spreads equally as wide. Both the silvery-gray stems and the lacy silver foliage have a sagelike aroma. Although individual blue flowers are only ¼ inch wide, they bloom in dense spikes that give the plant a cloudlike effect. Zones 5–8.

Petunia
Potato family
Solanaceae

Pe-too'ni-a. An important group of branching garden annuals and perennials comprising about 30 species, nearly all from Argentina. The leaves have smooth margins and are fuzzy and sticky. The funnel-shaped flowers are single or double and bloom in all colors from early summer to frost.

How to Grow

Plant petunias in full sun or light shade and average, well-drained soil. Petunias are drought resistant and can grow in pure sand. To grow them from seeds, start seeds indoors 10–12 weeks before the last spring frost; seeds are tiny and need light during germination, so don't cover them. Set plants into the garden 8–12 inches apart after the last frost; they will tolerate light frost. Fertilize at planting time; no further feeding

is necessary. Pinch young plants to encourage
bushiness. If plants become scraggly over the
summer, cut them back; this is often not
necessary with the new hybrids. If soil is
heavy, poor, or alkaline, plant single-
flowered rather than double-flowered
varieties.

Uses
Plant petunias in beds, borders, and all types
of containers. They tolerate seashore
conditions.

× *hybrida* p. 85
Common Garden Petunia. Plants grow 8–18
inches high and spread to 2 feet wide. The
flowers are 2–5 inches wide, sometimes
fringed or wavy, and come in every color of
the rainbow. Some flowers are solid colored,
others are splashed, striped, veined, starred,
or edged in white. Grandiflora petunias have
large flowers; multiflora petunias have
smaller but more numerous flowers and are
more disease resistant. Tender perennials
grown as half-hardy annuals.

Phalaris
Grass family
Gramineae

Fal′ar-is. About 15 species of both annual
and perennial ornamental grasses found in
the north temperate zone. They have flat
leaves that often have attractive variegation.
Tall stems bear narrow panicles of flattened
spikelets in the fall.

How to Grow
Ribbon Grass, the species listed below,
tolerates a wide variety of growing
conditions. Soil can be poor and either moist
or dry. It will grow in full sun, but the leaves
often bleach out if it is too hot. It will also
grow in full shade, but the growth will be
lanky and sparse. The clumps spread widely
and rapidly and should be divided when they
become crowded.

Uses
Ribbon Grass is a good accent plant that can
also be used as a ground cover where growing
conditions are less than ideal. Its attractive
foliage combines well with flowers and
darker-colored leaves.

arundinacea picta p. 143
Ribbon Grass; Gardener's-Garters. This perennial grass has large mounded clumps of leaves that are 12 inches long and ¾ inch wide. They are striped in green and white and sometimes pink. The 4- to 6-inch seed heads are white or pale pink and appear on 3-foot stems. Zones 4–10.

Phellodendron
Citrus family
Rutaceae

Fell-o-den'dron. Corktree. A genus of eight or nine species of deciduous Asiatic trees. Corktrees grow rapidly when young, developing into shapely round-headed trees that are wide-spreading with age. The decorative dark green foliage turns yellow in fall but drops quickly. Leaves are compound, the leaflets arranged feather-fashion. The flowers are greenish yellow, male and female flowers on separate trees, and although they are not showy, they are followed by clusters of black fruits that hang on for several months and are interesting in winter.

How to Grow
Amur Corktree, the species listed below, endures drought once it is established. Plant it in full sun in almost any type of soil except soggy or very dry soil. Prune trees when they are young to shape them; they need little pruning after that. This species transplants easily.

Uses
Amur Corktree is a good lawn specimen or shade tree.

amurense pp. 226, 227
Amur Corktree. This tree grows 40–50 feet high and has deeply fissured corky gray bark. Branches become massive and grow horizontally as the tree ages. Leaves are 10–15 inches long and are divided into 5–13 oval leaflets each 2–4 inches long. They have an aroma something like that of turpentine when bruised. The yellow-green flowers are small and insignificant. Zones 4–7.

Philadelphus
Saxifrage family
Saxifragaceae

Fill-a-del'fus. Mock-Orange. The mock-oranges are a genus of about 60 North American and Eurasian deciduous shrubs; most are erect, but some have long arching or drooping branches. The leaves of some species have marginal teeth. Fragrant, single or double white flowers bloom in late spring or early summer.

How to Grow
Mock-oranges are easy to grow in full sun or partial shade in any well-drained soil. The species below, Little Leaf Mock-Orange, is native to the southwestern U.S. and Mexico and tolerates drought and poor soil. Plants tend to become leggy, so prune them yearly immediately after they flower. Propagate from cuttings, from seeds, by layering, or from suckers.

Uses
Plant Little Leaf Mock-Orange in a shrub border or a hedge or use it as an accent plant. Plant it in a spot where its fragrance can be enjoyed.

microphyllus p. 164
Little Leaf Mock-Orange. This multibranched shrub usually grows 4 feet tall in a rounded shape. The reddish-brown bark shreds into thin strips. The 1-inch white flowers are pineapple scented; the oval to lance-shaped 1¼-inch leaves turn yellowish in the fall. Zones 6–10.

Phlox
Phlox family
Polemoniaceae

Flocks. Phlox. A genus of herbaceous annuals and perennials, most of North American origin. The plants are trailing or erect, depending on the species. They have lance-shaped leaves and showy clusters of small single flowers. Some bloom in spring, others in summer.

How to Grow
While most phlox prefer rich, moist soil, Ground Pink, the species listed below, likes poor, sandy, average to dry soil that is

neutral to alkaline and well drained. Some phlox tolerate partial shade, but Ground Pink prefers full sun. It is easy to propagate from seeds or cuttings or by division. Set plants 12 inches apart. Shear plants after they have flowered to promote dense growth.

Uses
Combine Ground Pink with spring-flowering bulbs in a flower border or rock garden or use it as a ground cover. These plants are subject to powdery mildew, so make sure they have adequate air circulation.

subulata p. 116

Ground Pink; Moss Pink; Mountain Pink. This evergreen perennial grows in a dense mat 6 inches high and 24 inches wide. The stems root as they creep along the ground. This garden favorite is easy to distinguish from other low-growing phlox by its inch-long needlelike leaves. Dense clusters of white, bright pink, blue, lavender, or red flowers with notched petals cover the plants in mid-spring. There are many cultivars in all of these colors. Zones 4–10.

Physocarpus
Rose family
Rosaceae

Fy-so-kar'pus. Ninebark. All of the 10 species of these attractive, spirea-like deciduous shrubs are native to North America except one, which is Asian. The shreddy or peeling bark gives the genus its common name. The leaves are toothed and often lobed. Red to brown inflated pods with shining yellowish seeds form in clusters.

How to Grow
Ninebark grows in sun or partial shade in any well-drained soil. It prefers acid soil and tolerates drought. Pinch young plants to encourage bushy growth. Prune plants during winter or early spring; pruning after the plants flower will eliminate the attractive seedpods. To encourage new growth, cut old wood down to the base of the plant. Propagate from seeds or softwood cuttings or by dividing existing plants.

Uses
Plant ninebark in a shrub border or hedge.

***opulifolius** p. 170*
Common Ninebark. Plants grow 5–10 feet high in an erect or arching habit. Leaves are oval to round, 2–3 inches long, and turn red in the fall. Small flowers bloom in late spring in dense terminal clusters that are 2 inches wide. They are white tinged in pink. 'Luteus', Goldenleaf Ninebark, is similar, except the leaves are yellow when they open and look like flowers from a distance; they change to green in summer. Zones 3–8.

Picea
Pine family
Pinaceae

Py-see′a or Py′see-a. Spruce. A genus of usually majestic, sometimes gigantic needleleaf evergreen trees of great horticultural importance that are also used for timber and paper. There are 45 known species, all from the Northern Hemisphere, most from cool, moist regions. The spruces are without doubt the most versatile cultivated conifers and come in a wide range of sizes and habits from small shrubby plants to huge forest specimens. Most have single unbranched trunks with tiers or whorls of branches; their outline is often in the shape of a candle flame. The needlelike leaves are spirally arranged around the branches. The flowers are insignificant; the cones generally hang down from the branches.

How to Grow
Most spruces like moist, light, sandy, well-drained soil, but the species listed below tolerate wind, heat, and drought. Plant them in full sun or light shade. Mulch to retain moisture and protect the shallow roots. They require little pruning other than the removal of dead or diseased wood. Spruce hedges should be wider at the bottom so the lower branches receive sunlight. Shear or prune spruces in late summer when they are dormant. Propagate from cuttings or seeds.

Uses
Because of their dense habit, spruces are excellent choices for hedges and windbreaks and can be used as lawn specimens as well.

***glauca** pp. 236, 237*
White Spruce. This tree grows 60–70 feet tall and has ascending branches and drooping

branchlets. The ¾-inch needles are bluish green with a white tinge. The cylindrical cones are 1½–2 inches long; they appear during fall and winter. Zones 3–6.

pungens pp. 234, 235
Colorado Spruce. This beautiful tree can reach 150 feet in the wild but usually grows 30–100 feet in cultivation. The whorls of branches are stiffly horizontal; the stiff, sharp 1¼-inch needles are dull green to bluish. The cones are 3–4 inches long; they appear in fall to winter. Blue-foliaged forms are called Blue Colorado Spruces. 'Hoopsii', Hoops' Blue Colorado Spruce, has silvery-blue needles. Zones 3–7.

Pinus
Pine family
Pinaceae

Py'nus. Pine. A genus of magnificent coniferous evergreen trees and shrubs of outstanding value as ornamental and timber plants. Nearly all of the approximately 90 known species are from the north temperate zone, although there are a few from Mexico, the West Indies, and Malaysia. More than 50 species of pine are grown in the United States. Most pines have a single trunk with tiers or whorls of branches. The needlelike leaves are borne in sheathed bundles; the sheaths are parchmentlike and enclose the base of the leaves. The new growth, which is called a candle, appears in spring. The flowers are insignificant; the cones are scaly.

How to Grow
Most pines need full sun and prefer light soil with excellent drainage; they will not tolerate wet soil. The species listed below are the most drought tolerant of the genus. Exposure and winter sun are the greatest enemies of pines. A drying wind in summer will turn foliage brown and do more damage than dry soil; strong winter sun will have the same effect. Avoid this type of damage by planting pines in a place where they will be protected from wind year-round and direct sun in winter. Control the size of pine trees by cutting the candle in half as it expands in spring. Propagate from cuttings or seeds.

Uses
Pines can be used as specimens, backgrounds
to other plantings, windbreaks, hedges, and
screens. Mugo Pine is a good choice in a rock
garden or as a ground cover.

flexilis pp. 236, 237
Limber Pine. This pine grows slowly and
may reach up to 75 feet in height. The stiff
2- to 3-inch leaves grow 5 to a sheath; they
are dark green. The cones are egg shaped and
grow 4–6 inches long. The branches are often
bare near the trunk, which has gray bark.
This species is one of the most tolerant of
wind and drought. Zones 4–7.

mugo mugo p. 235
Mugo Pine. This species, a popular, lower
variety of *P. mugo* (p. 234), is a mounded
shrub that grows 2–6 feet high and up to 12
feet across. It has medium to dark green 1½-
inch needles that grow 2 to a sheath. The
oval cones are ¾–1½ inches long. This is
one of the few species of pine that will grow
in light shade. It is sometimes sold as *P. mugo
mughus*. Zones 2–7.

nigra pp. 238, 239
Austrian Pine. This broadly conical tree
grows rapidly up to 100 feet tall but usually
to 60 feet or less. The dark green leaves are
4–6 inches long and grow 2 to a sheath. The
3-inch-long cones are egg shaped or conical.
This species and Japanese Black Pine
(*P. thunbergiana*) are the best pines for city
conditions. Zones 4–8.

ponderosa pp. 238, 239
Ponderosa Pine; Western Yellow Pine. This
dense, fast-growing pine can reach heights of
150 feet in the wild but usually reaches only
50–60 feet in the garden. The yellow-green
to dark green needles grow in bundles of 3
and are 5–11 inches long. The cones are oval
to oblong, 3–6 inches long, and prickly.
Zones 6–8.

Pistacia
Cashew family
Anacardiaceae

Pis-tash′i-a. Pistachio. A genus of aromatic
shrubs or trees, both deciduous and
evergreen. Most of the 10 species are
Eurasian. They have compound leaves, the
leaflets arranged feather-fashion. The male

and female flowers are on separate plants and
are inconspicuous; small but showy berries
form in the fall on the female plants. The
species *P. vera* is the source of pistachio nuts.

How to Grow
Chinese Pistache, the species listed below,
withstands drought and wind well. Plant it
in full sun; it prefers well-drained soil and
tolerates poor, dry soil. Prune plants when
they are young to develop a symmetrical
shape. Propagate from seeds or by budding or
grafting.

Uses
Chinese Pistache is effective as a shade tree,
lawn specimen, street tree, or windbreak.

chinensis pp. 218, 219
Chinese Pistache. This deciduous tree,
growing 30–60 feet high, has a rounded
crown. The leaves have 10–12 lance-shaped
leaflets and turn bright red to orange in the
fall. The flattened ¼-inch berries are scarlet
at first and turn bluish purple. Zones 7–9.

Polygonum
Knotweed family
Polygonaceae

Pol-lig'o-num. Smartweed; Knotweed. A
variable genus of annuals and perennials from
all over the world, containing erect, trailing,
and vining plants. Their common
characteristics are aggressive growth, angled
stems with swollen joints, and small, usually
white or pink flowers that bloom in loose,
showy spikes.

How to Grow
Smartweeds like full sun or light shade; most
prefer moist, well-drained soil, but the
species listed below, Himalayan Fleeceflower
and Silver-Lace Vine, are drought resistant.
They prefer poor soil and may become very
weedy in soil that is too rich. Grow new
plants from seeds or cuttings or by dividing
roots in spring. If necessary, cut back Silver-
Lace Vine severely in late winter to keep its
vigorous growth within bounds.

Uses
Himalayan Fleeceflower, because of its
aggressive growth, is best used as a ground
cover in large areas. Silver-Lace Vine can also

be grown as a ground cover but is more
spectacular climbing on fences, walls, and
trellises.

affine p. 125

Himalayan Fleeceflower. These creeping
perennials produce a mat of brownish-green
basal leaves that grow 4 inches long or
longer. Dense, 2- to 3-inch-long spikes of
bright rose-pink flowers bloom on leafless
18-inch stems during late summer and fall.
'Superbum' has dense spikes of deep pink
flowers. Zones 4–7.

aubertii p. 103

Silver-Lace Vine; Fleece-Vine. This rapid-
growing vine grows to 25 feet high and
spreads by underground stolons. Light green,
oval to heart-shaped leaves cover the plants,
which are at their best when the showy
panicles of white flowers open in late summer
to fall. Zones 4–7.

Populus
Willow family
Salicaceae

Pop'you-lus. Poplar; Aspen; Cottonwood.
About 30 to 40 species of trees that are
widely distributed across the Northern
Hemisphere. The leaves are mostly broad;
the flowers appear in catkins before the leaves
open. The seed capsules are covered with
copious hairs. There are separate male and
female plants.

How to Grow

Quaking Aspen, the species described below,
grows best in full sun and deep, moist, well-
drained soil but tolerates drought, air
pollution, and salt spray. It will grow only in
cool areas with very cold winters. Propagate
from cuttings, suckers, or seeds. Prune when
necessary during the summer.

Uses

Use Quaking Aspen in a woodland planting,
as a specimen, or as a windbreak.

tremuloides pp. 206, 207

Quaking Aspen. This large tree grows 40–90
feet high and has a 20- to 30-foot spread. It is
narrow and pyramidal when young and more
rounded at maturity. The bark is white. The
3-inch-long leaves are triangular, pointed,

and finely toothed; they turn yellow in the fall. The plant's common name refers to the way the leaves constantly shimmer in the breeze. Zones 1–5.

Portulaca
Purslane family
Portulacaceae

Por-tew-lak′a. Purslane. A genus of low-growing, mostly trailing, mostly annual plants comprising about 100 species from tropical and temperate regions. The stems are soft and fleshy and often reddish. The small thick leaves are needle or spoon shaped and grow 1–2 inches long. The flowers appear at the ends of the branches and open only in the sunlight. They are single or double and usually brightly colored.

How to Grow
Plant purslane in full sun and dry, sandy or gravelly soil that is well drained. They grow best in high temperatures and need little watering. Seeds are fine and may wash away if sown directly into the garden; instead, start seeds indoors 8–10 weeks before the last spring frost. Set plants in the garden when the soil is warm, spacing them 12–15 inches apart. Use little or no fertilizer. Flowers fall cleanly from the plant, and seeds self-sow easily.

Uses
Plant purslane on dry banks and in rock gardens or use it as a ground cover or an edging plant.

grandiflora p. 113
Garden Portulaca; Rose Moss. These trailing plants grow 4–6 inches high and 12–18 inches across. The 1- to 2-inch flowers are white, rose, orange, pink, yellow, red, or purple, blooming from early summer until frost. Tender annual.

Potentilla
Rose family
Rosaceae

Po-ten-till′a. Cinquefoil. A genus of perennial herbs and shrubs, rarely annuals, comprising more than 500 species found in

the Arctic and temperate regions, mostly in
the North. They are grown for their dense
rounded shape and long-blooming flowers.
The stems are creeping or erect; the creeping
species root at the stem joints. Leaves are
compound and are more or less hairy. The
flowers are single and cup shaped and bloom
in numerous small loose clusters. They are
yellow, white, or red and have many
stamens.

How to Grow
Cinquefoils grow well in full sun and fertile,
dry, well-drained soil. They tolerate
alkalinity and are suitable for clay loam soils.
Prune plants in early spring to keep them
compact; cut a third of the stems to the
ground in winter or very early spring to
renew plants. Spring Cinquefoil can be
mowed each spring. Propagate cinquefoils
from softwood cuttings.

Uses
Spring Cinquefoil is a handsome ground
cover, rock garden plant, and cover for spring
bulbs.

tabernaemontani *p. 113*
Spring Cinquefoil. This perennial herb is a
dainty, tufted creeping plant that grows 2–6
inches high and 18–24 inches across. The
bright green leaves are divided into 5 leaflets.
The ½-inch-wide golden-yellow flowers
bloom in clusters of 3–5 in spring. Also
known as *P. verna*. Zones 4–10.

Prunus
Rose family
Rosaceae

Proo'nus. A large and immensely important
genus of deciduous and broadleaf evergreen
trees and shrubs, nearly all from the north
temperate zone, a few reaching into the
Andes. The genus comprises more than 400
species, including the cherries, plums,
apricots, peaches, nectarines, and almonds.
In addition to the fruit trees, the genus
contains the superb Japanese flowering
cherries and many other flowering shrubs and
trees, the fruit of which is generally inedible.
Leaves of all species are sharply toothed. The
single or double flowers are white, pink, or
red, and are borne along the branches in
spring.

How to Grow

Plants in the *Prunus* genus need full sun. Most prefer moist, well-drained soil; the species below are the most drought tolerant of the group. Most are fairly short-lived plants, surviving for 20–30 years, and are highly susceptible to insects and diseases. Apply an organic mulch to help retain soil moisture. During periods of prolonged drought, water deeply. Prune out weak, damaged, or diseased branches in the early spring. Propagate from cuttings.

Uses

The species listed below have a variety of uses in the garden. Wild Plum grows in a thicket and makes a good screen or barrier plant. Sand Cherry is handsome in massed plantings, especially at the seashore, and attracts wildlife. European Bird Cherry is a popular ornamental shade tree. Use Schubert Chokecherry as an accent plant, in a grouping, or for a colorful screen planting.

americana pp. 222, 223

Wild Plum; Yellow Plum. This coarse shrub or tree grows 20–30 feet high and has shaggy gray bark. The branchlets are often thorny. Leaves are oval to lance shaped and grow 2½–4 inches long; they turn yellow in the fall. The fragrant white 1-inch flowers bloom in clusters before the leaves open. The fruits, which are ¾ inch or more wide, are yellow or red. They are edible but quite tart. Zones 4–8.

besseyi p. 191

Sand Cherry; Hansen Bush Cherry. This low shrub grows 4–6 feet high and often has spreading stems. The leathery 1- to 2-inch-long leaves are narrowly elliptic to oval. The ⅓-inch white flowers bloom in small clusters of 2–4. The fruit is nearly round, measures ½ inch in diameter, and is black. Edible and sweet, it is usually cooked in pies and jellies. Zones 3–7.

padus pp. 202, 203

European Bird Cherry. A deciduous tree that grows up to 40 feet high, this species has elliptic to oblong, 3- to 5½-inch leaves that are gray on the undersides. The flowers are fragrant, white, and ½ inch wide; they bloom in finger-shaped, drooping, 3- to 6-inch clusters. The ½-inch fruit is black; it is not edible and has little ornamental value. This is one of the first trees to leaf out in the spring. It has attractive peeling bark. The wood of this species is used for furniture. Zones 4–7.

***virginiana* 'Schubert'** *pp. 218, 219*
Schubert Chokecherry. A small deciduous tree with a rounded outline, this species grows rapidly when young, reaching 25–30 feet at maturity. The bark is red. The leaves are usually elliptic and grow 3 inches long. They are green at first and turn reddish purple for the summer and orange in the fall. The ⅓-inch flowers are white and bloom in narrow 4- to 8-inch clusters. The ¼-inch fruits are red at first and turn to purple. They are sour but edible and are used in cooking. Zones 3–5.

Ptelea
Rue family
Rutaceae

Tee′lee-a. A genus consisting of three species of shrubs or small trees from North America, including the Common Hop-Tree, listed below, which is planted for ornament. The leaves are usually divided into leaflets and are strongly aromatic. The greenish-white flowers bloom in clusters in early summer; they are highly fragrant.

How to Grow
Plant Common Hop-Tree in partial shade and porous, fertile, well-drained soil. It grows in moist or dry soil. Propagate from seeds or cuttings or by layering.   .

Uses
Hop-trees are useful as barrier plants, large hedges, and screens.

trifoliata *pp. 214, 215*
Common Hop-Tree; Stinking Ash; Wafer Ash. This species is a spreading plant that grows rapidly to 25 feet tall and has chestnut-brown bark. Its compound leaves are oval to elliptic; leaflets are 2½–4 inches long. They are dark green on the top and turn yellow in the fall. The flowers are inconspicuous. They are followed by dense green clusters of waferlike winged seeds similar to those of an elm. The seeds are sometimes used as a substitute for hops. The bark and the leaves emit a strong aroma when bruised. Zones 5–8.

Pyracantha
Rose family
Rosaceae

Py-ra-kan'tha. Fire Thorn. A small genus of thorny evergreen Asiatic shrubs that are upright or spreading, depending on the species. Most are grown for their fine foliage and the bright red or orange berries that persist throughout the winter. The small single white flowers bloom in clusters in spring; they are not especially showy.

How to Grow
For good fruit production, plant fire thorns in full sun in fertile, well-drained soil. They will tolerate drought and air pollution once established but need protection from winter wind. Plants tend to develop long, awkward branches, especially when they are young, and need pruning several times a year to keep the shape attractive. Propagate from seeds or hardwood cuttings or by layering.

Uses
The long thorns make these plants useful as hedges and barrier plants. They may also be trained against northern and eastern walls (heat reflected off southern and western walls is too strong) and used for espaliers.

coccinea p. 189
Scarlet Fire Thorn. This shrub grows 10–15 feet high and has toothed, oval 1- to 1½-inch leaves. The flower clusters are small and hairy. The ⅓-inch berries are bright red and appear in large showy clusters. This is the best-known species in cultivation. 'Lalandei' has deeply toothed leaves and bears orange-red fruit. It is hardier and more vigorous than the species. Zones 6–10.

Quercus
Beech family
Fagaceae

Kwer'kus. Oak. This genus includes some of the finest timber and ornamental trees in the temperate world. There are about 450 species of oaks, most from the north temperate zone, but a few from the tropics. The Asiatic species are evergreen, but the group as a whole is deciduous in North America. Many hang on to their withered leaves all winter. The leaves are variously lobed, toothed, or divided in most species. The flowers, which appear in early spring, are insignificant. The fruit, the acorn, is a true nut.

How to Grow
Oaks grow best in full sun but will tolerate light shade. They like rich, deep soil and will not tolerate compaction or grade changes around the root zone. Most oaks prefer moist acid soil; the species described below require only occasional watering. Scrub Oak grows in infertile, poor, sandy soil. Most oaks have a single main trunk extending their entire length, so pruning should be restricted to heading back lateral branches. Propagate from cuttings or seeds.

Uses
Oaks are handsome specimens, shade trees, and street trees. Scrub Oak is a good plant for woodland areas, naturalistic gardens, and along the seashore where little else will grow.

gambelii pp. 212, 213
Scrub Oak; Gambel Oak; Rocky Mountain White Oak. This species may develop several main trunks and grow as a shrub. Its mature height is 15–25 feet. The bark is scaly. The foliage has round lobes and is glossy on the top, hairy underneath, and turns orange in the fall. Zones 6–8. *Q. ilicifolia,* also known as Scrub Oak, is also a multibranched shrub or small tree. Its lobed, bristly toothed 4½-inch leaves are white and hairy on the undersides. Zones 5–8.

macrocarpa pp. 212, 213
Bur Oak; Mossy-Cup Oak. Growing 60–100 feet tall, this oak is a rugged-looking tree that tolerates adverse growing conditions. Its leaves are 4–10 inches long, rounded and broad on the tips, and deeply lobed. They are glossy green on top, white on the undersides, and turn yellow or reddish in the fall. The acorns are up to 1½ inches long and form in a fringed cup. The dark gray bark is thick and deeply furrowed. Zones 2–8.

Raphiolepis
Rose family
Rosaceae

Ra-fi-ol′e-pis. Handsome, dense evergreen Asiatic shrubs widely planted in warm areas for their leathery green foliage and showy

flower clusters. The leaves are thick and
fleshy; the single white or pink flowers
bloom in terminal clusters. Flowers are
followed by bluish-black or purplish-black
berries.

How to Grow
Indian Hawthorn, the species listed below,
tolerates drought once it is established. It is
easy to grow in full sun or partial shade in a
variety of soils, though flowering will be less
profuse in the shade. It may occasionally, but
not reliably, tolerate frost. After the plant
flowers, prune it to keep it compact.
Propagate from seeds or hardwood cuttings.

Uses
Indian Hawthorn is effective in borders and
hedges and as a large ground cover. It also
grows well in a container.

indica pp. *159, 173*
Indian Hawthorn. This shrub reaches a
maximum height and width of 3–5 feet. Its
oblong to narrow, 2- to 3-inch leaves are
pointed at the tip and bluntly toothed. The
pinkish-white ½-inch flowers appear in loose
clusters in spring. There may be a second
bloom in the fall. Zones 8–10.

Ratibida
Daisy family
Compositae

Rat-i-bid′a. Coneflower. Five species of
rough, hairy perennial or biennial herbs with
finely divided leaves. The drooping yellow or
purplish flowers surround cylindrical brown
centers; they bloom one to a stem.

How to Grow
Coneflowers thrive in full sun and rarely need
watering; they prefer good, well-drained soil.
Propagate from seeds; plants have a long
taproot and are difficult to divide.

Uses
Plant coneflowers in a flower border or
wildflower garden. They are excellent cut
flowers.

columnifera p. *77*
Prairie Coneflower; Mexican Hat. This
species, also known as *R. columnaris,* is a
multistemmed perennial or biennial that

grows 1–3½ feet tall. There are 7–9 lobes
per leaf; the lobes are linear to narrowly lance
shaped. The cylindrical to conical center of
the flower is ½–1½ inches high, as long or
longer than the bluntly toothed yellow
petals, which makes the flowers look
something like sombreros. When the flower
starts to bloom, it looks like there is a
hatband at the base of the cone. Flowers
bloom all summer. Zones 4–10.

Rhamnus
Buckthorn family
Rhamnaceae

Ram′nus. Buckthorn. A large group of
medically significant, mostly deciduous trees
and shrubs. Most of the 150 known species
are from the north temperate zone, a few
from Brazil and South Africa. The cultivated
species are chiefly shrubs grown for their
form and lustrous foliage. Plants are often
thorny. The small greenish flowers often have
no petals and are never showy. The showy
fruit is berrylike.

How to Grow
Plant buckthorns in full sun to partial shade
in well-drained soil. All species are easy to
grow and will thrive in moist soil but tolerate
drought and wind. Alder Buckthorn, the
species described below, must have extremely
well-drained soil. Prune or shear plants at
any time; often the only pruning necessary is
to control plant height. Propagate from seeds
or cuttings or by grafting. Plants spread
rapidly from seeds dropped by birds.

Uses
Buckthorns are effective hedges and
windbreaks. *R. frangula* 'Columnaris',
described below, is particularly useful as a
dense screen.

frangula p. 177
Alder Buckthorn. A shrub or small tree, this
species grows 10–18 feet high and is the
most ornamental of the buckthorns. Its
ovalish glossy dark green leaves are 1–3
inches long and half as wide. Berries are red
when they first appear, soon darkening to
black; they form during the summer while
plants are still in flower. The variety
'Asplenifolia', Feathery Buckthorn, is a shrub
or small tree that grows 10–12 feet high. Its

narrow wavy-margined leaves are cut and have a feathery look. 'Columnaris', Tallhedge Buckthorn, is a narrow shrub that grows 10–15 feet high. Its oval leaves are broad at the tip and grow 1½–2½ inches long; they turn bright yellow in the fall. Zones 3–9.

Rhus
Cashew family
Anacardiaceae

Rus. Sumac. A large genus of 150 species of deciduous and evergreen shrubs and trees, scattered very widely. The cultivated sumacs are of great decorative value in the fall when their compound foliage turns a more brilliant red than that of almost any other shrub or tree. The small greenish flowers are single and usually not particularly showy. The clustered red fruits, however, are very handsome. Most shrubby sumacs spread by suckers. Although they are related to Poison Sumac and Poison Ivy, the cultivated sumacs are not irritating or poisonous.

How to Grow
Sumacs are easy to grow in full sun in any garden soil; they will even grow in dry sand, poor soil, and on rocky hillsides. Those planted in partial shade will be less colorful in fall. Prune plants in early spring to control their size. Cut old overgrown plants to the ground to renew them. Sumacs can be raised from seeds and root cuttings.

Uses
Sumacs are plants for large areas and can serve as tall ground covers on hillsides, flat areas, and along roadsides. They are very useful in areas needing erosion control.

glabra pp. 186, 187
Smooth Sumac. This large shrub or small tree grows 8–20 feet high and spreads by underground roots to form large thickets. The fernlike leaves are divided into 11–31 toothed narrow leaflets that are 2–5 inches long and are dark green above and white underneath. This species blooms in summer; its flowers are more prominent than those of most sumacs. The erect and conically clustered berries last well into the winter. Both male and female plants are often needed to produce berries. The variety 'Laciniata' has lacy, finely divided foliage. Zones 3–10.

trilobata p. 186

Threeleaf Sumac; Skunkbush; Lemonade
Sumac. This sumac grows 4–6 feet high. Its
leaves are divided into 3 coarsely toothed 1-
inch leaflets that turn bright orange in the
fall. The flowers bloom in clustered spikes in
spring before the leaves open. This is one of
the most drought-resistant sumacs but it can
be foul smelling. Zones 4–10.

Ribes
Saxifrage family
Saxifragaceae

Ry'beez. A large genus of sometimes prickly
shrubs, most from the temperate regions.
There are more than 140 deciduous and
evergreen species, including the currants and
gooseberries, but not all *Ribes* are in
cultivation. Both the fruiting species and the
related shrubs grown for ornament are of
horticultural importance. The leaves are
usually lobed; the flowers greenish,
yellowish, or reddish, the sepals usually
larger than the petals. Juicy berries form in
midsummer after the spring flowers fade.
Both male and female plants are needed to
produce berries. The gooseberries are the
species with thorns; the currants are those
without.

How to Grow
Ornamental species of ribes are easy to grow
in sun or shade in any soil. They tolerate dry,
sandy, and alkaline soil. Prune plants in late
spring after the season's growth is completed,
cutting the oldest branches to the ground to
encourage new growth. Propagate by
layering or from cuttings or seeds.

Uses
Squaw Currant, the species described below,
is best used in hedges and massed plantings.

cereum p. 166
Squaw Currant; White-Flowered Currant.
This multibranched deciduous shrub grows 3
feet high. Its fragrant greenish-white flowers
bloom in drooping clusters in early summer
and are followed by tasty red berries. The
leaves turn yellow in the fall. Zones 5–10.

Robinia
Pea family
Leguminosae

Ro-bin'ee-a. Locust. A small genus of deciduous trees and shrubs native to North and Central America. They have compound leaves, usually have thorns, and have drooping clusters of white, rose, or pink pealike flowers that are similar to those of wisteria. The fruits are flat dried pods; the leaves have little fall color. The branches are often brittle and break easily.

How to Grow
Grow locusts in full sun in any well-drained soil; they tolerate poor soil and are also well adapted to heat and drought. Prune the shrubby forms in early spring to shape them and control their size. Black Locust needs pruning to shape it only when it is young. Propagate locusts from seeds, stolons, or cuttings, the cultivars by grafting or budding.

Uses
The locust species listed below have various uses in the garden. Rose Acacia is effective on dry rocky slopes, as a ground cover in large areas, and in massed plantings. Use New Mexico Locust in large hedges or as a screen. Black Locust is a handsome lawn, street, or shade tree.

hispida p. 160
Rose Acacia; Pink Locust. Growing 3–7 feet high, this species spreads by underground stolons and can become invasive. It will grow, however, where many other plants will not, in drought, heat, poor soil, and air pollution. The leaves are divided into 7–13 oblong to round, 1- to 2½-inch leaflets. The flowers are rose-pink to pale purple, blooming in late spring in 2- to 3-inch clusters. The young branches are covered with red bristles and the seedpods are 3 inches long. Zones 5–10.

neomexicana pp. 196, 197
New Mexico Locust; Thorny Locust. A multibranched shrub or small tree, this species grows 10–25 feet high. Each leaf has numerous lance-shaped 1½-inch leaflets. The fragrant flowers are rose colored and bloom in summer. Smooth 4-inch seedpods that remain on the tree all winter follow. Zones 3–10.

pseudoacacia pp. 196, 197

Black Locust; Yellow Locust; False Acacia.
This species is a tree growing to 75 feet tall
in an upright and open habit. Its drooping 3-
to 8-inch clusters of fragrant white flowers
bloom in early summer. The leaves are
divided into 7–19 oval 1- to 2-inch leaflets.
The seedpods are 3–4 inches long and remain
on the plants during the winter. The
attractive bark is dark brown and deeply
furrowed. Zones 3–10.

Romneya
Poppy family
Papaveraceae

Rom'nee-a. This genus contains two species
of perennials or subshrubs native to
California and Mexico. Both have spreading
roots and branching stems. Their broad
lance-shaped leaves are deeply lobed. White
flowers with prominent golden-yellow
stamens bloom in late summer at the tops of
the stems.

How to Grow
These striking garden plants are difficult to
grow unless they are started in pots and
transplanted carefully without disturbing the
long taproots. Set plants 3 feet apart in full
sun in dry, infertile, sandy soil that is well
drained. Although they will tolerate rich,
moist soil, they become too invasive for most
home gardens when grown under those
conditions. Cut plants to the ground in fall.
Winter protection is recommended in the
colder limits of their hardiness.

Uses
California Tree Poppy, the species listed
below, can be planted on hillsides—it will
help control soil erosion—along roadsides, or
at the back of the flower border, or used as a
screening plant.

coulteri p. 164

California Tree Poppy. Flowers of these 8-
foot-tall multibranched plants are 6 inches
across and have a sweet fragrance. Like all
poppies, they have crinkled petals. The gray-
green 3- to 4-inch-long leaves are deeply
divided and toothed. Zones 7–10.

Rosa
Rose family
Rosaceae

Ro′za. Rose. A genus of shrubs and climbing plants comprising all the true roses, from naturally occurring species roses to the complex hybrids grown in the garden and raised for cutting. Most roses have thorns, and some have more than others. All roses have compound leaves. The flowers vary from single blooms with 5 petals to double blooms with up to 100 petals. Blooms may appear one to a stem or in clusters. Many roses, but not all, are fragrant. Some roses bloom only once a year, others bloom from early summer until mid-fall. In fall, seedpods called hips form; they are bright red or orange.

How to Grow
Roses, almost without exception, need full sun. While the hybrids prefer rich, moist, well-drained soil, many of the species roses tolerate dry, sandy soil. Species roses require less pruning than hybrids; simply cut the oldest canes to the ground each year and trim the rest of the plant after it flowers. Propagate species roses from cuttings or seeds.

Uses
The roses described below can be mixed in a shrub border, used in a hedge, or planted as barrier plants. Rugosa Rose is also very useful at the seashore, as it tolerates salt spray and holds sand dunes in place.

foetida bicolor p. 154
Austrian Copper. This species is a tall lanky plant that can reach heights of 6–8 feet. It is a sport of *R. foetida,* which has a strong, sometimes unpleasant odor but was the original source of yellow in today's modern hybrids. The variety *bicolor* has 2- to 2½-inch single flowers that are orange-red with yellow on the outsides of the petals. Plants bloom in early summer and do not bloom again during the season. The canes are moderately thorny and have small medium green leaves. Zones 6–10.

rubrifolia pp. 158, 159
Redleaf Rose. This species, sometimes called *R. glauca,* grows 6 feet tall. Its single pink 1½-inch flowers bloom in small clusters in early summer. Its main landscape assets are its narrow bluish-green leaves, which are

tinged in reddish plum, and its oval scarlet-red hips. Redleaf Rose tolerates more shade than most roses. Zones 2–10.

rugosa pp. 156, 157

Rugosa Rose; Saltspray Rose. This species grows 4–6 feet high and spreads as much as 10–20 feet across. The stems are densely thorny. Each leaf is divided into 5–9 elliptic 1- to 2-inch leaflets that are rough, shiny, and prominently veined. The flowers, nearly 3½ inches wide, are red, pink, or white; they bloom all summer. Most are single, but there are double varieties. The brick-red hips are 1 inch wide. Zones 3–10.

Rosmarinus
Mint family
Labiatae

Ros-ma-ry′nus. Rosemary. A few species of aromatic evergreen shrubs or herbaceous perennials native to the Mediterranean region, one widely cultivated as a culinary herb. The ½- to 1-inch-long leaves are needle shaped and are darker above and woolly white on the undersides. The fragrant tubular blue flowers bloom in upright clusters in the leaf axils.

How to Grow

Rosemary grows best in full sun and soil that is not too rich but has excellent drainage. Be careful not to over-water rosemary, as it grows best in dry soil, and do not fertilize it. Rosemary tolerates heat, drought, and poor growing conditions. Prune after it flowers to improve its appearance and prevent excess woodiness. Propagate from stem cuttings or by division or layering. In areas where rosemary is not hardy, it can be grown as an annual or a container plant.

Uses

Rosemary is an excellent plant for a seashore garden and is one of the most popular herb-garden plants. It can also be used as an informal hedge and in a massed planting. Trailing Rosemary makes a good ground cover and is very attractive cascading over a wall.

officinalis p. 124

Rosemary. Rosemary grows upright and can reach heights of 2–6 feet, depending on the climate. The aromatic leaves are grayish green on the upper sides and white beneath. The light blue or white flowers are ½ inch wide. They appear in late winter and early spring in areas where rosemary is grown as a perennial and in summer when it is grown as an annual. Zones 8–10. The variety 'Prostratus', Trailing Rosemary, grows in a mound 6–24 inches high and 4 feet wide, rooting as it spreads. Zones 7–10.

Rubus
Rose family
Rosaceae

Roo'bus. Bramble. More than 400 species of shrubs, most of them thorny, and nearly all from the north temperate zone. The genus includes the wild brambles, blackberry, raspberry, loganberry, dewberry, and other fruiting and ornamental species. Most of them have biennial canes, which grow leaves the first year and flower, fruit, and die the second year. They have compound leaves and white flowers (pinkish-purple in a few) that usually bloom in clusters. The fruits form along the canes in summer after the flowers fade.

How to Grow
Plant Rocky Mountain Flowering Raspberry, the species described below, in full sun or light shade and average, dry, well-drained soil; it needs only occasional watering. After each cane has flowered and fruited, cut it to the ground. Propagate from seeds, from cuttings, or by removing suckers.

Uses
Use Rocky Mountain Flowering Raspberry as a hedge or screening plant.

deliciosus p. 165
Rocky Mountain Flowering Raspberry; Boulder Raspberry. This species is an upright shrubby plant that grows 6 feet high or more. Its spreading, arching canes are thornless. The leaves are round to oval with 3 or 5 shallow lobes. It is grown for its attractive white flowers, which are nearly 2 inches across and look like single roses; they appear in late spring. The fruits are dark purple to wine-red but are not tasty. Zones 6–10.

Rudbeckia
Daisy family
Compositae

Rood-beck′i-a. Coneflower. North American annual, biennial, and perennial herbs, comprising about 25 species. The leaves may be simple or compound and vary with the species. The daisylike flowers are generally yellow, usually with black or brown cone-shaped centers.

How to Grow
The most popular coneflower, Black-eyed Susan, will grow in rich, moist soil but is also very tolerant of heat and drought. Plant it in full sun or light shade in any well-drained garden soil. Sow seeds outdoors after all danger of frost has passed; in areas with a short growing season, start seeds indoors 8–10 weeks before the last spring frost. Move the plants to the garden after frost and set them 18 inches apart. Fertilize at planting time. Black-eyed Susan often reseeds and acts as a perennial.

Uses
Grow Black-eyed Susan in beds, borders, or wildflower gardens, or use it as an accent plant and for cut flowers.

hirta p. 79
Black-eyed Susan. These branching plants grow 1–3 feet high and are covered with short stiff hairs. Leaves are also rough and hairy. The flowers reach 2–3 inches across and are gold or yellow. Some are blotched or banded in a darker color; some are single, some double. Hybrids known as Gloriosa Daisies have been created with 2- to 6-inch flowers of yellow, gold, mahogany, or red. Perennial grown as a half-hardy annual.

Santolina
Daisy family
Compositae

San-to-ly′na. Originally from the Mediterranean, the eight species in this genus are evergreen, aromatic perennial herbs or subshrubs. The narrow, finely divided leaves form handsome mounds. Tiny yellow buttonlike flowers that have no petals bloom in summer. The major attraction of these plants is their foliage.

How to Grow

Plant santolinas in full sun. They will grow in any well-drained soil but like dry, infertile soil best. They are very tolerant of heat and drought. Cut plants back in early spring or after they flower to keep them compact. In northern climates, they may be grown as annuals; in the colder limits of their hardiness, they will need winter protection. Stem cuttings root easily, and plants also grow easily from seed. To make the best of the attractive foliage, shear the plants before they bloom.

Uses

Santolinas are valued ground cover or edging plants and are especially popular in herb gardens and seashore plantings.

chamaecyparissus p. 115

Lavender Cotton. Despite its common name, this silvery-gray evergreen is related to neither lavender nor cotton. Mounds of foliage grow 1–2 feet high and 2 feet across. The ¾-inch flowers are yellow and bloom on 6-inch stems. A close relative, Green Lavender Cotton, *C. virens*, is slower-growing and has thinner leaves that are dark green. Zones 6–9.

Saponaria
Pink family
Caryophyllaceae

Sap-o-nair′i-a. A genus of annuals and perennials from the Mediterranean region, some called soapworts. They have lance-shaped leaves and single flowers that bloom in showy loosely branched clusters. The flowers are pink or white and have notched or fringed petals.

How to Grow

Soapworts are easy to grow in full sun and sandy, average to dry, well-drained soil. Cut plants back after they have bloomed to keep them compact. Grow new plants from seeds or cuttings or by dividing existing plants in spring or fall. Space plants 12 inches apart.

Uses

Soapworts look spectacular when grown in rock walls or cascading from the tops of raised beds. They can also be used as ground covers and edging plants.

ocymoides p. 117

Rock Soapwort. These trailing perennial plants grow 4–8 inches high and spread to 2 feet across. The slender branches are clothed in small, downy evergreen or semievergreen leaves. The ½-inch flowers are bright pink and bloom in loose clusters in late spring and early summer. There is also a white-flowered variety. Zones 4–9.

Schinus
Cashew family
Anacardiaceae

Sky′nus. Pepper Tree. A genus of chiefly South American resinous trees comprising perhaps 28 species. Those commonly grown are broadleaf evergreen trees from semitropical climates. The leaves are sometimes compound. There are separate male and female plants. Small white flowers bloom in branched clusters; reddish berries form on the female plants. Some people have an allergic reaction to the pollen.

How to Grow
Brazilian Pepper Tree, the species listed below, is easy to grow in full sun in almost any soil. Feed and water infrequently to encourage deep roots. Young plants may need early staking and pruning to encourage a single trunk; otherwise they will grow into multibranched shrubs. Shorten long limbs and thin branches out so wind can pass through them to reduce the chance of storm breakage. Propagate from seeds or cuttings.

Uses
Use Brazilian Pepper Tree as a lawn specimen, shade tree, or accent plant.

terebinthifolius pp. 228, 229

Brazilian Pepper Tree; Christmasberry Tree. A small evergreen tree, this species grows to 30 feet high and is umbrella shaped. Its leaves are divided into 5–9 leaflets that are 2 inches long and dark green on the top. The flowers are yellowish and not attractive. The ¼-inch berries, which persist all winter, are bright red. Zones 9–10.

Sedum
Stonecrop family
Crassulaceae

See'dum. Stonecrop. Erect or trailing
perennials comprising about 600 species
found throughout the temperate and colder
regions of the Northern Hemisphere. The
fleshy succulent leaves sometimes overlap one
another. In some species they grow along the
branches, in others they appear in basal
rosettes. Tiny star-shaped single flowers
bloom in showy clusters at the ends of the
stems; the bloom time depends on the
species.

How to Grow
Stonecrops are easy-to-grow plants happy in
full sun or partial shade. They will grow in
average soil and tolerate poor, dry, sandy soil
as well. As is true with most succulents,
over-watering is destructive to stonecrops;
drainage must be excellent, especially in
winter. Propagate from seeds, from leaf or
stem cuttings, or by division. Space new
plants 12 inches apart.

Uses
Plant stonecrops in borders and rock gardens
or use them as edgings and ground covers.
Include them in your garden if you want to
attract butterflies.

cauticola p. 120
Shortleaf Stonecrop. Trailing stems arising
from a central crown grow 3 inches high and
8 inches long. The ½-inch leaves are round
and gray and grow scattered along the stems.
The ½-inch-wide flowers are bright pink and
bloom in late summer on 6-inch stems. This
species is very similar to *S. sieboldii,* but
S. cauticola blooms earlier and is therefore a
better plant for colder climates because it will
bloom before being killed by frost.
Zones 5–10.

kamtschaticum p. 110
Orange Stonecrop. This species grows in an
erect habit, 6–12 inches high and 12–18
inches across. Yellow-orange ¾-inch flowers
bloom in midsummer. The bright green oval
leaves have toothed margins. Zones 4–10.

spectabile p. 118
Showy Stonecrop. This upright-growing
species reaches 2 feet high and has gray-green
leaves up to 3 inches long. Pink ½-inch

flowers bloom in large dense heads in late summer to fall. Varieties include 'Brilliant', 18 inches tall with raspberry-red flowers, and 'Meteor', 18 inches high with deep red flowers. Zones 4–10.

spurium p. 119
Two-row Stonecrop. This creeping evergreen perennial grows 3–6 inches high and 12–24 inches across. Its inch-long, coarsely toothed oval leaves turn red in winter. The flowers are red to pale pink, blooming in flat, 2-inch-wide clusters in midsummer. Also sold as *S. stoloniferum*. Zones 6–10.

Senecio
Daisy family
Compositae

Sen-ee′si-o. Groundsel; Ragwort. A genus of more than 2,000 species of perennials, shrubs, vines, and small trees found throughout the world. Some are grown for their daisylike flowers; others for their foliage.

How to Grow
Like most plants with silver or gray leaves, Dusty Miller, the species described below, is very drought resistant. It grows best in warm to hot climates. Start seeds indoors 8–10 weeks before the last frost; do not cover the seeds because they need light during the 10- to 24-day germination period. Move plants to the garden 2–3 weeks before the last frost, spacing them 12 inches apart, in full sun or light shade and sandy, light, well-drained soil. Fertilize at planting time. If plants become leggy, cut them back.

Uses
Plant Dusty Miller in beds, borders, or rock gardens or use it as an edging. It is very effective as a buffer between strong colors and in gardens viewed at night.

cineraria p. 136
Dusty Miller. The plants grow 2½ feet high and are covered with long, white matted hairs. The leaves are thick and have narrow rounded lobes or finely divided segments. Small yellow or cream-colored flowers bloom in terminal clusters in long growing seasons but they are insignificant, and the plant is grown for its foliage. There are other plants

with white, gray, or silver foliage that are also known as Dusty Miller, but this is one of the more common species. Perennial grown as a half-hardy annual.

Solidago
Daisy family
Compositae

Sol-i-day'go. Goldenrod. These coarse perennials are often thought of as weeds, but some members of the genus make attractive garden plants. All but a handful of the 130 known species are from the New World. Plants are often branched or arching and usually have toothed leaves. The flowers, which are usually yellow, are small but bloom in large plumed clusters in late summer and fall. Goldenrod does not cause hayfever—it is ragweed that makes you sneeze.

How to Grow
Goldenrods tolerate considerable dryness and are easy to grow in full sun or partial shade in well-drained soil. In rich soil, they grow more foliage than flowers. Divide plants in spring or fall, setting them 18–24 inches apart. Goldenrods readily self-sow and may become invasive in fertile soil.

Uses
Goldenrod grows well on hillsides, in meadows, in informal borders, and in wildflower gardens.

speciosa p. 73
Noble Goldenrod. One of the most attractive for the garden, this species grows 3–6 feet tall and has narrow lance-shaped leaves. The flower clusters are slightly arching. Zones 6–10.

Spartium
Pea family
Leguminosae

Spar'shi-um. A single species, called Spanish Broom, of essentially leafless shrubs from southern Europe, related to the genus *Genista*. It is widely planted in warm climates for its profusion of yellow flowers, which bloom in terminal clusters. After the flowers, a flat seedpod forms.

How to Grow

Plant Spanish Broom in full sun in dry, well-drained soil. It grows best with infrequent watering and tolerates poor, rocky soil. It grows naturally in an open form; prune it in spring to make it grow more densely. Propagate from seeds or softwood cuttings.

Uses

Spanish Broom is a handsome ground cover especially effective on rough slopes.

junceum p. 148

Spanish Broom; Weaver's Broom. This shrub has numerous grooved rushlike stems and grows 6–8 feet high. It sometimes does not produce leaves, but the stems remain green all year, giving it the appearance of an evergreen. The flowers are fragrant, pealike, and very showy, blooming in 18-inch racemes. Plants flower summer to fall, and all year in California. The seedpod is hairy and grows 3–4 inches long. All parts of the plant are poisonous. Zones 8–10.

Stachys
Mint family
Labiatae

Stack'iss. Betony; Woundwort. About 300 species of annuals and perennials distributed throughout the world but chiefly from the temperate zones. They have hairy silvery leaves that grow in basal clumps and along the squarish stems. Tubular inch-long flowers bloom in loose whorled spikes at the tips of the stems.

How to Grow

Plant betony in full sun or light shade in sandy, dry, average to infertile soil that is well drained. Plants must have excellent drainage and dry soil during the winter. They grow best in low humidity. In early spring, cut back leaves that were damaged over the winter. Propagate by dividing plants in spring or fall (replant divisions 12–18 inches apart) or sowing seeds in early spring.

Uses

Lamb's-Ears, the species listed below, is valued for its attractive foliage, not its flowers, in rock gardens, herb gardens, and edgings.

byzantina p. 133

Lamb's-Ears. Mats of woolly silvery-gray leaves grow 8 inches high and spread to 3 feet wide. The individual leaves grow 4–6 inches long. Purple or pink flowers bloom on 18-inch stems in summer. Plants are evergreen in mild climates. Also sold as *S. lanata* and *S. olympica*. Zones 5–10.

Symphoricarpos
Honeysuckle family
Caprifoliaceae

Sim-for-i-kar'pos. A genus of hardy deciduous shrubs, all American, except for one Chinese species. They are ornamental but more showy in fruit than in flower. The flowers are small and bloom in clusters in the leaf axils or at the ends of the branches. The berries are produced in pairs or in clusters and remain on the plant well into winter.

How to Grow
Plant the species listed below, known as coralberries, in full sun or partial shade in any fertile, well-drained soil; they prefer slightly alkaline soil. Chenault Coralberry is extremely drought resistant; Indian Currant is moderately drought resistant. Prune in early spring if necessary to shape the plants. Propagate from softwood cuttings.

Uses
Plant coralberries in mixed borders, under trees and larger shrubs, or in massed plantings. Coralberries are very tolerant of city growing conditions.

× *chenaultii* p. 191
Chenault Coralberry. This multibranched shrub grows 3–6 feet high in an erect habit. The elliptic ¾-inch leaves are hairy on the undersides. The small tubular flowers are pinkish and bloom in spikes in spring; the fruit is white, turning pink to coral on the side exposed to the sun. Zones 5–10.

orbiculatus p. 190

Indian Currant; Coralberry. This species is a shrub 3–5 feet high, with erect branches. The leaves are elliptic to oval, 1½–2½ inches long, and pale and hairy on the undersides; they turn red in the fall. The ⅓-inch tubular flowers are white and appear in summer. The profuse berries are red and

are very attractive in fall. The variety
'Leucocarpus' has greenish-yellow flowers and
white fruit. It thrives in poor soil and partial
shade. Zones 3–10.

Syringa
Olive family
Oleaceae

Sir-ring'a. Lilac. A large group of decorative
deciduous shrubs and small trees from the
Old World. Lilacs have long been popular for
their fragrant late-spring blossoms, which
appear in conical clusters. The tubular
blooms are white, pink, lavender, or purple-
blue. The leaves are often heart shaped.

How to Grow
Lilacs like full sun and must have good air
circulation to avoid powdery mildew disease.
They grow best in well-drained, neutral to
alkaline soil but will also grow in slightly
acid soil. Most lilacs prefer moist soil; the
species listed below tolerate dry soil; Meyer
Lilac is the more drought tolerant of the two.
Fertilize lilacs every 2 years. Remove old
blossoms as soon as they fade. Prune at any
time during late winter or very early spring
by removing all weak wood that does not
bear large flower buds or that still carries the
previous year's fruit. Propagate from
softwood cuttings.

Uses
Lilacs are handsome plants for shrub borders,
hedges, or specimens. Situate them where
their fragrance can be enjoyed.

meyeri p. 160
Meyer Lilac. A handsome lilac with a dense
broad, mounded habit, this species grows 4–
8 feet high. The flowers are violet to purple
and appear in 4-inch clusters. This is one of
the most floriferous lilacs. 'Palibin' is a
compact form that is usually sold as *S. meyeri*.
Zones 4–8.

× *persica* p. 161
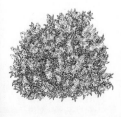
Persian Lilac. This species is a compact shrub
with slender arching branches that usually
grows 5–6 feet high, occasionally higher.
The 2½-inch-long leaves are lance shaped
and sometimes lobed or divided. The
fragrant flowers are pale lilac and bloom in
short, broad 3-inch clusters. Zones 4–8.

Tanacetum
Daisy family
Compositae

Tan-a-see'tum. Tansy. A genus of somewhat
weedy perennials or shrubs, all of the 50
known species from the north temperate
zone. The dark green leaves are large and
sometimes divided and fernlike. The yellow
flowers are small and buttonlike.

How to Grow
Plant tansy in full sun or partial shade in soil
that is well drained. Tansy can be invasive
but is less so if grown in dry, infertile soil.
Plants spread rapidly by underground
runners and can be divided in spring or fall;
plant divisions 18–24 inches apart. Tansy
also grows from seeds.

Uses
Tansy is a popular plant in herb gardens. It
was once used in cooking, but its safety is
questionable and ingesting it is no longer
recommended. Instead, use it in dried
arrangements, potpourris, and to repel
insects. Tansy is attractive in mixed borders,
more for its foliage than its late-blooming
flowers.

vulgare p. 126
Common Tansy. This dramatic plant has
heavily dissected leaves and grows 2–3 feet
tall. The ⅓-inch flowers bloom in small
clusters in late summer to early fall. The
variety *crispum* has more finely divided leaves.
Zones 4–10.

Taxus
Yew family
Taxaceae

Tacks'us. Yew. A small genus of handsome,
slow-growing coniferous evergreen shrubs
and trees. Depending on the species, plants
are upright, mounded, or spreading in habit.
The arrangement of the needles on the
branches also varies with the species. Some
needles spiral around the branches, some lie
in a flat plane, and others form a V. All have
short dark green needles that are lighter
green on the bottom. The bark is reddish
brown and flaky. Female plants produce red
berries; the seed inside the berry, not the
pulp, is toxic, as are the leaves and the bark.

How to Grow

Yews grow well in full sun or partial shade. They grow best in fertile, slightly acid to neutral soil with excellent drainage. Yews will develop root rot in poorly drained soil and will not survive in very wet soil. In cool climates they tolerate dry soil, but in hot climates the soil must be kept moist during the summer. Plant yews in an area shielded from winter wind and sun. Prune or shear them at any time to shape the plants and keep them compact. Be careful not to injure the bark with the lawn mower. Propagate yews from seeds or cuttings or by grafting.

Uses

Yews have a variety of roles in the garden, depending on the species. They will serve as hedges, as ground covers, and in foundation or massed plantings. They can be clipped into definite shapes for use in formal gardens.

baccata pp. *192, 193*

English Yew. This yew has shiny, slightly curved needles that have 2 pale green stripes on the bottom. Needles are usually arranged in a flat plane. Most cultivated English Yews are upright-growing plants reaching 2–12 feet high; an exception is the variety 'Repandens', Spreading English Yew, which grows 2 feet high, spreads to 6 feet across, and has a flat top. Zones 6–8.

cuspidata pp. *192, 193*

Japanese Yew. The needles of this species are soft and dull green with 2 yellowish-white stripes on the undersides. They are usually arranged in a V shape. Most Japanese Yews are spreading plants growing 1–12 feet tall; the variety 'Capitata', Cap Yew, is an exception; it grows in a broad pyramid 15–20 feet tall. Zones 5–8.

Tecomaria
Trumpet-vine family
Bignoniaceae

Teck-o-mair′i-a. A small genus of African woody vines or scrambling shrubs. The leaves are often whorled around the branches and are divided feather-fashion. The yellow, orange, or red flowers are funnel shaped, with a curved tube, and bloom in clusters at the ends of the branches.

How to Grow
Cape Honeysuckle, the species described
below, tolerates drought, wind, heat, and
salt air. It will grow in full sun to partial
shade in any soil as long as it has good
drainage. Prune as needed in early spring.
Increase plants from cuttings or seeds.

Uses
Cape Honeysuckle is a good ground cover for
hot, dry slopes and can be trained on a trellis,
fence, or arbor, or into an espalier or a hedge.

capensis p. 83
Cape Honeysuckle. This handsome evergreen
grows to 20 feet high as a supported vine or
to 6 feet tall when pruned as a scrambling
shrub. The shiny leaves are divided into 7–9
toothed oval leaflets. The flowers are 2 inches
long and bloom in showy clusters most of the
year. Zones 9–10.

Teucrium
Mint family
Labiatae

Too'kri-um. Germander. A genus of
perennials or subshrubs comprising about
300 species, some grown for ornament or
fragrance. Their leaves decrease in size near
the top of the plants. The tubular flowers
bloom in loose showy spikes.

How to Grow
Germander is easy to grow in full sun or
partial shade in average, well-drained soil.
Water it deeply but infrequently. It tolerates
poor soil but not drying winds. Plants can be
clipped into formal hedges at any time of
year. Those left to grow naturally can be
pruned in early spring. Propagate by
division, from cuttings, or from seeds. Space
plants 2 feet apart.

Uses
Wall Germander is a neat edging plant, low
hedge, or ground cover, and is commonly
used in herb knot gardens.

chamaedrys p. 122
Wall Germander. This evergreen perennial
grows 10–24 inches high and spreads to
2 feet across by underground stems. The
small, shiny dark green leaves are toothed
and covered with white or silver hairs. The

¾-inch flowers are pink or purplish red and bloom in summer. Plants clipped into formal hedges will not bloom. Wall Germander needs winter protection in northern areas. Zones 5–10.

Thermopsis
Pea family
Leguminosae

Ther-mop'sis. About 20 species of perennials from North America and Asia grown for their showy flowers. The leaves are compound; the flowers are yellow and pealike and bloom in erect spikes.

How to Grow
Carolina Lupine, the species listed below, is quite drought resistant. It grows well in most soils, even poor or infertile ones, but does best in light, well-drained soil. Plant it in full sun, spacing plants 2–3 feet apart. It is hard to transplant because it has deep roots. New plants grow easily from cuttings and seeds. Cut flowering stems back as soon as the blooms fade.

Uses
Carolina Lupine is best used at the back of a border, as an accent plant, or for cut flowers.

caroliniana *p. 72*
Carolina Lupine; Carolina Thermopsis. These plants resemble the lupines *(Lupinus)* and are a good substitute in areas where those stout, showy garden plants, which require moist, cool soil, will not grow. Carolina Lupine's flowering stems grow 3–5 feet high and are covered with blue-green leaves divided into 2- to 3-inch leaflets. The yellow flowers bloom in dense 8- to 10-inch spikes at the tops of the stems. Also sold as *T. villosa.* Zones 3–9.

Thymus
Mint family
Labiatae

Ty'mus. Thyme. A genus of pleasantly aromatic woody perennials or small shrubs comprising about 100 species primarily from the Mediterranean region. Several are widely grown for their ornamental value and one is grown for its fragrant leaves, which are used for seasoning. Plants are low-growing and often prostrate. The leaves are small and diminish in size to leaflike bracts near the flower cluster. The flowers, which may be pink, lilac, or purple, are fragrant and bloom in showy clusters in summer. They are very attractive to bees.

How to Grow
Thyme prefers a sunny location in well-drained soil that is not too rich. It likes dry soil and tolerates heat. Cut plants back in early spring or after they flower to keep them compact. Thyme is easy to grow from cuttings, by division, or from seeds.

Uses
While all thymes are fragrant, Common Thyme *(T. vulgaris)* is the species most ofen grown in the herb garden for culinary use. The others are at home in rock gardens, as edgings, as ground covers, or between stepping stones.

pseudolanuginosus p. 121
Woolly Thyme. This creeping perennial or subshrub forms a mat 1 inch high and 18 inches wide, rooting as it grows along the ground. The soft tiny leaves and the stems are covered with dense gray hairs. The flowers are pink but sparse. Zones 4–10.

serpyllum p. 124
Creeping Thyme; Mother-of-Thyme. This perennial forms a mat up to 4 inches high and 18 inches wide. The tiny dark green leaves are leathery and needle shaped. Purple flowers appear in rounded clusters on 4-inch stems. There are varieties with pink, rose, o white flowers. Many experts believe that thi is the same plant as *T. praecox arcticus,* whic is also called Mother-of-Thyme. Zones 4–10

Tradescantia
Spiderwort family
Commelinaceae

Tray-des-kan'ti-a. Spiderwort. About 20 species from North and South America of weak-stemmed and juicy perennials with prominent joints. Leaves are either long and narrow or oval and stalkless. The three-petaled flowers are white, blue, purple, or pink, and last only one day.

How to Grow
Spiderworts tolerate a wide variety of growing conditions. They will perform well in full sun or partial shade. They thrive in rich, moist soil with good drainage but, depending on the species, are almost as satisfactory in poor, dry soil or soil that is not well drained. In poor, dry soil they are not as aggressive and their bloom is diminished somewhat. Grow spiderworts from seeds, from stem cuttings separated at a joint, or by dividing established plants in spring. Space plants 12 inches apart.

Uses
Plant spiderworts in a natural border, a wildflower garden, or under trees and shrubs.

hirsuticaulis p. 96
Spiderwort. This is the most drought resistant of the spiderworts. Plants grow in clumps 12 inches high and wide and have narrow strap-shaped leaves covered with stiff hairs. The 1-inch flowers are bluish purple and bloom in small clusters at the tops of the stems in late spring or early summer. After the flowers fade, the foliage dies down but it reappears in fall and lasts through the winter. Zones 6–9.

Ulmus
Elm family
Ulmaceae

Ul′mus. Elm. A genus of 18 mostly deciduous trees, all from the north temperate zone of North America, Europe, and Asia. They are broadly upright, often vase shaped, and high branching, creating a canopy of dappled shade. The species described below is resistant to Dutch elm disease, which has destroyed the American Elm, *U. americana*. Elms are tall trees with double-toothed leaves. The flowers are inconspicuous and are followed by a compressed nut that is surrounded by a flat, often hairy wing. The bark is furrowed and gray.

How to Grow
Elms will grow in various soils except extremely wet or extremely dry. Siberian Elm is the most drought-resistant species but it needs occasional watering. It needs full sun to light shade and tolerates poor soil and heat. Prune young trees to minimize narrow

crotches that are prone to split in later years.
Propagate from seeds, by layering, or from
cuttings.

Uses
Elms are excellent shade trees and street
trees. Because of its hardiness, its strong root
system, and its drought resistance, Siberian
Elm is useful in the Great Plains and can be
used as a windbreak and to control soil
erosion.

pumila pp. 214, 215
Siberian Elm. A medium to large tree, this
elm may reach 75 feet in height. It has rough
bark and forked branches. The leaves are
smooth and grow 1–3 inches long. The flat
circular nut is ½ inch across but is not
ornamental; it appears in early summer. The
cultivar 'Coolshade' is a slower-growing tree
that is more resistant to breakage in ice
storms than the species. Zones 3–9;
semihardy in zone 2.

Vaccinium
Heath family
Ericaceae

Vak-sin′i-um. More than 150 species of erect
or ground-hugging shrubs whose native
habitats range from the Arctic Circle to the
summits of tropical mountains. Some are
grown for ornament, others, such as the
blueberry and the cranberry, for their fruit.
Small urn-shaped flowers bloom in spring in
clusters at the ends of the branches; they
often are not showy. The edible berries form
by early summer and ripen over the season.

How to Grow
Some species in this genus prefer wet or even
boggy soil, but Low-Bush Blueberry,
described below, likes dry soil and tolerates
heat. It will grow in light shade but produce
better flowers and berries in full sun. The soil
should be sandy or rocky, rich, acid, and well
drained. Increase from cuttings or by
division. Shear plants at any time to keep
them low and dense.

Uses
Plant Low-Bush Blueberry in a rock garden
or at the front of a shrub border or use it as an
edging.

angustifolium p. 127

Low-Bush Blueberry. A twiggy deciduous shrub, this plant grows 1–2 feet high and has small, narrow elliptic leaves that turn bright red in fall. The flowers are white, often with reddish lines. They are followed by ½-inch blue-black berries that are covered with a whitish powder. They ripen in July. Zones 3–9.

Viburnum
Honeysuckle family
Caprifoliaceae

Vy-bur'num. A large and valuable genus of shrubs and small trees, many of the 225 known species cultivated for their attractive, usually highly fragrant spring flowers and their often showy berries. They are chiefly deciduous shrubs of the north temperate zone. The small bell-shaped flowers usually are white and bloom in showy terminal clusters. The berries are brightly colored and are a favorite food of birds.

How to Grow

Viburnums are popular because they are easy to grow in full sun or partial shade. Most prefer moist, well-drained, slightly acid soil, but the species described below is drought resistant. Prune plants after they flower if necessary. Propagate from seeds or cuttings or by layering. To ensure heavy berry production, plant at least 2 plants of the same species.

Uses

Plant viburnums in an informal hedge, a screen, or in the shrub border. They will attract birds to the garden.

lantana pp. 172, 185

Wayfaring-tree Viburnum. A treelike deciduous shrub, this viburnum grows 10–15 feet high. The broadly ovalish gray-green leaves are 3–5 inches long, hairy on both sides, and coarsely toothed. They sometimes, but not always, turn red in the fall. The flat flower clusters are nearly 4 inches wide and appear in late spring. The oblong berries are red, later turning black. The variety 'Mohican' grows to only 6 feet high, and its fruit stays orange-red. Zones 4–8.

Xylosma
Indian plum family
Flacourtiaceae

Zy-los'ma. A genus of more than 100 species
of shrubs and trees, all tropical, some grown
for their shiny yellow-green foliage. The
flowers are small and inconspicuous, without
petals.

How to Grow
Xylosma is easy to grow in full sun or partial
shade in most soils. It looks best with
occasional watering but tolerates heat and
drought. It responds well to pruning and can
be trained into an espalier. Xylosma is
somewhat difficult to propagate but can
usually be found in containers at nurseries.

Uses
Xylosma is effective in hedges, as a ground
cover, as an accent plant, and as an espalier.

congestum p. 180
Xylosma. This species is a shrub that grows
8–10 feet high and wide. Unpruned, the
main stem of these plants zig-zags as it
grows, and the side branches arch or droop.
Plants have hairy brown twigs and sharp
slender spines in the leaf axils. The 3½-inch
evergreen leaves are ovalish, pointed, and
bluntly toothed on the margins. They are
bronzy in color when young. Xylosma
survives light frost although it may lose its
leaves. Zones 9–10.

Yucca
Agave family
Agavaceae

Yuck'a. About 40 species of evergreen
perennials and shrubs, chiefly of Mexican
desert origin, grown in the garden for their
striking flower clusters. Most are stemless
plants with a large basal rosette of tough,
leathery sword-shaped leaves that grow 2–3
feet long. The white or off-white flowers are
waxy, bell shaped, and often slightly fragrant
at night. They bloom in showy erect clusters

How to Grow
All yuccas do best in full sun, although they
will tolerate light shade. Soil should be sandy
and fast draining. They are desert plants and
withstand considerable drought. The roots

are strong and deep and make yuccas difficult to transplant. Propagate from seeds or by removing the suckers that grow at the base of the plant. Set them in groups, spacing plants 2–3 feet apart. Not all plants will bloom every year, so planting them in groups is recommended.

Uses
Plant yucca in the garden where an accent or bold, dramatic touch is needed. It will help control soil erosion.

filamentosa p. 139
Adam's Needle. This is the most common yucca in Eastern gardens. The green or variegated leaves are thready along their margins. The flower stalk can reach a height of 15 feet but usually grows 3–5 feet high. Flowers are creamy white and 2 inches long. Zones 5–10.

glauca p. 138
Soapweed. The leaves of this species are gray-green to blue-green and are narrower than those of Adam's Needle (only ½ inch wide). They are edged in white or pale gray and are thready along the margins. Greenish-white 2-inch-long flowers bloom on 3-foot stems. Zones 5–10.

Appendices

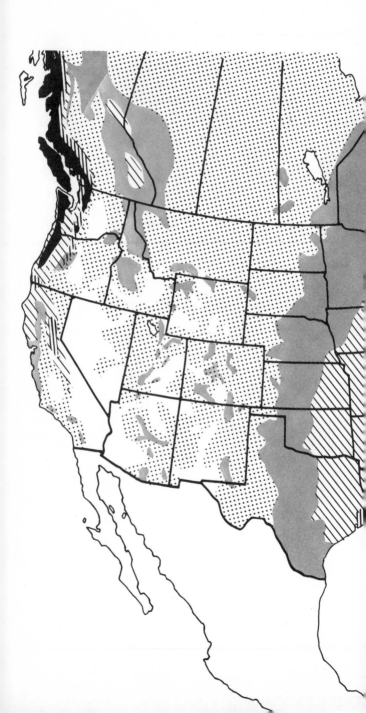

The map below indicates average amounts of annual precipitation in the United States and southern Canada. To save water in the garden, discover the water needs of the plants you are considering and determine whether they will be met by rainfall in your area. The captions in the color plates give a description of relative drought tolerance for each plant. Consult the key on page 49 to see how those translate into measured amounts of water needed.

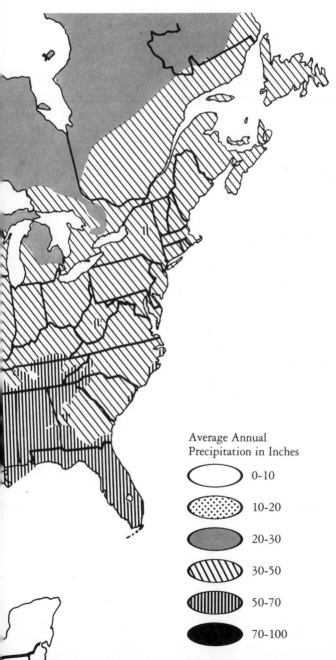

Average Annual
Precipitation in Inches

0-10

10-20

20-30

30-50

50-70

70-100

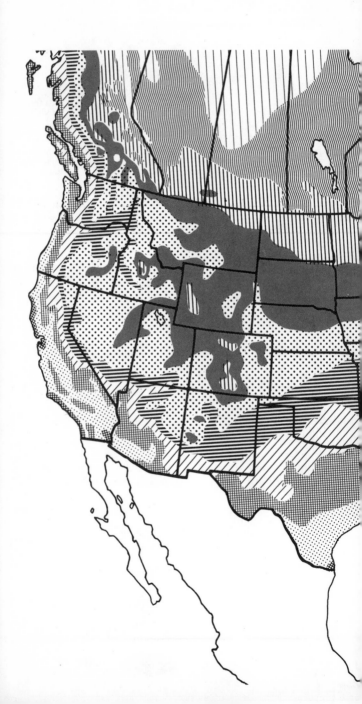

This map was compiled
by the United States
Department of
Agriculture as a
broad guideline to
temperature extremes
in your area.

The key below gives
you the average
minimum temperatures
of the ten zones.
Determine if your
area corresponds to
its zone allocation
by comparing your

coldest temperatures
with those given in
the key.

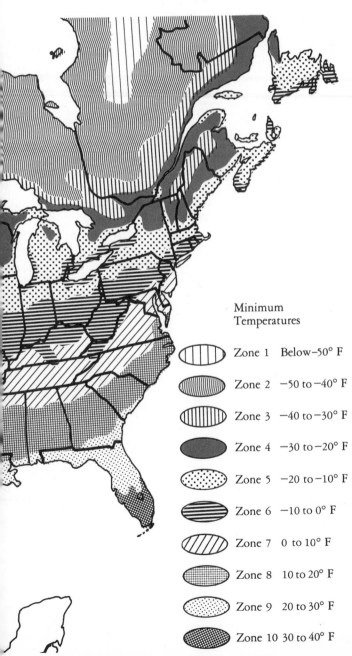

Minimum
Temperatures

Zone 1   Below−50° F

Zone 2   −50 to −40° F

Zone 3   −40 to −30° F

Zone 4   −30 to −20° F

Zone 5   −20 to −10° F

Zone 6   −10 to 0° F

Zone 7   0 to 10° F

Zone 8   10 to 20° F

Zone 9   20 to 30° F

Zone 10   30 to 40° F

Frost-Date Map

This map is based on freeze data tabulations made by the United States Weather Bureau.

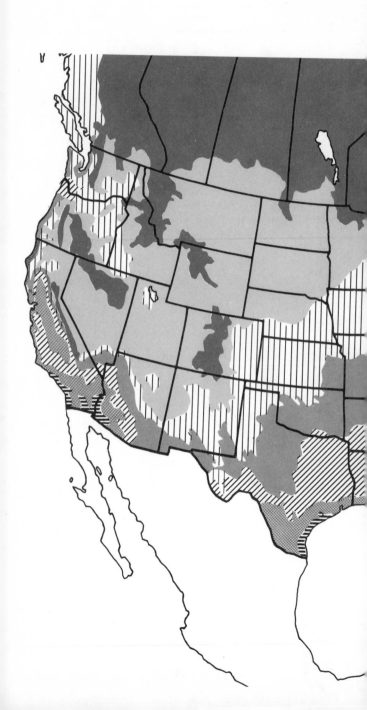

*he key below shows
e average dates of the
st spring frost and
e average length of
e growing season in
ven frost zones. The
owing season is the* *period between the
spring and fall frosts,
often referred to as the
frost-free days.*

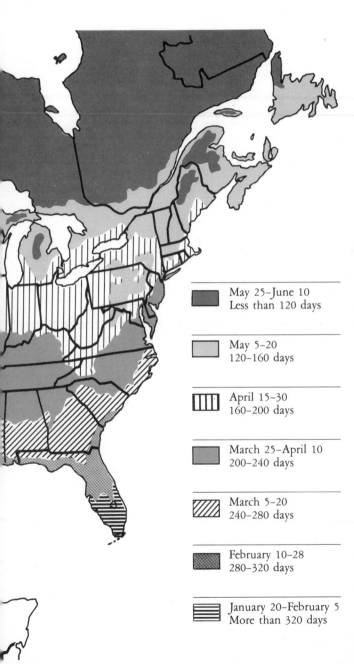

May 25–June 10
Less than 120 days

May 5–20
120–160 days

April 15–30
160–200 days

March 25–April 10
200–240 days

March 5–20
240–280 days

February 10–28
280–320 days

January 20–February 5
More than 320 days

Gardening Tips

Most of the information in this guide is provided on the assumption
that the reader has had some experience in planting a garden.
However, there is no reason why a beginner shouldn't plant a first
garden that is water efficient. If you have never picked up a spade, it i
a good idea to consult a basic guide in conjunction with this one; an
of the Taylor's Guides listed on the back cover will help you get
started.

The following pages provide a brief overview of some basic gardenin
terms and tasks. Reading through them will let you know what is
involved in planting various types of plants and should help pinpoin
areas in which you may need more help.

Plant Hardiness

The key to success in gardening is to choose the right plants for you
environment. Some plants are so tolerant that they can survive almos
anywhere; others can live only within certain temperature or humidit
ranges.

Plant hardiness is based on three factors: temperature, availability of
water, and soil conditions. Of these, temperature is the most
important. The U.S. Department of Agriculture has devised a map
that divides North America into ten zones based on minimum winte
temperatures. (See pages 410–411.) Zone 1 is the coldest, with winte
lows of −50°F; zone 10 is the warmest, with winter minimums of 30
to 40°F, and is often frost free. Knowing the zone in which you live i
particularly useful when you buy a plant you have never grown before
If the description in this book says "Zones 4–7," it means that the
plant will survive in zones 4, 5, 6, and 7 but will not generally surviv
winters colder than those north of zone 4 or summers warmer than
those south of zone 7.

Within each zone, conditions can fluctuate because of variations in
temperature, rainfall, or soil type. The resulting microclimates can
occur within states, cities, or even on a small plot of land. For
example, temperatures may be colder on the north side of your house
than they are elsewhere. Similarly, colder-than-normal temperatures
often occur at the bottoms of hills or on ground that is exposed to
wind. Areas that receive plenty of sun are usually warmer than those
that do not, as are areas that are protected from the wind and those
that receive reflected heat in the winter.

Successful gardening is based, in part, on understanding how these
variations affect your garden. By learning to recognize the
microclimates on your land, you will be able to grow a wider variety o
plants than if you based all your plant choices on zone. It is also usefu
to understand microclimates in order to create favorable ones in your
garden. For example, one of the "tricks" of water-saving gardening i
to provide a windbreak, which will protect a particular planting from
moving air that can rob it of needed moisture.

for Beginners

Annuals

The plants in the section of color plates called Flowers are of two types—annuals and perennials. An annual plant grows, flowers, sets seed, and dies in the same year, while a perennial blooms for more than one year. A perennial's flowers die back to the ground in winter, but its roots remain alive and the plant is renewed in the spring.

Depending on their tolerance of heat or cold, flowering annuals fall into one of three classes: tender annuals, half-hardy annuals, and hardy annuals. Tender annuals are subject to damage from frost; they are planted in warm soil in spring after all danger of frost has passed. In warm regions, a second planting can be made in midsummer for a fall display of color. Half-hardy annuals are those that will tolerate cool weather but will not withstand heavy frost. They can be planted in spring several weeks before the anticipated date of the last frost. Hardy annuals are not killed by frost. They can be planted in spring as soon as the soil can be worked. In mild climates, they can be planted in fall for early bloom the next year.

The term "annual" is also loosely applied to certain tender perennials that cannot survive the winter outside of very mild climates. These flowers can be grown in cooler areas during the summer as if they were annuals. Thus, you will sometimes see in a plant's description a term such as "Tender perennial grown as a tender annual."

The planting dates for tender and half-hardy perennials grown as annuals depend on the individual plant. Some can be planted in early spring or mid-spring; others grow better in warm soil and should be planted after danger of frost has passed. The individual plant accounts in the encyclopedia section tell you to which class the annuals belong; the How to Grow section gives the proper planting time.

Before you make a planting schedule for annual flowers, refer to the frost-date map on pages 412-413. The map divides the country into seven areas, based on the average date of the last spring frost and the number of days in the growing season. These dates are, of course, approximations; they can change slightly with your microclimate or fluctuate from year to year with differences in weather.

Do not plant tender annuals before the date given on the map; if you have had a particularly cold spring, wait a little longer beyond the date. An unexpected late frost could kill tender plants. Half-hardy annuals can generally be planted two to four weeks before the last frost date. Hardy annuals can be planted one to two months before the last frost date. In mild climates, if you are making a planting for fall color, count backwards three months or more from the date of the first fall frost to determine the planting date.

Starting Annuals Outdoors from Seed

It is easier, especially for beginning gardeners, to buy annuals that have been started in pots, but many people like to start their own plants from seed. Some annuals cannot be seeded directly into the garden because the seeds are too fine or the growing season is too short;

Gardening Tips for Beginners

many others, however, grow quickly if planted from seed outdoors. Before you sow seeds outdoors, prepare the soil in the way described in the essay called Water-Saving Fundamentals, then rake it level and moisten it lightly. Follow the directions in the plant accounts or on seed packets regarding spacing and planting depth; a general rule of thumb is to sow seeds twice as heavily as the suggested final spacing of the plants, and no deeper than the thickness of the seed.

You can sow seeds in rows or scatter them, depending on your garden design; bear in mind, however, that randomly sown seedlings are often hard to distinguish from weeds. Keep the soil bed evenly moist at all times until the seeds have germinated. Once they sprout, water then daily until the seedlings have four to six leaves and then gradually decrease watering until you can water about once a week.

When the plants are several inches high, thin them to the final spacing given on the seed packet or in the plant accounts in this book. Make sure the soil is moist before thinning and take care not to disturb the roots of the plants that remain.

Starting Annuals Indoors from Seed

Annuals that need a head start on the growing season, and those whose seeds are very small, should be started indoors. The first thing you need is some type of container—which you can purchase or make yourself from milk cartons or aluminum trays. Be sure the container is between 2½ and 4 inches deep, that it has drainage holes, and that it is clean. Before using plastic or metal containers, wash them in a solution of 10 percent chlorine bleach to make sure they are sterile, and rinse them thoroughly.

Next, you'll need a germinating medium. You can purchase a mixture at your garden center or make your own, using 50 percent fine peat moss and 50 percent fine perlite or vermiculite. Never use garden soil; it is too heavy and contains insects, diseases, and weed seeds.

Fill the container with moistened medium to within 1 inch of the top and sow the seeds in rows. Do not cover small seeds during germination; simply press them into the surface of the medium. Bury larger seeds to a depth about equal their width. Cover the container with a plastic bag until the seeds germinate; they should not need watering during this period.

When your seeds have sprouted, water as soon as the medium starts to dry out. Watering from the bottom is the recommended method, because it will not dislodge small seedings. When the seedlings have developed two sets of true leaves, thin them so they are about 1 inch apart. Start feeding them weekly with one-quarter-strength soluble fertilizer, following the directions on the package.

If you transplant your seedlings into individual cells or pots when they are about 1 inch high, you will make transplanting into the garden easier later on. To avoid burning the tender roots, do not fertilize for two weeks after transplanting.

Grow seedlings on a sunny windowsill or under fluorescent lights; if you grow them under lights, keep the lights 6 inches above the tops of the seedlings and leave them on for 12 to 14 hours a day once the seeds have germinated. Experienced gardeners have found that fluorescent lights give better results than windowsill gardening.

About a week before moving plants into the garden, it is time to start a process called "hardening off," which gradually accustoms seedlings to their new environment. On the first day, move the plants outside into a shaded position out of the wind and bring them back inside at night. Repeat this procedure for several days, and then move the seedlings to a spot where the light they receive will be equivalent to the sunlight in their final home. Leave them outdoors unless a cold night threatens. Plants can also be hardened off in a cold frame, which is a box with a glass or plastic "skylight" on top.

Plant annual seedlings in the garden in the same way you would perennial seedlings; that procedure is described below.

Perennials

Perennials are rewarding flowers to plant because they bloom year after year, repaying you richly for the time and effort you've invested. Perennials make low-maintenance flower gardens a reality, yet they offer unlimited opportunities for the gardener who wants to spend time at a hobby.

Technically, trees and shrubs are perennials, but most people use the term to denote the herbaceous perennials, whose flowers die back to the ground in winter. The hardiness of perennials is expressed in terms of the zones described above; you'll find a range of appropriate zones listed for each perennials (and shrub and tree) in the Encyclopedia.

Ground Covers

An important part of any garden, ground covers are a diverse group of low-growing plants; they may be shrubs, vines, perennials, or annuals. When chosen carefully and used creatively, these practical plants can add considerable interest to your surroundings.

No single ground cover can fill every need, but many choices exist. Some ground covers are evergreen; others are deciduous, losing their leaves in winter. Ground covers with tenacious roots can help prevent erosion of steep banks; others can be used on slopes where mowing grass would be difficult. Many ground covers thrive in poor soil or areas that bake in the sun—places where a lawn would not grow well. Most important in terms of saving water in the landscape, ground covers are a practical and attractive alternative to large expanses of lawn that require large amounts of water to maintain.

Planting Perennial Flowers and Ground Covers

Most gardeners buy perennials either from local garden centers and specialty nurseries or by mail order. Price alone is not a reliable criterion for choosing one plant source over another, since cost is not always an indication of plant size or quality. If possible, try to get recommendations from another gardener.

Gardening Tips for Beginners

Because perennials live for many years in the same spot, it is worth the effort to prepare the soil well before you plant them. Doing so allows plants to establish good root systems. Most perennials prefer soils that are loamy, well drained, high in organic matter, and slightly acid to neutral in pH level. A soil's pH level measures its degree of acidity or alkalinity, factors that influence the uptake of secondary and micronutrients. The pH scale ranges from 1 to 14, with 7 representing a neutral level. The lower numbers indicate acidity, the higher ones alkalinity. Adding lime to the soil will make it more alkaline, and sulfur or peat moss will make it more acid. To determine the pH level of your soil, buy a soil test kit or send a sample to a local soil-testing lab.

One of the goals of water-saving gardening is to use as little fertilizer as possible, because it takes extra water to make fertilizers work and because selecting plants to match conditions in your garden should make adding fertilizers virtually unnecessary. Since it is helpful, however, to give newly installed plants a boost, there are several things you should know about fertilizers.

A complete fertilizer contains nitrogen, phosphorous, and potassium. The percentage of each of these elements in the mixture is described by three numbers on the package, such as 5–10–5, 10–10–10, or 10–6–4. Most perennials grown for their flowers do best with a fertilizer that is relatively low in nitrogen, because too much nitrogen encourages the growth of foliage at the cost of flowers. (See also the recommendations in the essay on water-saving fundamentals.)

Fertilizer can be applied in a granular form when the bed is prepared, as a liquid after planting, or in time-release pellets.

To prepare a new planting bed, first turn the soil over to a depth of one spade (about 18 to 20 inches). Next, spread a layer of compost, peat moss, or other organic material over the soil surface. The amount of granular fertilizer you should add depends upon soil test results, and if your soil is very acid you may want to add lime. Incorporate the organic material, fertilizer, and lime into the soil by turning them in with a spade or by Rototilling. Finally, rake the ground smooth.

To reduce transplanting shock, it is best to put your plants in the ground on a cloudy day or late in the afternoon, if possible. Carefully remove the plants from their cell packs or pots, keeping the root ball intact to avoid damage. Examine the roots; if they are very compact, loosen them slightly before planting.

Dig a hole slightly larger than the root ball, set the plant in the ground at the same level at which it was growing in the pot, and carefully firm the soil around the roots. Space the plants according to the instructions in the plant accounts. Water after planting and daily until new growth appears.

Shrubs and Trees

Both shrubs and trees are woody (as opposed to herbaceous) perennial plants. There is no strict distinction between a tree and a shrub, but plants are usually called shrubs if they are smaller than most trees and have several trunks or stems. Many shrubs, however, grow with only one trunk. Most shrubs survive winters without dying back. Some die to the ground over winter and produce new stems in spring. Shrubs and trees may be deciduous, evergreen, or semievergreen.

Shrubs and trees add distinctive silhouettes to a landscape, whether they are planted in groups or stand alone in the lawn. Because most shrubs and trees are long-lived and relatively expensive, it pays to do some careful research before choosing one.

Planting Shrubs and Trees

Mail-order nurseries and some local garden centers sell shrubs and trees in a form called bare-root, meaning that the plants are dormant and have no soil around their roots. These can be planted in early spring in any climate and in fall in fairly mild climates. If you plant in the fall, do it six to eight weeks before the ground freezes so the roots become established before severe cold sets in. Never let the roots of a bare-root shrub or tree dry out.

Shrubs and trees sold in containers or balled and burlapped (with the roots enclosed in soil and held together in a piece of burlap) can be planted from early spring until six to eight weeks before the ground freezes. Keep them in their containers or wraps until you are ready to plant them; in any case, it pays to plant shrubs and trees as soon as possible after you've brought them home.

Experts disagree about how and to what degree you should improve your soil before planting large shrubs and trees. Refer to the section called Soil Improvement on page 11 for more on the topic. Create a planting hole about three times wider than the spread of the plant's roots, whether they are bare or in a root ball, but no deeper. The plant's crown, or the juncture of roots and stem, should rest at or slightly above soil level—never deeper. Lightly loosen the soil on the sides of the hole before planting. If the plant is balled and burlapped, place it in the hole, cut any strings around the root ball, and loosen the burlap and pull it back slightly, but do not completely remove it. For a container plant, water the medium in the container and, no matter what it is made of, remove the container. This prevents roots from becoming compacted, which could eventually kill the plant. If the roots are tightly encircling the root ball, loosen them, or cut several slits into the root ball to encourage new growth. Lower the plant into the hole, fill the hole halfway with soil, and water it. Let the water drain, then fill the hole completely and water it again.

Taking Care of Plants

A well-planned water-saving garden needs relatively little care once it becomes established. Some tips on maintenance are given in the essays in the front of this book; you should refer to guides on growing particular plants for more detailed information. You'll find that gardening is a pleasurable challenge, one that rewards you constantly with beautiful results.

Plant Sources

The list below includes just a sampling of the many suppliers of drought-resistant plants, as well as the names of several directories in which you'll find other sources. Many suppliers carry only native plants, while others also offer adapted species. If a particular supplier cannot help you, ask him or her to refer you to a more appropriate source who has knowledge of water-saving gardening in your local area.

Nurseries

Bernardo Beach
Native Plant Farm
1 Sanchez Road
Veguita, NM 87062
Retail Outlet: 520 Montano NW
Albuquerque, NM
(505) 345-6248

Botanicals, Inc.
P.O. Box 436
Wayland, MA 01778
(508) 358-4846

Green Horizons
218 Quinlan, Suite 571
Kerrville, TX 78028
(512) 257-5141

Massachusetts Horticultural
Society
Horticulture Hall
300 Massachusetts Avenue
Boston, MA 02115
(617) 536-9280

Old Farm Nursery
5550 Indiana Street
Golden, CO 80401
(303) 278-0754

Plants of the Southwest
1812 Second Street
Santa Fe, NM 87501
(505) 983-1548

Schichtel Nursery, Inc.
c/o 4555 Eldridge Street
Golden, CO 80403
(303) 279-5060

Stock Seed Farms, Inc.
R.R. 1, Box 112
Murdock, NE 68407
(402) 867-3771

Tree of Life Nursery
P.O. Box 736
San Juan Capistrano, CA 92693
(714) 728-0685

Directories

Nursery Sources of Native Plants and Wildflowers ($3.50 ppd.)
New England Wildflower Society
Garden in the Woods
Hemenway Road
Framingham, MA 01701

Source of Native Plants ($3.50 ppd.)
Soil Conservation Society of America
7515 Ankenny Road NE
Ankeny, IA 50021

Texas Native Plant Directories
Texas Department of Agriculture
P.O. Box 12847
Austin, TX 78711

Irrigation

The first step in designing a water-saving garden is to select plants that will require little more water than your region receives as precipitation. But since it is virtually impossible to create a garden that will never need extra water, the next step is to decide how to irrigate the plants in the most efficient way possible.

There are two ways to irrigate your landscape—through portable, hose-end systems and through fixed, in-ground systems. Some of the best examples of both types are described in the chart that follows; advantages and disadvantages are listed to help you decide which may be best for your garden.

Portable, Hose-End Systems

There are a variety of ways to water your plants by simply attaching a device to your outdoor spigot. The chief advantage of these hose-end systems is that they cost less than more complicated built-in irrigation lines. A major disadvantage is that they require more attention from the user, who must set them up and remember to turn them on and off. Nonetheless, hose-end methods are useful in many situations; in a water-saving garden, they are especially valuable in getting plants off to a good start and giving them an occasional boost during dry spells. The four systems detailed in the chart serve a range of needs; there are many others from which to choose.

Fixed, In-Ground Systems

Permanent, built-in irrigation systems are usually made of plastic pipe connected to the main water supply and buried a few inches below the soil's surface. They may be controlled manually, by turning on valves, or electronically, through master switches connected to the supply lines. There are also sophisticated, computer-controlled systems equipped to shut off when it rains or when soil moisture is adequate. In-ground systems cost more than hose-end methods, but in many situations they pay for themselves over time through savings of water and maintenance time. They also offer convenience to the user.

Various styles of spray heads are available to meet the needs of different areas and types of vegetation. Four of the most popular are described in the chart; check with an irrigation-system supplier to determine the best choices for areas of your landscape.

Portable, Hose-End Systems	Description
Hand-held spray nozzle 	Screw on to ordinary garden hose and squeeze trigger to spray. A variety of types are available, some of which provide high-pressure water streams or have spring-loaded shut-off handles.
Perforated hose 	A garden hose with small holes that emit water in a trickle or a fine spray, depending on the water pressure. (A similar system, the soaker hose, is made of porous material through which water seeps.)
Oscillating sprinkler 	Device with sprinkler bar that tips back and forth, delivering fine spray across a large area.
Fan sprinkler 	A simple spray device that sends a fine half-circle of water in one direction.

Advantages	Disadvantages
Offers good control over amount and direction of water flow. Especially helpful in giving newly planted trees and shrubs a good soaking. Can save water because operation requires the user's close attention.	Does not work unattended. User may apply water with too much or too little force, thus injuring or over- or under-watering plants.
Excellent to soak newly seeded areas. Flexible enough to serve areas of different shapes and sizes. Slow discharge rate reduces runoff waste. Inexpensive and can be left unattended for a period of time. Works in a way similar to drip irrigation (see next page).	Wears out quickly. Fine spray evaporates easily or is blown by wind. Irrigation pattern can be uneven.
Covers large square or rectangular area. Useful for watering trees, shrubs, turf, or ground covers. Allows for slow penetration of water into soil.	Throws water high into the air, where it can be lost through evaporation or carried away by winds. Less expensive models may be unreliable and give uneven spray patterns.
Soft spray makes it especially useful for watering delicate flowers and ground covers. Single direction allows for fairly accurate aim. Device has a long life.	If used with high water pressure, misting and evaporation occurs. High-volume output can cause runoff.

Fixed, In-Ground Systems	Description
Pop-up spray head 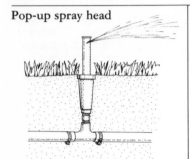	A high-volume system in which water pressure forces a riser out of its buried housing. Then water is distributed through a spray head on the riser. Discharges 1–3 gallons per minute.
Fixed-riser spray head 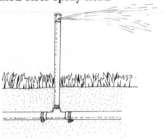	High-volume system similar to pop-up spray heads, with fixed heads that remain above ground
Low-volume spray 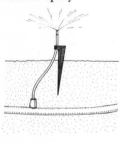	Narrow plastic tubing connecte to supply lines and topped wit a small spray cap rises above ground to distribute a fine spra 4–15 feet in radius. Discharge rates are $1/10$–$3/4$ gallon per minute.
Drip irrigation 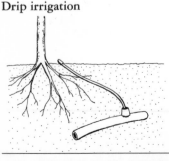	Narrow tubing runs from suppl line directly to base of plant an discharges water very slowly.

Advantages	Disadvantages
Excellent for areas of turf or ground cover because the risers (available in various heights) clear the tops of plants. Buried risers do not obstruct lawn mowers and are unobtrusive. Offer low trajectory so little water is lost through evaporation.	May discharge water faster than soil can absorb it. One head every 10 feet is required. (Similar devices called pop-up impact heads and gear-driven stream rotors require fewer heads.) Makes it fairly difficult to rearrange planting area once installed.
Less expensive than high-rise pop-up head but offers similar advantages. Requires lighter digging to install.	Risers are always in view, make mowing difficult, and can be tripped over. Other disadvantages similar to those of pop-up head, above.
Slow application rate is excellent for ground covers, shrubs, and trees and for small areas. Permits deep penetration of water. Various spray heads offer different coverage patterns; system may use pop-up or fixed risers. Easy to install and unobtrusive.	Pressure-reducing device is required. Narrow tubing may become clogged. Fixed risers are easily damaged.
Subject to little evaporation and minimal runoff; excellent for use on slopes and for establishing new plantings. Emitters can be buried under mulch to keep them out of sight. Very inexpensive and easily changed.	Requires use of pressure-reducer and strainer between supply line and emitter. Difficult to verify operation if tubes are out of sight.

Reading List

Water-saving gardening is still just catching on in some areas. As more and more communities begin to promote similar concepts, it will become easier to find information that is specific to your region. The following reading list will point you toward sources of good, general written information.

Borland, James N., Sylvia Brockner, and Jeanne R. Janish. *Native Plants of Genesee*. Golden, CO: Genesee Foundation, 1987.

Coates, Margaret. *Perennials for the Western Garden*. Boulder, CO: Pruett Press, 1976.

Creasy, Rosalind. *Complete Book of Edible Landscaping*. San Francisco: Sierra Club, 1982.

Damrosch, Barbara. *Theme Gardens*. New York: Workman Publishing, 1982.

Donselman, H., and T.K. Broschat. *Xeriscape Plant Guide*. West Palm Beach: South Florida Water Management District, 1987.

Foley, Daniel J. *Gardening by the Sea*. Philadelphia: Chilton Books, 1965.

Hillier, H.G. *Hillier's Colour Guide of Trees and Shrubs*. North Pomfret, VT: David and Charles, Inc., 1981.

Huddleston, Sam, and M. Hussey. *Grow Native: Landscaping with Native and Adapted Plants of the Rocky Mountains*. Boulder, CO: Pruett Press, 1988.

Jarmusch, Ann. "Natives to the Rescue." *Organic Gardening Magazine*, Vol. 35, No. 11 (1988), pp. 62–67.

Jones, Patricia Wellingham. "The Dry Garden Comes of Age." *Garden*, Vol. 10, No. 4 (1986), pp. 12–32.

Jones, Warren, D., and Mary Rose Duffield. *Plants for Dry Climates: How to Select, Grow & Enjoy*. Tucson, AZ: H.P. Books, 1981.

Kelly, George. *Rocky Mountain Horticulture*. Boulder, CO: Pruett Press, 1967.

Landscaping. Menlo Park, CA: Lane Publishing, 1984.

Landscaping for Privacy. Menlo Park, CA: Lane Publishing, 1985.

Landscaping for Water Conservation: Xeriscape! CO: City of Aurora Utilities Department and Denver Water Department, 1989.

Lemontre, Sue. "California Green'n." *Organic Gardening Magazine*, Vol. 35, No. 11 (1988), pp. 62–67.

Martin, Kent. "Dry Times." *Organic Gardening Magazine*, Vol. 35, No. 11 (1988), pp. 56–61.

Matlock, G., *Water Harvesting for Urban Landscapes*. AZ: Tucson Water Department, 1985.

Nelson, John O. "Water Conserving Landscapes Show Impressive Savings." *Journal: American Water Works Association*, March 1987, pp. 35–42.

Nierling, Arno. *Easy Gardening with Drought Resistant Plants*. New York: Hearthside Press, Inc., 1968.

Organic Gardening. Emmaus, PA: Rodale Press, 1988.

Phillips, Judith. *Southwestern Landscaping with Native Plants*. Santa Fe, NM: Museum of New Mexico Press, 1987.

Robinette, Gary O. *Landscaping Planning for Energy Conservation*. Reston, VA: Environmental Design Press, 1988.

---. *Water Conservation in Landscape Design and Management*. New York: Van Nostrand Reinhold Co., 1984.

Smith, Ken L. *Home Landscaping in the Northeast and Midwest*. Los Angeles: H.P. Books, 1985.

Smyser, Carol. *Nature's Design: A Practical Guide to Natural Landscaping*. Emmaus, PA: Rodale Publishing, 1982.

Sunset Western Garden Book, 4th ed. Menlo Park, CA: Lane Publishing, 1979.

Sweezey, Lauren. "It uses 63% less water than the average Denver garden." *Sunset*, July 1986, pp. 182b & c.

Taylor's Guide to Garden Design. Boston: Houghton Mifflin Company, 1988.

Drip Irrigation for the Home Garden and Landscape. Berkeley: University of California, 1976.

Waterwise Gardening. Menlo Park, CA: Lane Publishing Co., 1989.

Network List

For more information on programs about landscape water conservation in your area, contact your local cooperative extension program, or the following:

Arkansas

City of Fort Smith
3900 Kelley Highway
Fort Smith, AR 72904
(501) 785-2801

Arizona

City of Flagstaff
Community Development
Department
211 West Aspen Avenue
Flagstaff, AZ 86001
(602) 779-7650

City of Glendale
5850 West Glendale Avenue
Glendale, AZ 85301
(602) 435-4090

City of Mesa
P.O. Box 1466
Mesa, AZ 85201
(602) 644-2011

Arizona Municipal Water
Users Association
505 North Second Street
Suite 385
Phoenix, AZ 85004
(602) 256-0999

Water Conservation
and Resources
City of Phoenix
455 North Fifth Street
Phoenix, AZ 85004
(602) 256-3370

City of Scottsdale
Water Resources
3939 Civic Center Plaza
Scottsdale, AZ 85251
(602) 994-7093

Tucson Water
P.O. Box 27320
Tucson, AZ 85726
(602) 791-3242

California

Mojave Water Agency
P.O. Box 1089
Apple Valley, CA 92307
(619) 240-9201

City of Fresno
Water Conservation Program
1910 East University
Fresno, CA 93703
(209) 498-1016

Hesperia Water District
9393 Santa Fe Avenue
Hesperia, CA 92345
(619) 244-6154

Indian Wells Valley
Water District
P.O. Box 399
Ridgecrest, CA 93556
(619) 375-5086

California Department
of Water Resources
Office of Water Conservation
1416 Ninth Street, Room 804
Sacramento, CA 95814
(916) 323-0859

San Diego County
Water Authority
3211 Fifth Avenue
San Diego, CA 92103
(619) 297-3218

Tree of Life Nursery
P.O. Box 736
San Juan Capistrano, CA 92693
(714) 728-0685

City of Santa Monica
1685 Main Street
Santa Monica, CA 90401
(213) 458-8229

Sonoma County Water District
P.O. Box 11628
Santa Rosa, CA 95406
(415) 897-4133

City of Santee
10765 Woodside Avenue
Santee, CA 92071
(619) 258-0206

Colorado

City of Arvada Utilities Division
8101 Ralston Road
Arvada, CO 80002
(303) 431-3035

City of Aurora
Water Utilities Department
1470 South Havana, Suite 400
Aurora, CO 80012
(303) 695-7387

City of Boulder Utilities Division
P.O. Box 791
Boulder, CO 80306
(303) 441-3200

Town of Castle Rock
Parks Department
118 Fourth Street
Castle Rock, CO 80104
(303) 660-1052

American Water Works Association
6666 West Quincy Avenue
Denver, CO 80235
(303) 794-7711

City of Fort Collins
Water Utilities Department
P.O. Box 580
Fort Collins, CO 80522
(303) 221-6681

City of Lakewood
Parks Department
445 South Allison Parkway
Lakewood, CO 80226
(303) 987-7800

Florida

Southwest Florida Water
Management District
2379 Broad Street
Brooksville, FL 34609
(904) 796-7211

City of Cape Coral
Parks and Recreation Department
P.O. Box 150027
Cape Coral, FL 33915
(813) 945-1588

Coral Springs Parks
and Recreation
9551 West Sample Road
Coral Springs, FL 33065
(305) 344-1125

City of Fort Pierce Department
of Public Works
P.O. Box 1480
Fort Pierce, FL 34954
(407) 464-5600

Northwest Florida Water
Management District
Route 1, Box 3100
Havana, FL 32333
(904) 539-5999

Town of Highland Beach
3614 South Ocean Boulevard
Highland Beach, FL 33487
(407) 997-7234

City of Melbourne
Water Conservation
900 East Strawbridge Avenue
Melbourne, FL 32901
(407) 727-2900

South Brevard Water Authority
P.O. Box 360382
Melbourne, FL 32936
(407) 242-6524

General Development
Utilities, Inc.
111 South Bayshore Drive
Miami, FL 33131
(305) 859-4331

City of Tamarac
7525 NW 88th Avenue
Tamarac, FL 33321
(305) 722-5900

Board of County Commissioners
Brevard County
Titusville, FL 32780
(407) 269-8141

Palm Beach County
Planning, Zoning, and
Building Department
3400 Belvedere Road
West Palm Beach, FL 33406
(305) 471-3500

Georgia

Cobb County Marietta
Water Authority
1660 Barnes Mill Road
Marietta, GA 30062
(404) 426-8788

Hawaii

Board of Water Supply
630 South Bretania Street
Honolulu, HI 96843
(808) 527-6199

Kansas

Botanica/The Wichita Gardens
701 Amidon
Wichita, KS 67203
(316) 264-0448

Water Department
Water Pollution Control
455 North Main Street
Wichita, KS 67202
(316) 268-4504

Maryland

Department of Utilities
7409 Baltimore and Annapolis
Boulevard NW
Glen Burnie, MD 21061
(301) 760-7740

Massachusetts

Massachusetts Water
Resources Authority
Charlestown Navy Yard
100 First Avenue
Boston, MA 02129
(617) 242-0230

New Mexico

City of Albuquerque
Parks Management Department
P.O. Box 1293
Albuquerque, NM 87103
(505) 768-3550

County of Los Alamos
P.O. Box 30
Los Alamos, NM 87544
(505) 662-8150

Santa Fe Metropolitan
Water Board
P.O. Box 276
Santa Fe, NM 87504
(505) 984-5010

Nevada

Las Vegas Valley Water District
3700 West Charleston Boulevard
Las Vegas, NV 89153
(702) 258-3205

New York

Long Island Water Corp.
733 Sunrise Highway
Lynbrook, NY 11563
(516) 593-1000

Cooperative Extension Association
1425 Old Country Road
Building J
Plainview, NY 11803
(516) 454-0906

Oregon

City of Portland
Bureau of Water Works
1120 SW Fifth Avenue, 6th Floor
Portland, OR 97204
(503) 796-7483

Rhode Island

Water Resources
Coordinating Council
265 Melrose Street
Providence, RI 02907
(401) 277-2656

Texas

City of Arlington
Water Office
P.O. Box 20
Arlington, TX 76004
(817) 275-5931

South Austin Growth Corridor
8870 Business Park Drive, #500
Austin, TX 78759
(512) 343-9388

Texas Water Development Board
P.O. Box 13231 Capitol Station
Austin, TX 78711
(512) 463-7955

City of Brownsville
Public Utilities Board
P.O. Box 3270
Brownsville, TX 78520
(512) 544-3882

City of College Station
P.O. Box 9960
College Station, TX 77842
(409) 764-3570

City of Corpus Christi
Public Utilities, Parks,
and Recreation Department
P.O. Box 9277
Corpus Christi, TX 78469
(512) 880-3476

The NXC

The National Xeriscape Council, Inc., was established in 1986 in response to growing interest about water-efficient landscaping across the United States. It is a nonprofit public-service and educational organization whose board of directors includes volunteers from the landscape industry, municipal water agencies, and universities.

Goals of the Council
The council and its members work to assist any community, or any interested individual, in finding means to improve the quality of their landscapes while reducing their requirements for water. Through a network of professionals, it helps communities begin conservation programs, develop educational materials, organize conferences and seminars, and plan other activities to create greater public awareness of and participation in water-saving landscape efforts.

Xeriscape
The idea of popularizing water-saving landscape practices was conceived in Denver, Colorado, in 1981. A cooperative effort by the landscape industry and the Denver Water Department resulted in the coinage of the trademark name "Xeriscape," the creation of a logo, and the development of a simplified system of water-efficient horticultural and landscape principles, based on seven fundamentals. The concept grew rapidly in popularity and acceptance across the nation, and the council was formed to encourage the continued growth of public interest.

As of the publication of this book, more than 100 communities in over 15 states have initiated Xeriscape programs; the states include Colorado, Washington, California, Hawaii, Arizona, Nevada, New Mexico, Wyoming, Texas, Kansas, Georgia, Florida, Massachusetts, New York, New Jersey, and Rhode Island. One of the major results of the council's efforts has been the creation of demonstration gardens in most communities that have active Xeriscape programs. Visitors to these gardens can learn about water-saving gardening and see its effect firsthand.

Xeriscape is much more than landscaping with xeric, or drought-tolerant, plants. It is a system of basic principles encompassing planning, design, irrigation, using appropriate plants, and maintaining an efficient landscape. Applying all these practices at once can result in great savings of water, money, and maintenance time.

To receive more information about Xeriscape and to learn of programs in your area, contact your nearest water-supply agency, USDA cooperative extension office, or local government office. To contact the NXC, write or call any of the charter members listed here.

City of Austin
P.O. Box 1088
Austin, TX 78767
(512) 462-6265

City of Colorado Springs, Water Division
30 South Nevada, Suite 603
P.O. Box 1103
Colorado Springs, CO 80947

Denver Water Department
1600 West 12th Avenue
Denver, CO 80254
(303) 628-6000

Lower Colorado River Authority
P.O. Box 220
Austin, TX 78767
(512) 473-4069

South Florida Water Management District
P.O. Box 24680
West Palm Beach, FL 33416
(305) 686-8800

Toro County—Irrigation Division
P.O. Box 489
Riverside, CA 92502
(714) 688-9221

Rain Bird Corp.
145 North Grand Avenue
Glendora, CA 91740
(818) 963-9311

Photo Credits

*The letter after each
page number refers to
the position of the color
plates. A represents the
picture at the top and
B the picture at the
bottom.*

Judy Glattstein
136B, 156B

Bruce Hamilton
236A

Pamela J. Harper
73B, 75B, 77A, 78B, 79B, 83A, 83B, 86B, 88B, 89A, 90A, 91A, 91B,
93A, 93B, 94A, 95A, 96B, 97A, 97B, 99A, 101B, 103A, 103B, 104B,
105A, 105B, 106A, 111A, 112A, 112B, 113B, 115A, 115B, 117A,
118A, 119A, 120A, 121B, 126B, 128A, 129A, 129B, 134B, 135A,
139B, 141A, 147A, 152A, 152B, 153A, 155A, 162B, 167B, 181B,
182B, 184B, 185A, 190B

Robert E. Heapes
Cover, 50, 77B, 104A, 108, 114B, 119B, 126A, 149B, 223B

Walter Hodge
106B, 107A, 117B, 121A, 140B, 144, 148A, 148B, 149A, 154A,
163B, 173B, 186A, 191B, 201A, 205A, 207B, 211A, 237A

Saxon Holt
62, 66, 68, 99B, 238A

Philip E. Keenan
202B, 203B, 210B, 226A

Jim Knopf
173A

Robert Kourik
2

Ken Lewis, Jr.
84A, 239B

John A. Lynch
31B

John A. Lynch, PHOTO/NATS
3A

Robert E. Lyons, PHOTO/NATS
89B, 209A, 211B

Robert F. McDuffie, PHOTO/NATS
40A

Fred McGourty
114A, 120B, 128B, 131A, 132B

Gary Mottau
58

Julie O'Neal, PHOTO/NATS
137B

Muriel Orans, Horticultural Photography
100A, 151A, 218B, 222A, 228A

Jerry and Joanne Pavia
70, 89B, 94B

Marv Poulson
171B, 196B, 197B

Ann Reilly, PHOTO/NATS
122B, 123B

Richard Simon
76A

John J. Smith
127B

John J. Smith, PHOTO/NATS
113A, 166B, 169B

Doug Sokell, Visuals Unlimited
212A, 213A, 233A

Joy Spurr
80A, 98A, 130B, 139A, 147B, 175A, 187B, 225A, 236B, 237B, 239A

Alvin E. Staffan
225B

Steven M. Still
72A, 74A, 74B, 78A, 80B, 85A, 86A, 87A, 90B, 92A, 95B, 96A, 98B,
100B, 102B, 107B, 110A, 116A, 116B, 122A, 123A, 125A, 125B,
127A, 131B, 134A, 135B, 136A, 137A, 138A, 138B, 143A, 151B,
155B, 160B, 169A, 170B, 171A, 172A, 172B, 177A, 177B, 178B,
179A, 179B, 180A, 182A, 191A, 197A, 207A, 208B, 209B, 212B,
213B, 214A, 215A, 216A, 217A, 218A, 219A, 219B, 220A, 221A,
226B, 227A, 227B, 230A, 230B, 232B, 234B, 235B

David M. Stone, PHOTO/NATS
167A, 181A, 188B

George Taloumis
4, 64, 142B, 143B, 176B, 189A, 192A, 193A, 224A, 235A

Brooking Tatum, Visuals Unlimited
99A

Allan R. Taylor
8A, 168A, 175B, 176A, 178A, 186B

Thomas K. Todsen
174A, 174B

Connie Toops
96A

Valerie Wilkinson, Valan Photos
64A

Index

Numbers in boldface
refer to pages on which
color plates appear.

Chanticleer Press

Publisher: Andrew Stewart
Senior Editor: Ann Whitman
Series Editor: Carol M. Healy
Project Editor: Amy K. Hughes
Editorial Assistant: Katherine Jacobs
Production: Kathy Rosenbloom,
    Karyn Slutsky
Project Design: Paul Zakris
Photo Library: Tim Allan